AUTOMOBILE INDUSTRY:
CURRENT ISSUES

AUTOMOBILE INDUSTRY: CURRENT ISSUES

LEON R. DOMANSKY
EDITOR

Novinka Books
New York

For permission to use material from this book please contact us:
Telephone 631-231-7269; Fax 631-231-8175
Web Site: http://www.novapublishers.com

NOTICE TO THE READER

LIBRARY OF CONGRESS CATALOGING-IN-PUBLICATION DATA
Available upon request

ISBN 1-59454-686-X

Published by Nova Science Publishers, Inc. ✛ *New York*

CONTENTS

PREFACE

Like it or not, the automobile industry is now and will remain an overwhelming factor in the lives of most people. If not an owner and driver, then as a pedestrian or a breather of air which is being polluted by the gas-guzzling and vile-air belching monsters created for our individual hedonistic pleasure. This book presents issues of current interest to those who cannot ignore their presence.

In: Automobile Industry: Current Issues   ISBN: 1-59454-686-X
Editor: L. R. Domansky, pp. 1-15   © 2006 Nova Science Publishers, Inc.

Chapter 1

MODERN GLOBAL AUTOMOBILE INDUSTRY[*]

Business References Service

SUMMARY

Today, the modern global automotive industry encompasses the principal manufacturers, General Motors, Ford, Toyota, Honda, Volkswagen, and DaimlerChrylser, all of which operate in a global competitive marketplace. It is suggested that the globalization of the automotive industry, has greatly accelerated during the last half of the 1990's due to the construction of important overseas facilities and establishment of mergers between giant multinational automakers [1].

Industry specialists indicate that the origins in the expansion of foreign commerce in the automobile industry, date back to the technology transfer of Ford Motor Company's mass-production model from the U.S. to Western Europe and Japan following both World Wars I and II [2]. The advancements in industrialization led to significant increases in the growth and production of the Japanese and German markets, in particular. The second important trend in industrial globalization was the export of fuel efficient cars from Japan to the U.S. as a result of the oil embargo from 1973 to 1974.

---

[*] Extracted from http://www.loc.gov/rr/business/BERA/issue2/industry.html

ADVERTISEMENT FOR FORD CABRIOLET

Advertisement for Ford cabriolet from the Wittemann Collection (Library of Congress). Reproduction number: LC-USZC4-2697

Increasing global trade has enabled the growth in world commercial distribution systems, which has also expanded global competition amongst the automobile manufacturers. Japanese automakers in particular, have instituted innovative production methods by modifying the U.S. manufacturing model, as well as adapting and utilizing technology to enhance production and increase product competition.

There are a number of trends that can be identified by examining the global automotive market, which can be divided into the following factors [3].

Global Market Dynamics - The world's largest automobile manufacturers continue to invest into production facilities in emerging markets in order to reduce production costs. These emerging markets include Latin America, China, Malaysia and other markets in Southeast Asia.

Establishment of Global Alliances - U.S. automakers, "The Big Three" (GM, Ford and Chrysler) have merged with, and in some cases established commercial strategic partnerships with other European and Japanese automobile manufacturers. Some mergers, such as the Chrysler Daimler-Benz merger, was initiated by the European automaker in a strategy to strengthen its position in the U.S. market. Overall, there has been a trend by the world automakers to expand in overseas markets.

Industry Consolidation - Increasing global competition amongst the global manufacturers and positioning within foreign markets has divided the world's automakers into three tiers, the first tier being GM, Ford, Toyota, Honda and Volkswagen, and the two remaining tier manufacturers attempting to consolidate or merge with other lower tier automakers to compete with the first tier companies.

1st Tier Company Mergers - Volkswagen-Lamborgini; BMW-Rolls Royce
2nd Tier Company Mergers - Chrysler-Mercedes Benz; Renault-Nissan-Fiat
3rd Tier Company Mergers - Mazda-Mitsubishi; Kia-Volvo

This section presents literature that examines three major automotive markets in North America, Europe and East Asia. This material is intended to provide a thorough examination of industry trends, structure, and the effects of global market dynamics of the automotive industry within each region, as well as their interrelationships, followed by literature researching the East Asian automotive market.

RESEARCH ON THE MODERN GLOBAL AUTOMOBILE INDUSTRY

Hiraoka, Leslie. S. Global Alliances in the Motor Vehicle Industry. Westport, CT: Quorum Books, 2001.
LC Call Number: HD9710.A2 H57 2001
LC Catalog Record: 00037269

This study examines the origins, consequences, and trends of globalization in the motor vehicle industry, with chapters on transplants from Japan, US recovery, the DaimlerChrysler merger NAFTA, Mercosur, and the development of the motor vehicle industry in China and India. Book review by Book News, Inc.

Lung, Yannick. Cars, Carriers of Regionalism. Houndsmills, Basingstoke, Hampshire; New York: Palgrave MacMillan, 2004.
LC Call Number: HE5611 .C279 2004
LC Catalog Record: 2003068747

This highly topical book brings together some of the world's leading specialists on the global car industry who discuss the ins and outs of the faster lane of regionalism at a time that the world is reassessing the ins and outs of globalization. It provides a thorough and up-dated mapping of the worldwide geography of the car industry, in the triad regions (Europe, North America and Japan), and in the emerging countries and regions. Review by Books In Print.

Industry and Trade Summary: Motor Vehicles. U.S. ITC Publication 3545, September 2002. Washington, D.C.: U.S. International Trade Commission, 2002.
ftp://ftp.usitc.gov/pub/reports/studies/PUB3545.PDF

An analysis of the basic factors affecting trends in consumption, production, and trade in the motor vehicle industry, as well as competiveness of the U.S. motor vehicle industry in domestic and foreign markets. This report covers the period 1997-2001.

Maxton, Graeme P. Time for a Modle Change: Re-engineering the Global Automobile Industry for the 21st Century. New York: Cambridge University Press, 2004.
LC Call Number: HD9710.A2 M3863 2004 (in process as of November 2004)
LC Catalog Record: 2004045634

This work examines the automotive industry, making recommendations for change and improved industry performance. Review by Books In Print.

Shimokawa, Koichi. Reorganization of the Global Automobile Industry and Structural Change of the Automobile Component Industry. International Motor Vehicle Program at MIT.
http://imvp.mit.edu/papers/99/shimokawa.pdf

This paper examines the global reorganization of the automobile industry and the direction of its global strategies; The role of economies of scale in the global reorganization and the production sytems of various models and quantities; and the direction of global structural change in the automobile component industry.

North American Automotive Market

The automobile manufacturing industry is one of the largest industries within the U.S., and is a vital engine for the U.S. economy contributing greatly to employment and productivity. Reports indicate that motor vehicle production represents over 5 % of the U.S. private sector GDP [4]. The U.S. is the world's largest producer and consumer of motor vehicles with production reaching 12.2 million units in 2002 [5]. The U.S. automotive industry continues to experience on-going organizational and technological change, and have taken steps to increase its global presence by expanding global alliances and seeking greater collaboration with other U.S. automakers.

The Big Three U.S. automakers makeup approximately 76 % of U.S. passenger vehicle production, while Japanese automakers, Toyota, Honda, Nissan, Mitsubishi, Subaru, Isuzu represents 18 %, and European automakers, BMW and Mercedes (division of Daimler-Chrysler) make up nearly 2 % [6].

Unlike the Japanese and European automotive markets, the U.S. does not rely significantly on foreign exports. The U.S. auto trade relies mostly on its own domestic market, and to some degree on the Canadian market. Canada is the largest market for U.S. vehicle exports with subsidiaries of U.S. automakers accounting for most of the imports. Integration of the U.S. and Canadian automotive industry dates back to the U.S.-Canadian Automotive Products Trade Agreement established in 1965.

The U.S. Big Three automakers continue to invest billions of dollars into the Canadian market, which has resulted in Canada becoming a global leader in automotive engineering. All of Canada's passenger vehicle production is located in Ontario due to its close proximity to Detroit.

Research on the North American Automotive Market

Encyclopedia of American Cars: A Comprehensive History of the Automakers and the Cars they Built. Lincolnwood, IL: Publications International, © 2002.
LC Call Number: TL23 .E53 2002
LC Catalog Record: 2002727235

A comprehensive, and authoritative encyclopedia that covers American cars from 1930 to 2002 and includes Chrysler, Ford, and GM, plus major independents, such as Duesenberg, Hudson, Checker, Shelby, and others. Also includes more than 3,500 photographs. The publication provides a comprehensive portrait of the workers and machines that contributed to developments in American automotive history.

Keenan, Philip T. and Paich, Mark. Modeling General Motors and the North American Automobile Market. March 24, 2004. Prepublication draft.
http://www.xjtek.com/files/papers/modelinggeneralmotors2004.pdf

This study discusses General Motor's North American Enterprise Model, a system dynamics model of the North American automotive market, and examines the corporation and its marketplace, as well as production functions, such as engineering, manufacturing, marketing, and external competition.

Klepper, Steven. The Evolution of the U.S. Automobile Industry and Detroit as its Capital. Danish Research Unit for Industrial Dynamics Conference Paper, November 2001.
http://www.druid.dk/conferences/winter2002/gallery/klepper.pdf

Author examines the evolution of the U.S. automobile industry and industry consolidation. The paper focuses on the developments leading up to the concentration of the U.S.'s Big Three firms around Detroit, Michigan.

Ramey, Valerie A. and Vine, Daniel J. Tracking the Source of the Decline in GDP Volatility: An Analysis of the Automobile Industry. NBER Working Paper No. 10384, March 2004.
Abstract: http://www.nber.org/papers/W10384
Full text (Pdf): http://papers.nber.org/papers/w10384.pdf

This study identifies a dramatic decline in volatitlity of U.S. GDP growth beginning in 1984, and attempts to correlate various sources of the decline in volatility, specifically by studying the U.S. automobile industry.

Rubenstein, James M. The Changing U.S. Auto Industry. London; New York: Routledge, 2002.
LC Call Number: HD9710.U52 R83 1992 (Library has the 1992 edition only)
LC Catalog Record: 91016821

Drawing on rarely used archive material and recent interviews with industry officials, this book examines the radical changes which have affected automobile production in recent years. Review by Books in Print
Also available online to patrons onsite at the Library of Congress via netLibrary.

Tuman, John P. Reshaping the North American Automobile Industry: Restructuring, Corporatism, and Union Demoracy in Mexico. New York: Continuum, 2002. LC Call Number:
LC Catalog Record: 2002073315

This book examines the responses of unions and workers to regional integration and restructuring in the automobile industry in North and South America.

European Automotive Market

The European Union is made up of 15 member states, and any European country applying for membership. The EU is the world's largest automotive manufacturing region and the world's largest market [7]. The European automotive industry represents approximately 9 % of the EU manufacturing sector [8]. The European automotive industry is considered a leader in the global market with integrated operations consisting of: research, design, development, production and sales. The European automotive market is comprised of a concentrated and sophisticated global network, which includes joint-ventures, cooperatives, productions and assembly sites [9]. EU automotive industry producers have a combined output that exceeds that of the U.S. and Japan, however no one individual EU country produces more than its U.S. or Japanese competitor.

The importance of the automotive industry on the economies of individual EU countries varies country to country. According to recent reports, Germany, Sweden, France and Spain automobile production represents approximately 10 % of total manufacturing, while the average for the EU is about 8 % [10]. The EU's largest automotive producer is Germany estimated at 30 % of EU's total production, followed by France at 19 % and Spain at 17 %, and the United Kingdom at 10 %. [11] These countries are the largest automotive markets in the region.

There are over 20 vehicle manufacturers in the EU, with the largest automakers producing multiple brands, such as General Motors, Ford, DaimlerChrysler, Volkswagen, Fiat and Peugot Citroen. There are also independent automakers, such as Porsche, BMW and Bertione. The last 10 years has shown an overall increase in vehicle production for the EU auto industry, along with Extra-EU exports accounting for approximately 20 % of total production [12].

Like the other markets in the global automobile industry trade, the EU auto industry has experienced significant restructuring and consolidation, which includes mergers, such as ChryslerDaimler-Benz; GM acquisition of Saab; Ford's acquisition of Jaguar and Volvo's passenger car division; BMW's take over and then sale of Rover; and Volkswagen's acquisition of Bentley, Lamborgini, SEAT and Skoda [13]. There continues to be co-production efforts and supply arrangements among the EU automakers, as well as with foreign partners outside of the European Union.

Research on the European Automotive Market

Automotive Sector, Sectoral Issues. Europa Trade Issues. Official homepage of the European Union:

http://europa.eu.int/comm/trade/issues/sectoral/industry/auto/index_en.htm

This report is accessible on the European Union website EUROPA, and provides an overview of the automotive sector for the EU market. The information includes facts and figures, and a general analysis of the EU auto market.

Brenkers, Randy and Verboven, Frank. Liberalizing a Distribution System: The European Car Market. Research Paper, European University Insitute, September 2002.
http://www.iue.it/Personal/Motta/forum/Brescia2-4-04/verboven.pdf

This paper quantifies the competitive effects of removing vertical restraints, based on the recent proposals to liberalize the selective and exclusive distribution system in the European automobile market.

Freyssenet, Michael and Shimizu, Koichi. Globalization or Regionalization of the European Car Industry? New York: Palgrave Macmillan, 2003.
LC Call Number: HD9710.E82 G58 2003
LC Catalog Record: 2002030791
Publisher Description:
http://www.loc.gov/catdir/description/hol041/2002030791.html

This publication presents a systematic description and analysis of the internationalization of strategies that are being pursued by European automobile manufacturers, suppliers, and dealers.

Lung, Yannick. "The Changing Geography of the European Automobile System." International Journal of Automotive Technology and Management, Vol. 4, No. 2/3, 2004.
https://www.inderscience.com/offer.php?id=5324

McLauglin, Andrew M. The European Automobile Industry: Multi-Level Governance, Policy and Politics. London: New York: Routledge, 1999.
LC Call Number: HD9710.E82 M34 1999
LC Catalog Record: 98031831

This work presents an analysis of some of the changes that have transformed the automobile industry in the last 30 years illustrating some of the most significant consequences of globalization. Review by Books In Print.

Motor Business Europe. London: Economist Intelligence Unit. (Quarterly)

This quarterly publication provides analysis and forecasts of vehicle sales and production for each of the 17 countries, analysis of vehicle manufacturers and markets, interviews with leaders of Europe's auto industry and producitivity trends.

Stephen, Roland Francis. Vehicle of Influence: Building a European Car Market. Ann Arbor: University of Michigan Press, c2000.

An examination of the political aspects of the integration of the European automobile industry. The book also discusses the role the European automakers played in role influencing the institutions of the European Union. Synopsis by Books In Print.

East Asian Automotive Market

The Asian motor vehicle market is comprised of three 'core' markets, Japan, South Korea and China. The Korean and Chinese automotive markets continue to grow rapidly, with many analysts predicting that the Korean and Chinese markets will surpass that of Japan within a decade [14].

The Asian financial crisis during the late 1990's slowed down the demand and production of the auto industry, and did not reach pre-currency crisis levels until 2000. However, with the continued strong production growth of the automotive industry in Asia, analysts suggest that the Asia/Pacific region will be a driver of industry growth worldwide [15]. As the automotive manufacturing industry continues to grow in Asia, foreign investment has begun to increase substantially in Asia over the last several years. U.S. and European automakers have targeted the region to not only establish a greater presence in the Asian marketplace, but also to expand its production capacity in Asia. In addition, there have been undertakings by both the U.S. and European automakers to collaborate with Asian automakers.

Japan's Automobile Industry

The automotive industry represents a significant portion of Japan's economy, representing 13 % of its total manufacturing output and 10 % of employment [16]. Japan is home to 11 automobile manufacturers consisting of: Toyota Motor Corp., Honda, Nissan, Mazda Motor Corp., Isuzu Motors, Ltd., Suzuki Motor Corp., and Fuji Heavy Industries, Ltd., and Daihatsu Motor Co. Each of these automakers have manufacturing operations in the U.S. except Suzuki and Daihatsu. However, Suzuki is part of a joint-venture with GM, which is located in Canada.

Japan is also the third leading producer of motor vehicles after the U.S. and the EU. The U.S. is the largest market for Japanese vehicle exports, however, automobile production has fluctuated downward over the last several years in Japan [17]. Like the auto industries in the other regions, the industry has also experienced major restructuring, which is the a result of a downturn in domestic demand. Japanese automakers have responded to stagnate domestic economic conditions by reducing production capacity through plant closures, and have offered equity ownership to foreign automakers to receive financial and managerial assistance. GM has equity in Suzuki and Subaru and controlling interests in Isuzu; Ford has majority equity in Mazda; DaimlerChrysler has majority equity control in Mitsubishi; and Renault has controlling interests in Nissan [18].

The Japanese automotive industry relies heavily on exports with imports making up a much smaller percentage of auto trade. German automaker imports account for the greatest percentage of imports at nearly 70 % [19]. However, trade barriers on foreign automotive imports in Japan have often created problematic trade relations with U.S. automakers and U.S. trade policy officials.

South Korea's Automobile Industry

Presently in South Korea, there are seven automobile manufacturers, which include: Hyundai, Daewoo, Kia, Samsung, Asia Motors, Jinda, and Ssanyong. South Korea is the world's third largest automobile exporter, exporting 41 % of its total motor vehicle production, with roughly 35 % of the exports going to the U.S. [20]. South Korea is the 6th largest automobile market, however imports makeup less than 1 % of motor vehicle trade in the domestic market. Prior to 1987, foreign auto imports were prohibited and Japanese automotive imports were not permitted until 1999. South Korea's automotive industry has also experienced restructuring. In 1999, Hyundai acquired Kia and Asia Motors, and sold 10 % of its equity to DaimlerChrysler in 2000; Daewoo purchased 52 % equity in Ssanyong in

1998; and GM purchased 42 % equity of Daewoo; and in 2000, French automaker Renault purchased Samsung Motors.

Currently, South Korea has no independent auto manufacturers. DaimlerChrysler and Hyundai Motor Co., have formed an alliance in which DaimlerChyrsler will acquire a 10 % equity in Hyundai [21]. Korean automakers have made efforts to join in collaborative ventures with foreign automakers and sold significant portions of its equity in order to continue to operate in the domestic market, as well as receive financial assistance. Industry specialists suggests that in order to become more competitive and efficient in both the domestic and foreign markets, Korean automakers must consolidate platforms domestically and with foreign partners; create strategies that more efficiently utilize regional sourcing; and enhance production and production platforms, as well as supply networks [22].

China's Automobile Industry

China's automobile industry continues to grow rapidly. It is projected that by 2010, China will become one of the world's largest automobile markets with domestic production reaching 5 million units [23]. The automobile industry in China is composed of 120 vehicle manufacturers, employing nearly 2 million workers [24].

The FAW Group is China's first large-scale motor vehicle producer, which has an agreement with Volkswagen to produce Jetta's and Audi sedans. The second largest automaker is the Dong Feng Motor Corporation with three major production facilities in the Hubei province.

The Shanghai Motor Group, the third largest automotive producer in China, began producing cars during the 1960's. It established a joint-venture with Volkswagen in the 1980's that has contributed to the increase in automobile production in China's domestic market.

Government officials in China have initiated policies that are intended to encourage the continuing development of China's domestic automobile manufacturing industry. Nevertheless, there are significant trade barriers for foreign competitors in the way of tariff policies that are applied to foreign auto imports. This restrictive trade environment has contributed to the serious problem of illegal imports of foreign cars into China.

Despite China's growing auto industry, industry productivity lags behind the other Asian competitors, and it lacks the ability to conduct research and development, relying on its foreign partners to develop new vehicles. Chinese automakers are presently creating new policies and methods through foreign joint-ventures to continue the development of China's automotive industry, but at this stage, China's automotive industry still remains underdeveloped both technically and managerially. These conditions present a significant challenge for China's automotive industry, and it is expected to take a considerable amount of time before China becomes a global competitor in the automotive market.

Research on the East Asian Automotive Market

Busser, Rogier, and Sadoi, Yuri. Production Networks in Asia and Europe: Skill Formation and Technology Transfer in the Automobile Industry. London; New York: Routledge, © 2003.
LC Call Number: HD9710.J32 P76 2003 (in process as of November 2004)
LC Catalog Record: 2003005316

This book explores Japanese investment in Europe and Southeast Asia, in relation to the automobile industry.

Freyssenet, Michel, Shimizu, Koichi, and Volpato, Giuseppe. Globalization or Regionalization of American and Asian Car Industry? Hampshire; New York: Palgrave MacMillian in association with GERPISA, 2003.
LC Call Number: HD9710 U52 G54 2003
LC Catalog Record: 2002030787
Publisher Description:
    http://www.loc.gov/catdir/description/hol031/2002030787.html

This book argues that this is not entirely the case due to the heterogeneity of firms and the diversity of strategies pursued. It highlights the diversity and forms of internationalization and the preference for regionalization rather than globalization that has occurred over the past decade. This book looks specifically at the American and Asian car industry. Synopsis taken from OCLC's WorldCat database.

Gallagher, Kelley Sims. "Foreign Technology in China's Automobile Industry: Implications for Energy, Economic Development, and Environment." China Environment Series, Issue 6. Washington, D.C.: Woodrow Wilson International Center for Scholars.
http://wwics.si.edu/topics/pubs/2-feature_1.pdf

This paper explores the role of foreign automakers - particulary the Big Three (General Motors, Ford, and DaimlerChrysler) - in transferring technology, which have helped in modernizing China's automobile industry.

Motor Business Asia-Pacific: The Automotive Industry Within Asia-Pacific. London: Economist Intelligence Unit. (Quarterly)
LC Call Number: HD9710.A782 M68
LC Catalog Record: 97649920

A quarterly publication that provides analysis on the vehicle and components industries of China, India, South Korea, Malaysia, Indonesia, Phillipines, Taiwan, Thailand and Vietnam.

Veloso, Francisco, and Kumar, Rajiv. "The Automotive Supply Chain: Global Trends and Asian Perspectives." Economics and Research Department Working Paper Series No. 3. Manila: Asian Development Bank, 2002.
http://www.adb.org/Documents/ERD/Working_Papers/wp003.pdf LC Call Number: HC411 .E73 no. 3
LC Catalog Record: 2003318266

This report provides an overview of the major trends taking place in the automotive industry across the world, with an emphasis on the Asian market.

Yang, Xiaohua. Globalization of the Automobile Industry: The United States, Japan, and the People's Republic of China. Westport, CT: Greenwood Press, 1995.
LC Call Number: HD9710.A2 Y36 1995
LC Catalog Record: 94037887

Explains the seemingly contradictory trends toward global integration and national balkanization since World War II as a bifurcation of economic and political borders. The author examines the three countries' relationship involving government-economic relations, and the global automobile trade.

REFERENCES

[1] Hiroaka, Leslie S. Global Alliances in the Motor Vehicle Industry. Westport, CT: Quorum Books, 2001, p. 1.
[2] Ibid, p. 1.
[3] Ibid, p. 15.
[4] Industry and Trade Summary: Motor Vehicles. U.S. ITC Publication 3545, September 2002. Washington, D.C.: U.S. International Trade

Commission, p.3. Internet: ftp://ftp.usitc.gov/pub/reports/studies/ PUB3545.PDF

[5] Ward's Automotive Yearbook. Detroit: Ward's Report, Inc., 2003, p. 14.

[6] Ibid, p. 5.

[7] Lung, Yannick. "The Changing Geography of the European Automobile Systems." 10th GERPISA International Colloquium. Co-ordinating competencies and knowledge in the auto industry. Internet: http://cockeas.montesquieu.u-bordeaux.fr/Lung_WP4va.pdf

[8] Trade Issues, Automotive Sectors. Europa, Official Internet site of the European Union. Internet: http://europa.eu.int/comm/trade/issues/ sectoral/industry/auto/index_en.htm

[9] Ibid.

[10] Industry and Trade Summary: Motor Vehicles. U.S. ITC Publication 3545, September 2002. Washington, D.C.: U.S. International Trade Commission, p. 49. Internet: ftp://ftp.usitc.gov/pub/reports/studies/ PUB3545.PDF

[11] Ibid, p. 50.

[12] Ibid, p. 50.

[13] Ibid, p. 52.

[14] Automotive Supply Chain: Global Trends and Asian Perspectives. Manila: Asian Development Bank, 2002, p. 23. Internet: http://www.adb.org/Documents/ERD/Working_Papers/wp003.pdf

[15] Ibid, p. 22.

[16] Industry and Trade Summary: Motor Vehicles. U.S. ITC Publication 3545, September 2002. Washington, D.C.: U.S. International Trade Commission, p. 55. Internet: ftp://ftp.usitc.gov/pub/reports/studies/ PUB3545.PDF

[17] Ibid, p. 55.

[18] Ibid, p. 56.

[19] Ibid, p. 57.

[20] Industry and Trade Summary: Motor Vehicles. U.S. ITC Publication 3545, September 2002. Washington, D.C.: U.S. International Trade Commission, p. 55. Internet: ftp://ftp.usitc.gov/pub/reports/studies/ PUB3545.PDF

[21] Ibid, p. 60.

[22] Automotive Supply Chain: Global Trends and Asian Perspectives. Manila: Asian Development Bank, 2002, p. 30. Internet: http://www.adb.org/Documents/ERD/Wowrking_Papers/wp003.pdf

[23] Industry and Trade Summary: Motor Vehicles. U.S. ITC Publication 3545, September 2002. Washington, D.C.: U.S. International Trade Commission, p. 61. Internet: ftp://ftp.usitc.gov/pub/reports/studies/PUB3545.PDF

[24] Automotive Supply Chain: Global Trends and Asian Perspectives. Manila: Asian Development Bank, 2002, p. 28. Internet: http://www.adb.org/Documents/ERD/Working_Papers/wp003.pdf

In: Automobile Industry: Current Issues
Editor: L. R. Domansky, pp. 17-76

ISBN: 1-59454-686-X
© 2006 Nova Science Publishers, Inc.

Chapter 2

USING THE FUEL ECONOMY GUIDE[*]

The U.S. Environmental Protection Agency (EPA) and U.S. Department of Energy (DOE)

FUEL ECONOMY ESTIMATES

Each vehicle in this guide has two fuel economy estimates.

City represents urban driving, in which a vehicle is started in the morning (after being parked all night) and driven in stop-and-go rush hour traffic.

Highway represents a mixture of rural and interstate highway driving in warmed-up vehicles, typical of longer trips in free-flowing traffic.

EPA miles-per-gallon (MPG) estimates are based on lab testing and are adjusted to reflect real-world driving conditions for an average U.S. motorist. Vehicles are tested in the same manner to allow fair comparisons. For answers to frequently asked questions about fuel economy estimates, visit www.fueleconomy.gov/feg/info.shtml.

---

[*] Extracted from http://www.fueleconomy.gov/feg/FEG2006intro.pdf.

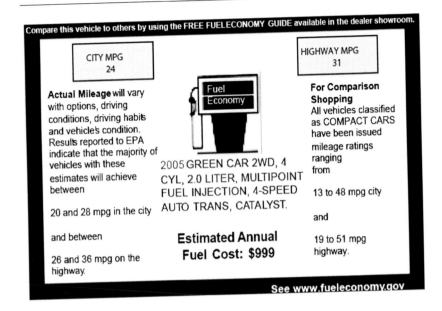

Compare this vehicle to others by using the FREE FUELECONOMY GUIDE available in the dealer showroom.

CITY MPG
24

HIGHWAY MPG
31

Actual Mileage will vary with options, driving conditions, driving habits and vehicle's condition. Results reported to EPA indicate that the majority of vehicles with these estimates will achieve between

20 and 28 mpg in the city

and between

26 and 36 mpg on the highway.

Fuel Economy

2005 GREEN CAR 2WD, 4 CYL, 2.0 LITER, MULTIPOINT FUEL INJECTION, 4-SPEED AUTO TRANS, CATALYST.

Estimated Annual Fuel Cost: $999

For Comparison Shopping All vehicles classified as COMPACT CARS have been issued mileage ratings ranging from

13 to 48 mpg city

and

19 to 51 mpg highway.

See www.fueleconomy.gov

Why Your Fuel Economy Can Vary

A vehicle's fuel economy is not a constant or fixed number; it varies among vehicles of the same make and model, and it will vary over time for an individual vehicle. Many factors affect a vehicle's fuel economy:

When, where, and how the vehicle is driven: Frequent acceleration and braking necessary in stop-and-go traffic and on hilly terrain hurt fuel economy, and aggressive driving (hard accelerating and braking) reduces it even more. Cold weather can reduce MPG, since your engine doesn't run efficiently until it is warmed up, and driving with a heavy load or with the air conditioner running can also reduce MPG.

Vehicle maintenance: A poorly tuned engine burns more fuel, so fuel economy will suffer if your engine is not in tune. Keeping tires at the correct pressure and changing the air filter on a regular basis can improve fuel economy. Also, new energy-saving motor oils can improve MPG.

Inherent variations in vehicles: Small variations in the way vehicles are manufactured and assembled can cause MPG variations among vehicles of the same make and model. Usually, differences are small, but a few drivers may see a noticeable deviation from the EPA estimates.

Refer to www.fueleconomy.gov for more detailed explanations and fuel economy tips.

Annual Fuel Cost Estimates

This guide provides annual fuel cost estimates for each vehicle. The estimates are based on the assumptions that you travel 15,000 miles per year (55% under city driving conditions and 45% under highway conditions) and that fuel costs $1.80/gallon for regular unleaded gasoline and $1.95/gallon for premium. Cost-per-gallon assumptions for vehicles that use other fuel types are discussed at the beginning of those vehicle sections.

UNDERSTANDING THE GUIDE LISTINGS

We hope you'll find the *Fuel Economy Guide* easy to use! Within each section of the guide, vehicles are first organized by class (see the table on page 2 for a listing of vehicle classes). Within each class, vehicles are listed alphabetically by manufacturer and model—vehicle models with different characteristics, including transmission type or engine size, are listed as different vehicles. Additional characteristics about the vehicle, such as valve or fuel system, may also be needed to distinguish between similar vehicles. This information is listed in the "Notes" column. Interior volume information is located in the index at the back of the Guide.

The diagram below explains the contents of a typical listing. The vehicle make and model are listed in the first column. Additional information on transmission type (e.g., automatic or manual) and the number of gears is listed in the second column, and information on the engine size (in liters) and the number of cylinders is listed in the third. This information is usually needed to correctly identify a specific configuration within a model type.

Column 4 shows EPA MPG estimates for city and highway driving. The most fuel-efficient automatic and manual vehicles per class are listed in green boldface type and highlighted by a gray bar. The most efficient vehicle in each class is marked with an arrow _. Alternative fuel vehicles are highlighted by a green bar, and those that can use two kinds of fuel, such as flexible fuel vehicles, have an entry for each fuel type. Annual estimated fuel cost is listed in column 5 (see the inside front cover for an explanation of how this is estimated). The final column ("Notes") contains additional information on engine and fuel system type, applicable taxes, and other useful information.

Vehicles with a "P" in the "Notes" column require premium-grade gasoline. Because premium is the most expensive grade of gasoline, these vehicles may have a higher annual fuel cost even though they have a slightly better fuel economy than other vehicles. A legend for all of the abbreviations is provided at the bottom of alternating pages.

Additional information on interior passenger and cargo volumes is included in the Index.

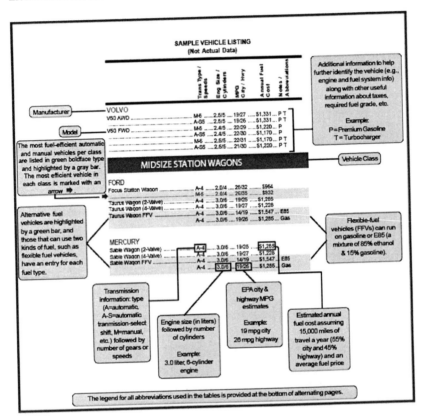

WHY SOME VEHICLES ARE NOT LISTED

- ◆ Vans, pickup trucks, and sport utility vehicles (SUVs) weighing more than 8,500 pounds gross vehicle weight (vehicle weight plus carrying capacity) are classified as heavy-duty vehicles. Fuel economy regulations do not apply to these vehicles, so they are not tested and fuel economy labels are not posted on their windows.

♦ Some vehicles' fuel economy information is not available in time to be included in the guide. However, you can usually find this information at www.fueleconomy.gov, which is updated regularly.

♦ The availability of some vehicles is restricted.

VEHICLE CLASSES USED IN THIS GUIDE

CARS (based on interior passenger and cargo volume)		TRUCKS (based on body style and load-bearing capacity)	
TWO-SEATER CARS SEDANS	Passenger and Cargo Volume	PICKUP TRUCKS	Gross Vehicle Weight Rating
Minicompact	Under 85 cubic feet	Small	Under 4,500 pounds
Subcompact	85 to 99 cubic feet	Standard	4,500 to 8,500 pounds
Compact	100 to 109 cubic feet	VANS	Under 8,500 pounds
Midsize	110 to 119 cubic feet	Passenger	
Large	120 or more cubic feet	Cargo	
STATION		MINIVANS	Under 8,500 pounds
WAGONS		SPORT UTILITY	Under 8,500 pounds
Small	Under 130 cubic feet	VEHICLES	
Midsize	130 to 159 cubic feet	SPECIAL PURPOSE	Under 8,500 pounds
Large	160 or more cubic feet	VEHICLES	

TAX INCENTIVES AND DISINCENTIVES

Tax Credits and Deductions

If you purchase a qualifying electric or "clean-fuel" vehicle in 2004-2005, you may be eligible for federal income tax incentives, such as tax credits and deductions. Clean fuel vehicles include qualified gasoline-electric hybrids, compressed natural gas (CNG) vehicles, liquefied propane gas (LPG) vehicles, and others powered by alternative fuels. Vehicles must go through an IRS qualification process before they are eligible for the hybrid deduction. Visit www.fueleconomy.gov for more detailed information on current incentives and the most up-to-date news on tax incentives under consideration.

Gas Guzzler Tax

The Energy Tax Act of 1978 requires auto companies to pay a gas guzzler tax on the sale of passenger cars with exceptionally low fuel economy. Such vehicles are identified in this guide by the word "Tax" in the "Notes" column. In the dealer showroom, the words "Gas Guzzler" and the amount of the tax are listed on the vehicle's fuel economy label. The tax does not apply to light trucks.

WWW.FUELECONOMY.GOV

Learn more and do more on-line at www.fueleconomy.gov!

◆ Download and print additional copies of the *Fuel Economy Guide.*
◆ Search for specific vehicles by class, manufacturer, and MPG and compare up to three vehicles at a time, side-by-side.
◆ View MPG, emissions, and safety information for used vehicles dating back to 1985.
◆ Learn about tax incentives for hybrid-electric, electric, and other alternative fuel vehicles.
◆ Read tips for improving the fuel economy of your current vehicle.
◆ Calculate your annual fuel cost.
◆ Learn what makes a gallon of gasoline cost what it does (e.g., refining, transportation, taxes, etc.).
◆ Learn about advanced technologies such as hybrid-electric and fuel cell vehicles.
◆ Find out how fuel economy ratings are determined.

WHY CONSIDER FUEL ECONOMY?

Save Money

You could save $300-$500 in fuel costs each year by choosing the most fuel-efficient vehicle in a particular class. This can add up to thousands of dollars over a vehicle's lifetime. Fuel-efficient models come in all shapes and sizes, so you need not sacrifice utility or size.

Each vehicle listing in the *Fuel Economy Guide* provides fuel cost information (described on the inside front cover). The fuel economy web site, www.fueleconomy.gov, features an annual fuel cost calculator, which allows you to insert your local gasoline prices and consider your driving preference to achieve the most accurate fuel cost information for your vehicle.

Strengthen National Energy Security

Buying a more fuel-efficient vehicle can help strengthen our national energy security by reducing our dependence on foreign oil. Half of the oil used to produce the gasoline you put in your tank is imported. The United States uses about 20 million barrels of oil per day, two-thirds of which is used for transportation. Petroleum imports cost us about $2 billion a week— that's money that could be used to fuel our own economy.

Protect the Environment

Burning fossil fuels such as gasoline or diesel adds greenhouse gases, including carbon dioxide, to the earth's atmosphere. Greenhouse gases trap heat and thus warm the earth because they prevent a significant proportion of infrared radiation from escaping into space.

Vehicles with lower fuel economy burn more fuel, creating more carbon dioxide. Every gallon of gasoline your vehicle burns puts 20 pounds of carbon dioxide into the atmosphere. You can reduce your contribution to global warming by choosing a vehicle with higher fuel economy.

By choosing a vehicle that achieves 25 miles per gallon rather than 20 miles per gallon, you can prevent the release of about 15 tons of greenhouse gas pollution over the lifetime of your vehicle.

Tips for Improving Fuel Economy

Keep Your Car in Shape

♦ Fixing a car that is noticeably out of tune can improve gas mileage by about 4%—repairing a faulty oxygen sensor can improve fuel economy by as much as 40%!

♦   Replacing a clogged air filter can improve gas mileage by as much as 10% (and protect your engine).

♦   Keeping your tires inflated to the recommended pressure and using the recommended grade of motor oil can save as much as 3–5¢/gallon. The manufacturer's recommended tire pressure can be found on the tire information placard and/or vehicle certification label located on the vehicle door edge, doorpost, or glove-box door, or inside the trunk lid.

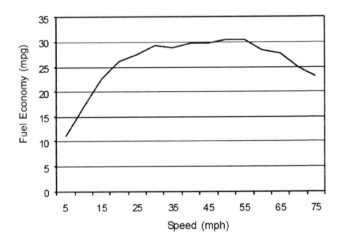

Plan and Combine Trips

♦   A warmed-up engine is more fuel efficient than a cold one. Many short trips taken from a cold start can use twice as much fuel as one multipurpose trip covering the same distance when the engine is warmed up and efficient. Trip planning not only saves fuel, but also reduces wear and tear on your car.

♦   For more tips and for more information about gasoline pricing, visit www.fueleconomy.gov.

Drive More Efficiently

♦   Aggressive driving (speeding and rapid acceleration and braking) can lower your gas mileage by as much as 33% at highway speeds and 5% around town (costing you as much as 49¢/gallon!).

- Observe the speed limit—each 5 miles per hour (mph) you drive over 60 mph is like paying an additional 10¢/ gallon.
- Avoid idling—idling gets 0 miles per gallon.

MODEL YEAR 2005 FUEL ECONOMY LEADERS

Listed below are vehicles with the highest fuel economy in the most popular classes, including vehicles with both automatic and manual transmissions. Please note that many vehicle models come in a range of engine sizes and trim lines, resulting in different fuel economy values.

	Transmission Type	MPG City/Hwy
TWO-SEATER CARS		
Honda Insight (hybrid)	manual	61/66
	automatic	57/56
MINICOMPACT CARS		
Mini Cooper	manual	28/36
	automatic	26/34
SUBCOMPACT CARS		
Volkswagen New Beetle (diesel)	manual	38/46
	automatic	36/42
COMPACT CARS		
Honda Civic Hybrid	automatic	48/47
	manual	46/51
MIDSIZE CARS		
Toyota Prius (hybrid)	automatic	60/51
Hyundai Elantra	manual	27/34
LARGE CARS		
Toyota Avalon	automatic	22/31
SMALL STATION WAGONS		
Volkswagen Jetta Wagon (diesel)	manual	36/43
	automatic	32/43
MIDSIZE STATION WAGONS		
Volkswagen Passat Wagon (diesel)	automatic	27/38
Ford Focus Station Wagon	manual	26/35
CARGO VANS		
Chevrolet Astro 2WD	automatic	16/22
GMC Safari 2WD	automatic	16/22
MINIVANS		
Honda Odyssey 2WD	automatic	20/28
PASSENGER VANS		
Chevrolet Astro 2WD	automatic	16/21
GMC Safari 2WD	automatic	16/21

	Transmission Type	MPG City/Hwy
SUV		
Ford Escape HEV 2WD	automatic	36/31
Toyota Rav4 2WD	manual	24/30
STANDARD PICKUP TRUCKS		
Ford Ranger Pickup 2WD	manual	24/29
	automatic	22/26
Mazda B2300 2WD	manual	24/29
	automatic	22/26

FUEL ECONOMY & ANNUAL FUEL COST RANGES FOR VEHICLE CLASSES

The graph below provides the fuel economy and annual fuel cost ranges for the vehicles in each vehicle class so that you can see where a given vehicle's fuel economy and cost fall within its class. Combined city and highway MPG estimates are used; these assume you will drive 55% in the city and 45% on the highway. You can visit www.fueleconomy.gov to calculate annual fuel cost for a specific vehicle based on your own driving conditions and per-gallon fuel costs.

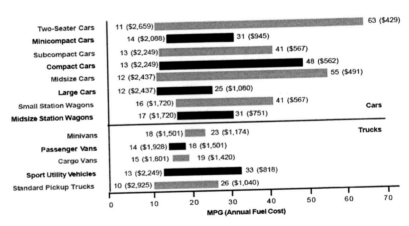

APPENDIX 1
2005 MODEL YEAR VEHICLES

This section contains the fuel economy values for 2005 model year vehicles. Alternative fuel vehicles are highlighted with a green bar, and those that can use two kinds of fuel, such as flexible fuel vehicles, have an entry for each fuel type. The most fuel-efficient automatic and manual vehicles per class are listed in green boldface type and highlighted by a gray bar. The most efficient vehicle in each class is marked with an arrow.

	Trans Type / Speeds	Eng Size / Cylinders	MPG City / Hwy	Annual Fuel Cost	Notes / Abbreviations
TWO SEATERS					
ACURA					
NSX	A-S4	3.0/6	17/24	$1,462...	P
	M-6	3.2/6	17/24	$1,462...	P
AUDI					
TT Roadster	A-S6	1.8/4	20/28	$1,272...	P T
TT Roadster Quattro	M-6	1.8/4	20/29	$1,272...	P T
	A-S6	3.2/6	19/25	$1,392...	P
BMW					
Z4 Roadster	M-5	2.5/6	20/28	$1,272...	P
	A-S5	2.5/6	21/28	$1,272...	P
	M-6	3.0/6	21/29	$1,220...	P
	A-S5	3.0/6	19/27	$1,331...	P
	A-S6	3.0/6	20/29	$1,272...	P
CADILLAC					
XLR	A-S5	4.6/8	17/25	$1,539...	P
CHEVROLET					
Corvette	A-4	6.0/8	18/26	$1,392...	P
	M-6	6.0/8	18/28	$1,392...	P
CHRYSLER					
Crossfire Coupe	A-5	3.2/6	21/28	$1,220...	P
	A-5	3.2/6	17/24	$1,462...	P S
	M-6	3.2/6	17/25	$1,462...	P
Crossfire Roadster	A-5	3.2/6	21/28	$1,220...	P
	A-5	3.2/6	17/24	$1,462...	P S
	M-6	3.2/6	17/25	$1,462...	P

	Trans Type / Speeds	Eng Size / Cylinders	MPG City / Hwy	Annual Fuel Cost	Notes / Abbreviations
DODGE					
Viper Conv	M-6	8.3/10	.. 12/20	$1,951...	P Tax
FERRARI					
360 Modena/Spider/Challenge	3.6/8	M-6	11/16	$2,249...	P Tax
	A-S6	3.6/8	10/16	$2,437...	P Tax
575 MM & SuperAmerica	M-6	5.7/12	.. 10/16	$2,437...	P Tax
	A-S6	5.7/12	.. 10/17	$2,437...	P Tax
F430	A-6	4.3/8	11/16	$2,249...	P Tax
	M-6	4.3/8	11/17	$2,249...	P Tax
FORD					
GT 2WD	M-6	5.4/8	13/21	$1,828...	P S Tax
Thunderbird	A-5	3.9/8	18/24	$1,462...	P
	A-S5	3.9/8	17/24	$1,462...	P
HONDA					
Insight	**A V**	**1.0/3**	**57/56**	**$483...**	**HEV**
	M-5	**1.0/3**	**61/66**	**$429...**	**HEV**
S̲2̲0̲0̲0̲	M-6	2.2/4	20/25	$1,331...	P
LAMBORGHINI					
L-140/141 Gallardo	M-6	5.0/10	..9/15	$2,659...	P Tax
	A-S6	5.0/10	.. 10/17	$2,437...	P Tax
L-147/148 Murcielago	M-6	6.2/12	.. 9/13	$2,659...	P Tax
	A-S6	6.2/12	.. 10/15	$2,437...	P Tax
LOTUS					
Elise/Exige	M-6	1.8/4	23/27	$1,170...	P
MASERATI					
Spyder Cambiocorsa/GT/90	M-6	4.2/8	12/17	$2,249...	P Tax
ANV	A-S6	4.2/8	12/17	$2,088...	P Tax
MAZDA					
MX-5 Miata	A-4	1.8/4	22/28	$1,220...	P
	M-5	1.8/4	23/28	$1,170...	P
	M-6	1.8/4	23/28	$1,170...	P
	M-6	1.8/4	20/26	$1,331...	P T
MERCEDES-BENZ					
SLR	A-S5	5.4/8	13/18	$1,951...	P S Tax
SL500	A-7	5.0/8	16/23	$1,626...	P Tax
SL55 AMG	A-S5	5.4/8	14/20	$1,828...	P S Tax
SL600	A-5	5.5/12..	13/19	$1,951...	P T Tax
SL65 AMG	A-S5	6.0/12..	12/19	$1,951...	P T Tax
SLK350	A-7	3.5/6	19/25	$1,392...	P

	Trans Type / Speeds	Eng Size / Cylinders	MPG City / Hwy	Annual Fuel Cost	Notes / Abbreviations
SLK350	M-6	3.5/6	18/25	$1,392...	P
SLK55 AMG	NA	5.4/8	16/22	$1,626...	P Tax
NISSAN					
350Z	M-6	3.5/6	20/26	$1,331...	P
	M-6	3.5/6	19/25	$1,331...	P DVVT
	A-S5	3.5/6	19/26	$1,392...	P
350Z Roadster	M-6	3.5/6	20/26	$1,331...	P
	A-S5	3.5/6	18/25	$1,392...	P
PORSCHE					
Carrera 2 911 GT3	M-6	3.6/6	15/23	$1,626...	P Tax
Carrera GT	M-6	5.7/10..	10/16	$2,437...	P Tax
Turbo 2 911 GT2	M-6	3.6/6	15/23	$1,626...	P T Tax
TOYOTA					
MR2	M-5	1.8/4	26/32	$932	
	M-6	1.8/4	26/33	$932	

MINICOMPACT CARS

	Trans Type / Speeds	Eng Size / Cylinders	MPG City / Hwy	Annual Fuel Cost	Notes / Abbreviations
ASTON MARTIN					
DB9	A-S6	5.9/12..	12/19	$1,951...	P Tax
DB9 Volante	A-S6	5.9/12..	13/18	$1,951...	P Tax
V12 Vanquish S	A-S6	5.9/12..	11/17	$2,249...	P Tax
AUDI					
TT Coupe	A-S6	1.8/4	21/29	$1,220...	P T
TT Coupe Quattro	M-6	1.8/4	20/29	$1,272...	P T
	A-S6	3.2/6	19/26	$1,331...	P
BMW					
325CI Conv	M-5	2.5/6	19/27	$1,331...	P
	A-S5	2.5/6	18/26	$1,392...	P
330CI Conv	M-6	3.0/6	19/28	$1,272...	P
	A-S5	3.0/6	18/25	$1,392...	P
	A-S6	3.0/6	19/27	$1,331...	P
M3 Conv	M-6	3.2/6	16/23	$1,626...	P Tax
M3 Conv (6-Mode)	A-S6	3.2/6	16/22	$1,626...	P Tax
JAGUAR					
XK8 Conv	A-6	4.2/8	18/26	$1,392...	P
XKR Conv	A-6	4.2/8	16/23	$1,626...	P S Tax
LEXUS					
SC 430	A-5	4.3/8	18/23	$1,462...	P
MINI					
Cooper	A V	1.6/4	26/34	$1,009...	P

	Trans Type / Speeds	Eng Size / Cylinders	MPG City / Hwy	Annual Fuel Cost	Notes / Abbreviations
	M-5	1.6/4	28/36	$945...	P
Cooper Conv	A V	1.6/4	26/33	$1,009...	P
	M-5	1.6/4	27/35	$974...	P
Cooper S	M-6	1.6/4	25/32	$1,082...	P
	A-S6	1.6/4	23/32	$1,082...	P
Cooper S Conv	M-6	1.6/4	25/32	$1,082...	P
	A-S6	1.6/4	23/32	$1,082...	P

MITSUBISHI

	Trans Type / Speeds	Eng Size / Cylinders	MPG City / Hwy	Annual Fuel Cost	Notes / Abbreviations
Eclipse Spyder	M-5	2.4/4	23/31	$1,040	
	A-S4	2.4/4	20/26	$1,174	
	M-5	3.0/6	20/29	$1,272...	P
	M-5	3.0/6	20/28	$1,272...	P VIS
	A-S4	3.0/6	20/28	$1,272...	P
	A-S4	3.0/6	20/27	$1,272...	P VIS

PORSCHE

	Trans Type / Speeds	Eng Size / Cylinders	MPG City / Hwy	Annual Fuel Cost	Notes / Abbreviations
Carrera 2 Cabriolet (new body style).	A-5	3.6/6	19/26	$1,392...	P
Carrera 2 Cabriolet	A-5	3.6/6	18/26	$1,392...	P
	M-6	3.6/6	18/26	$1,392...	P
Carrera 2 Cabriolet Kit	A-5	3.6/6	18/26	$1,392...	P
	M-6	3.6/6	18/26	$1,392...	P
Carrera 2 Coupe (new body style)	A-5	3.6/6	19/26	$1,392...	P
Carrera 2 Coupe	A-5	3.6/6	18/26	$1,392...	P
	M-6	3.6/6	18/26	$1,392...	P
Carrera 2 Coupe Kit	A-5	3.6/6	18/26	$1,392...	P
	M-6	3.6/6	18/26	$1,392...	P
Carrera 2 S Cabriolet	A-5	3.8/6	19/26	$1,392...	P
	M-6	3.8/6	18/26	$1,392...	P
Carrera 2 S Coupe	A-5	3.8/6	19/26	$1,392...	P
	M-6	3.8/6	18/26	$1,392...	P
Carrera 4 Cabriolet	A-5	3.6/6	17/23	$1,539...	P
	M-6	3.6/6	17/24	$1.539...	P
Carrera 4 Cabriolet Kit	A-5	3.6/6	17/23	$1,539...	P
	M-6	3.6/6	17/24	$1,539...	P
Carrera 4 S Cabriolet	A-5	3.6/6	17/23	$1,539...	P
	M-6	3.6/6	17/24	$1,539...	P
Carrera 4 S Cabriolet Kit	A-5	3.6/6	17/23	$1,539...	P
	M-6	3.6/6	17/24	$1,539...	P
Carrera 4 S Coupe	A-5	3.6/6	17/23	$1,539...	P
	M-6	3.6/6	17/24	$1,539...	P
Carrera 4 S Kit	A-5	3.6/6	17/23	$1,539...	P
	M-6	3.6/6	17/24	$1,539...	P

	Trans Type / Speeds	Eng Size / Cylinders	MPG City / Hwy	Annual Fuel Cost	Notes / Abbreviations
Targa	A-5	3.6/6	18/26	$1,392...	P
	M-6	3.6/6	18/26	$1,392...	P
Targa Kit	A-5	3.6/6	18/26	$1,392...	P
	M-6	3.6/6	18/26	$1,392...	P
Turbo 4 911	A-5	3.6/6	14/22	$1,720...	P T Tax
	M-6	3.6/6	15/22	$1,720...	P T Tax
Turbo 4 911 Cab	A-5	3.6/6	14/22	$1,720...	P T Tax
	M-6	3.6/6	15/22	$1,626...	P T Tax
Turbo 4 911 Cab Kit	A-5	3.6/6	14/22	$1,720...	P T Tax
	M-6	3.6/6	15/22	$1,626...	P T Tax
Turbo 4 911 Cab S	A-5	3.6/6	14/22	$1,720...	P T Tax
	M-6	3.6/6	15/22	$1,626...	P T Tax
Turbo 4 911 Kit	A-5	3.6/6	14/22	$1,720...	P T Tax
	M-6	3.6/6	15/22	$1,720...	P T Tax
Turbo 4 911 S	A-5	3.6/6	14/22	$1,720...	P T Tax
	M-6	3.6/6	15/22	$1,720...	P T Tax

VOLKSWAGEN

New Beetle Conv	M-5	1.8/4	25/30	$1,082...	P T
	A-S6	1.8/4	22/30	$1,170...	P T
	M-5	2.0/4	24/30	$1,040	
	A-S6	2.0/4	21/31	$1,080	

SUBCOMPACT CARS

ACURA

RSX	M-5	2.0/4	27/34	$899	
	M-6	2.0/4	23/31	$1,126...	P
	A-S5	2.0/4	25/34	$964	

AUDI

A4 Cabriolet	A V	1.8/4	23/30	$1,126...	P T
	A V	3.0/6	21/29	$1,220...	P
A4 Cabriolet Quattro	A-S5	3.0/6	18/26	$1,392...	P
S4 Cabriolet	M-6	4.2/8	15/21	$1,720...	P Tax
	A-S6	4.2/8	15/22	$1,626...	P Tax

BMW

325CI	M-5	2.5/6	20/29	$1,220...	P
	A-S5	2.5/6	19/27	$1,331...	P
330CI	M-6	3.0/6	20/30	$1,272...	P
	A-S5	3.0/6	19/27	$1,331...	P
	A-S6	3.0/6	20/29	$1,272...	P
645CI	M-6	4.4/8	17/25	$1,462...	P
645CI (3-Mode)	A-S6	4.4/8	18/26	$1,392...	P
645CI (4-Mode)	A-S6	4.4/8	16/24	$1,539...	P
645CI Conv	M-6	4.4/8	15/23	$1,626...	P Tax

	Trans Type / Speeds	Eng Size / Cylinders	MPG City / Hwy	Annual Fuel Cost	Notes / Abbreviations
645CI Conv (3-Mode)	A-S6	4.4/8	18/26	$1,392...	P
645CI Conv (4-Mode)	A-S6	4.4/8	15/22	$1,720...	P Tax
M3	M-6	3.2/6	16/24	$1,539...	P Tax
	A-S6	3.2/6	16/23	$1,539...	P Tax
CHEVROLET					
Cobalt	M-5	2.0/4	23/29	$1,170...	P S
	A-4	2.2/4	24/32	$999	
	M-5	2.2/4	25/34	$964	
FORD					
Mustang	A-5	4.0/6	19/25	$1,285	
	M-5	4.0/6	19/28	$1,228	
	A-5	4.6/8	18/23	$1,350	
	M-5	4.6/8	17/25	$1,350	
HYUNDAI					
Tiburon	A-4	2.0/4	22/30	$1,080	
	M-5	2.0/4	24/30	$1,040	
	A-4	2.7/6	19/26	$1,228	
	M-5	2.7/6	19/26	$1,228	
	M-6	2.7/6	18/26	$1,285	
JAGUAR					
XK8	A-6	4.2/8	18/26	$1,392...	P
XKR	A-6	4.2/8	16/23	$1,626...	P S Tax
MASERATI					
Coupe & Gransport	M-6	4.2/8	12/17	$2,249...	P Tax
	A-S6	4.2/8	12/17	$2,088...	P Tax
MAZDA					
RX-8	M-6	1.3/2	18/24	$1,462...	P
	A-S4	1.3/2	18/24	$1,462...	P
MERCEDES-BENZ					
CLK320	A-5	3.2/6	20/28	$1,272...	P
CLK320 Cabriolet	A-5	3.2/6	20/26	$1,331...	P
CLK500	A-7	5.0/8	17/25	$1,462...	P
CLK500 Cabriolet	A-7	5.0/8	17/25	$1,462...	P
CLK55 AMG	A-S5	5.4/8	16/22	$1,626...	P Tax
CLK55 AMG Cabriolet	A-S5	5.4/8	16/22	$1,626...	P Tax
MITSUBISHI					
Eclipse	A-4	2.4/4	21/28	$1,174	
	M-5	2.4/4	23/31	$1,040	
	A-S4	2.4/4	21/28	$1,174	

	Trans Type / Speeds	Eng Size / Cylinders	MPG City / Hwy	Annual Fuel Cost	Notes / Abbreviations
Eclipse	M-5	3.0/6	20/29	$1,272...	P
	M-5	3.0/6	20/29	$1,272...	P VIS
	A-S4	3.0/6	20/28	$1,272...	P
	A-S4	3.0/6	21/28	$1,272...	P VIS
SAAB					
9-3 Convertible	M-5	2.0/4	21/28	$1,220...	P T
	A-5	2.0/4	19/27	$1,392...	P T
SCION					
tC	A-4	2.4/4	23/30	$1,040	
	M-5	2.4/4	22/29	$1,080	
xA	A-4	1.5/4	31/38	$794	
	M-5	1.5/4	32/37	$794	
SUBARU					
Impreza AWD	A-4	2.0/4	19/26	$1,331...	P T
	M-5	2.0/4	20/27	$1,331...	P T
	A-4	2.5/4	22/28.	$1,080	
	M-5	2.5/4	23/30	$1,080	
	M-6	2.5/4	18/24	$1,462...	P T
TOYOTA					
Celica	A-4	1.8/4	29/36	$842	
	M-5	1.8/4	27/33	$932	
	M-6	1.8/4	24/33	$1,044...	P
	A-S4	1.8/4	25/31	$1,082...	P
VOLKSWAGEN					
New Beetle	M-5	1.8/4	25/30	$1,082...	P T .
	A-S6	1.8/4	22/30	$1,170...	P T
—	**M-5**	**1.9/4**	**38/46**	**$567...**	**D T**
	A-S6	**1.9/4**	**35/42**	**$611...**	**D T**
	M-5	2.0/4	24/31	$999	
	A-S6	2.0/4	22/31	$1,080	

COMPACT CARS

	Trans Type / Speeds	Eng Size / Cylinders	MPG City / Hwy	Annual Fuel Cost	Notes / Abbreviations
ACURA					
TSX	M-6	2.4/4	21/30	$1,220...	P
	A-S5	2.4/4	22/31	$1,170...	P
AUDI					
A4	A V	1.8/4	23/29	$1,170...	P T

	Trans Type / Speeds	Eng Size / Cylinders	MPG City / Hwy	Annual Fuel Cost	Notes / Abbreviations
A4	M-5	1.8/4	22/31	$1,170...	P T
	A V	2.0/4	24/32	$1,082...	P T
	M-6	2.0/4	23/34	$1,082...	P T
	A V	3.0/6	21/29	$1,220...	P
A4 Quattro	M-6	1.8/4	21/30	$1,220...	P T
	A-S5	1.8/4	20/29	$1,272...	P T
	M-6	2.0/4	22/31	$1,170...	P T
	A-S6	2.0/4	22/30	$1,170...	P T
	M-6	3.0/6	18/26	$1,392...	P
	A-S5	3.0/6	18/26	$1,392...	P
	A-S6	3.1/6	19/26	$1,392...	P
S4	M-6	4.2/8	15/21	$1,720...	P Tax
.	A-S6	4.2/8	15/23	$1,626...	P
BENTLEY					
Continental GT	A-S6	6.0/12	..11/18	$2,249...	P T Tax
BMW					
325I	M-5	2.5/6	20/29	$1,220...	P
	A-S5	2.5/6	19/27	$1,331...	P
	A-S6	2.5/6	21/30	$1,220...	P
325XI	M-5	2.5/6	19/27	$1,331...	P
	A-S5	2.5/6	19/26	$1,331...	P
330I	M-6	3.0/6	20/30	$1,272...	P
	A-S5	3.0/6	19/27	$1,331...	P
	A-S6	3.0/6	20/29	$1,272...	P
330XI	M-6	3.0/6	20/29	$1,272...	P
	A-S5	3.0/6	18/25	$1,392...	P
CHEVROLET					
Aveo	A-4	1.6/4	26/34	$932	
	M-5	1.6/4	27/35	$899	
Aveo 5	A-4	1.6/4	26/34	$932	
	M-5	1.6/4	27/35	$899	
Cavalier	A-4	2.2/4	24/34	$964	
	M-5	2.2/4	26/36	$899	
Optra	A-4	2.0/4	22/30	$1,080	
	M-5	2.0/4	22/30	$1,080	
Optra 5	A-4	2.0/4	22/30	$1,080	
	M-5	2.0/4	22/30	$1,080	
CHRYSLER					
Sebring	A-4	2.4/4	21/28	$1,126	
	M-5	2.4/4	24/32	$999	

	Trans Type / Speeds	Eng Size / Cylinders	MPG City / Hwy	Annual Fuel Cost	Notes / Abbreviations
Sebring	A-4	3.0/6	20/28	$1,272...	P
	M-5	3.0/6	21/29	$1,220...	P
	A-S4	3.0/6	20/28	$1,272...	P
Sebring Conv	A-4	2.4/4	22/30	$1,080	
Sebring Conv FFV	A-4	2.7/6	15/20	$1,455...	E85
	A-4	2.7/6	21/28	$1,174...	Gas
Sebring Conv FFV (2-Mode)	A-4	2.7/6	15/20	$1,455...	E85
	A-4	2.7/6	21/28	$1,174...	Gas
DODGE					
Neon/SRT-4/SX 2.0	A-4	2.0/4	25/32	$964	
	M-5	2.0/4	29/36	$842	
	M-5	2.4/4	22/30	$1,170...	P T
Stratus	A-4	2.4/4	21/28	$1,126	
	M-5	2.4/4	24/32	$999	
	A-4	3.0/6	20/28	$1,272...	P
	M-5	3.0/6	21/29	$1,220...	P
	A-S4	3.0/6	20/28	$1,272...	P
FORD					
Focus FWD	A-4	2.0/4	26/32	$964	
	M-5	2.0/4	26/35	$932	
	M-5	2.3/4	22/31	$1,080	
HONDA					
Civic	A V	1.7/4	30/34	$491...	CNG
	A V	1.7/4	35/40	$729...	LB
	A-4	1.7/4	29/38	$818	
	A-4	1.7/4	31/38	$794...	VTEC
	M-5	1.7/4	32/38	$794	
	M-5	1.7/4	36/44	$691...	LB
	M-5	1.7/4	32/37	$794...	VTEC
	M-5	2.0/4	26/31	$964	
Civic Hybrid	A V	1.3/4	47/48	$575...	HEV
	A V	**1.3/4**	**48/47**	**$562...**	**HEV LB**
	M-5	**1.3/4**	**46/51**	**$562...**	**HEV LB**
	M-5	1.3/4	45/51	$575...	HEV
HYUNDAI					
Accent/Brio	A-4	1.5/4	27/35	$899	
	M-5	1.5/4	28/36	$872	
	A-4	1.6/4	26/35	$899	
	M-5	1.6/4	29/33	$872	

	Trans Type / Speeds	Eng Size / Cylinders	MPG City / Hwy	Annual Fuel Cost	Notes / Abbreviations
INFINITI					
G35	M-6	3.5/6	19/26	$1,331...	P
	A-S5	3.5/6	18/25	$1,285	
	A-S5	3.5/6	17/24	$1,350	
	A-S5	3.5/6	18/25	$1,392...	P
JAGUAR					
X-Type	A-5	2.5/6	18/26	$1,392...	P
	M-5	2.5/6	19/28	$1,331...	P
	A-5	3.0/6	18/25	$1,462...	P
	M-5	3.0/6	18/28	$1,331...	P
KIA					
Rio	A-4	1.6/4	24/31	$999	
	M-5	1.6/4	25/31	$964	
LEXUS					
IS 300	M-5	3.0/6	18/25	$1,462...	P
	A-S5	3.0/6	18/24	$1,462...	P
MAZDA					
3	M-5	2.0/4	28/35	$899	
3	A-S4	2.0/4	26/34	$932	
	M-5	2.3/4	25/32	$964	
	A-S4	2.3/4	24/29	$1,040	
MERCEDES-BENZ					
C230 Kompressor	A-5	1.8/4	24/32	$1,082...	P S
	M-6	1.8/4	23/32	$1,126...	P S
C230 Kompressor Sports Coupe	A-5	1.8/4	23/32	$1,126...	P S
	M-6	1.8/4	23/31	$1,126...	P S
C240 4MATIC	A-5	2.6/6	19/25	$1,392...	P
C240 FFV	A-5	2.6/6	14/19	$1,547...	E85
	A-5	2.6/6	20/25	$1,331...	P
C320	M-6	3.2/6	19/26	$1,392...	P
C320 4MATIC	A-5	3.2/6	19/26	$1,331...	P
C320 FFV	A-5	3.2/6	14/19	$1,547...	E85
	A-5	3.2/6	20/26	$1,331...	P
C320 Sports Coupe	M-6	3.2/6	17/24	$1,462...	P
C320 Sports Coupe FFV	A-5	3.2/6	14/18	$1,651...	E85
	A-5	3.2/6	19/24	$1,392...	P
C55 AMG	A-S5	5.4/8	16/22	$1,626...	P Tax
CL500	A-7	5.0/8	16/24	$1,539...	P Tax
CL55 AMG	A-S5	5.4/8	14/22	$1,720...	P S Tax
CL600	A-5	5.5/12	.. 13/19	$1,951...	P T Tax
CL65 AMG	A-S5	6.0/12	.. 12/19	$1,951...	P T Tax

	Trans Type / Speeds	Eng Size / Cylinders	MPG City / Hwy	Annual Fuel Cost	Notes / Abbreviations
MITSUBISHI					
Lancer	A-4	2.0/4	25/31	$999	
	M-5	2.0/4	27/34	$899	
	A-4	2.4/4	22/28	$1,080	
	M-5	2.4/4	23/29	$1,040	
Lancer Evolution	M-5	2.0/4	19/26	$1,392...	P T
	M-6	2.0/4	19/26	$1,392...	P T
NISSAN					
Sentra	A-4	1.8/4	28/34	$899	
	M-5	1.8/4	28/35	$872	
	A-4	2.5/4	23/28	$1,080	
	M-6	2.5/4	23/29	$1,040	
PONTIAC					
G6	A-4	3.5/6	22/32	$1,040	
	A-S4	3.5/6	21/29	$1,126	
Grand Am	A-4	2.2/4	25/34	$964	
	A-4	3.4/6	20/29	$1,174	
GTO	M-6	6.0/8	17/25	$1,539...	P
	A-4	6.0/8	16/21	$1,626...	P Tax
Sunfire	A-4	2.2/4	24/34	$964	
	M-5	2.2/4	26/36	$899	
Wave	A-4	1.6/4	26/34	$932	
	M-5	1.6/4	27/35	$899	
Wave 5	A-4	1.6/4	26/34	$932	
	M-5	1.6/4	27/35	$899	
SAAB					
9-3 Sport Sedan	M-5	2.0/4	22/32	$1,170...	P T
	M-5	2.0/4	22/30	$1,080...	T
	A-S5	2.0/4	21/28	$1,220...	P T
	A-S5	2.0/4	21/31	$1,080...	T
SATURN					
Ion	M-5	2.0/4	23/29	$1,170...	P S
	A-4	2.2/4	24/32	$999	
	M-5	2.2/4	26/35	$899	
SUBARU					
Legacy AWD	M-5	2.5/4	19/25	$1,392...	P T
	M-5	2.5/4	23/30	$1,080	
	A-S4	2.5/4	22/30	$1,080	
	A-S5	2.5/4	19/25	$1,392...	P T

	Trans Type / Speeds	Eng Size / Cylinders	MPG City / Hwy	Annual Fuel Cost	Notes / Abbreviations
SUZUKI					
Aerio	A-4	2.3/4	25/31	$999	
	M-5	2.3/4	25/31	$999	
Aerio AWD	A-4	2.3/4	24/29	$1,040	
Forenza	A-4	2.0/4	22/30	$1,080	
	M-5	2.0/4	22/30	$1,080	
Reno	A-4	2.0/4	22/30	$1,080	
	M-5	2.0/4	22/30	$1,080	
Swift	A-4	1.6/4	26/34	$932	
	M-5	1.6/4	27/35	$899	
Swift +	A-4	1.6/4	26/34	$932	
	M-5	1.6/4	27/35	$899	
TOYOTA					
Camry Solara	A-4	2.4/4	23/32	$1,040	
	M-5	2.4/4	24/33	$999	
	A-S5	3.3/6	21/29	$1,126	
Camry Solara Conv	A-S5	3.3/6	20/29	$1,174	
Corolla	A-4	1.8/4	30/38	$818	
	M-5	1.8/4	32/41	$751	
	M-6	1.8/4	26/34	$1,009...	P
Echo	A-4	1.5/4	33/39	$751	
	M-5	1.5/4	35/42	$710	
VOLKSWAGEN					
Golf	M-5	1.9/4	38/46	$567...	D T
	A-S5	1.9/4	32/43	$646...	D T
	A-4	2.0/4	24/30	$1,040	
	M-5	2.0/4	24/31	$999	
GTI	M-5	1.8/4	24/31	$1,082...	P T
	A-S5	1.8/4	22/29	$1,170...	P T
	M-6	2.8/6	22/29	$1,220...	P
Jetta	M-5	1.8/4	24/31	$1,082...	P T
	M-6	1.8/4	21/29	$1,220...	P T
	A-S5	1.8/4	22/29	$1,170...	P T
	M-5	1.9/4	38/46	$567...	D T
	A-S5	1.9/4	32/43	$646...	D T
	A-S6	1.9/4	35/42	$611...	D T
	A-4	2.0/4	24/30	$1,040	
	M-5	2.0/4	24/31	$999	
	M-5	2.5/5	22/30	$1,080	
	A-S6	2.5/5	22/30	$1,080	
Passat 4MOTION	M-5	1.8/4	21/30	$1,170...	P T
	A-S5	1.8/4	20/29	$1,272...	P T

	Trans Type / Speeds	Eng Size / Cylinders	MPG City / Hwy	Annual Fuel Cost	Notes / Abbreviations
Passat 4MOTION	A-S5	2.8/6	19/26	$1,392...	P

VOLVO

S40 AWD	M-6	2.5/5	19/27	$1,331...	P T
	A-S5	2.5/5	20/27	$1,272...	P T
S40 FWD	M-5	2.4/5	22/29	$1,220...	P
	A-S5	2.4/5	22/30	$1,170...	P
	M-6	2.5/5	22/31	$1,170...	P T
	A-S5	2.5/5	21/30	$1,220...	P T
S60 AWD	A-S5	2.5/5	19/26	$1,331...	P T
S60 FWD	A-5	2.4/5	21/29	$1,220...	P
	M-5	2.4/5	22/29	$1,220...	P
	M-6	2.4/5	21/28	$1,272...	P T
	A-S5	2.4/5	21/29	$1,220...	P T
	A-5	2.5/5	21/30	$1,220...	P T
S60 R AWD	M-6	2.5/5	18/24	$1,392...	P T
	A-S5	2.5/5	18/24	$1,462...	P T

MIDSIZE CARS

ACURA

RL	A-S5	3.5/6	18/26	$1,392...	P
TL	M-6	3.2/6	20/29	$1,272...	P
	A-S5	3.2/6	20/29	$1,272...	P

AUDI

A6 Quattro	A-S6	3.1/6	19/26	$1,392...	P
A8	A-S6	4.2/8	18/24	$1,462...	P

BENTLEY

Arnage	A-4	6.8/8	10/14	$2,437...	P T Tax

BMW

525I	M-6	2.5/6	19/28	$1,331...	P
	A-S6	2.5/6	19/28	$1,331...	P
530I	M-6	3.0/6	20/30	$1,272...	P
530I (4-Mode)	A-S6	3.0/6	20/29	$1,272...	P
530I (3-Mode)	A-S6	3.0/6	19/29	$1,272...	P
545I	M-6	4.4/8	17/25	$1,462...	P
545I (3-Mode)	A-S6	4.4/8	18/26	$1,392...	P
545I (4-Mode)	A-S6	4.4/8	16/24	$1,539...	P

BUICK

Century	A-4	3.1/6	20/30	$1,126	
LaCrosse/Allure	A-4	3.6/6	19/27	$1,228	
	A-4	3.8/6	20/29	$1,174	

	Trans Type / Speeds	Eng Size / Cylinders	MPG City / Hwy	Annual Fuel Cost	Notes / Abbreviations
CADILLAC					
CTS	M-6	2.8/6	17/27	$1,285	
	A-5	2.8/6	18/27	$1,285	
CTS	A-5	3.6/6	18/27	$1,285	
	M-6	3.6/6	17/27	$1,350	
	M-6	5.7/8	15/23	$1,626...	P Tax
STS	A-S5	3.6/6	17/24	$1,350	
	A-S5	4.6/8	17/26	$1,462...	P
STS AWD	A-S5	4.6/8	16/22	$1,626...	P Tax
CHEVROLET					
Classic	A-4	2.2/4	25/34	$964	
Epica	A-4	2.5/6	20/28	$1,174	
Malibu	A-4	2.2/4	24/35	$964	
	A-4	3.5/6	22/32	$1,040	
Monte Carlo	A-4	3.4/6	21/32	$1,080	
	A-4	3.8/6	19/28	$1,331...	P S
	A-4	3.8/6	20/30	$1,126	
CHRYSLER					
Sebring 4-dr	A-4	2.4/4	22/30	$1,080	
Sebring 4-dr FFV	A-4	2.7/6	15/20	$1,455...	E85
	A-4	2.7/6	21/28	$1,174...	Gas
Sebring 4-dr FFV (2-Mode)	A-4	2.7/6	15/20	$1,455...	E85
	A-4	2.7/6	21/28	$1,174...	Gas
DODGE					
Stratus 4-dr	A-4	2.4/4	22/30	$1,080	
Stratus 4-dr FFV	A-4	2.7/6	15/20	$1,455...	E85
	A-4	2.7/6	21/28	$1,174...	Gas
Stratus 4-dr FFV (2-Mode)	A-4	2.7/6	15/20	$1,455...	E85
	A-4	2.7/6	21/28	$1,174...	Gas
FERRARI					
612 Scaglietti	M-6	5.7/12	..11/17	$2,249...	P Tax
	A-S6	5.7/12	..10/17	$2,437...	P Tax
HONDA					
Accord	A-5	2.4/4	24/34	$999	
	M-5	2.4/4	26/34	$932	
	A-5	3.0/6	21/30	$1,126	
	M-6	3.0/6	20/30	$1,126	
Accord Hybrid	A-5	3.0/6	29/37	$842...	HEV
HYUNDAI					
Elantra	A-4	2.0/4	24/32	$999	
	M-5	2.0/4	27/34	$899	

	Trans Type / Speeds	Eng Size / Cylinders	MPG City / Hwy	Annual Fuel Cost	Notes / Abbreviations
Sonata	A-4	2.4/4	22/30	$1,080	
	M-5	2.4/4	22/30	$1,080	
	A-4	2.7/6	19/27	$1,228	
	M-5	2.7/6	20/27	$1,174	
XG350	A-5	3.5/6	18/26	$1,285	
INFINITI					
Q45	A-S5	4.5/8	17/23	$1,462...	P
JAGUAR					
S-Type 3.0 Litre	A-6	3.0/6	18/26	$1,392...	P
	M-5	3.0/6	18/26	$1,392...	P
S-Type 4.2 Litre	A-6	4.2/8	18/28	$1,331...	P
S-Type R	A-6	4.2/8	17/24	$1,462...	P S
X-Type Sport Brake	A-5	2.5/6	19/26	$1,331...	P
	M-5	2.5/6	19/27	$1,331...	P
	A-5	3.0/6	18/24	$1,462...	P
	M-5	3.0/6	18/27	$1,392...	P
KIA					
Optima	A-4	2.4/4	22/30	$1,080	
	M-5	2.4/4	23/30	$1,080	
	A-4	2.7/6	20/27	$1,174	
	M-5	2.7/6	20/28	$1,174	
Spectra	A-4	2.0/4	24/34	$964	
	M-5	2.0/4	25/33	$964	
LEXUS					
ES 330	A-5	3.3/6	21/29	$1,126	
GS 300/GS 430	A-S5	3.0/6	18/25	$1,392...	P
	A-5	4.3/8	18/23	$1,462...	P
LINCOLN					
LS	A-5	3.0/6	20/26	$1,331.	P
	A-S5	3.0/6	20/26	$1,331.	P
	A-5	3.9/8	18/24	$1,462	P
	A-S5	3.9/8	17/24	$1,462	P
MERCURY					
Sable (2-Valve)	A-4	3.0/6	20/27	$1,174	
Sable (4-Valve)	A-4	3.0/6	20/27	$1,174	
Sable FFV	A-4	3.0/6	15/20	$1,455...	E85
	A-4	3.0/6	19/27	$1,228...	Gas
MAZDA					
6	M-5	2.3/4	23/31	$1,040	

	Trans Type / Speeds	Eng Size / Cylinders	MPG City / Hwy	Annual Fuel Cost	Notes / Abbreviations
6	A-S4	2.3/4	23/28	$1,080	
	M-5	3.0/6	19/26	$1,228	
	A-S6	3.0/6	20/27	$1,228	
MERCEDES-BENZ					
E320	A-5	3.2/6	20/28	$1,272	P
E320 4MATIC	A-5	3.2/6	19/25	$1,392	P
E320 CDI	A-5	3.2/6	27/37	$774.	D T
E500	A-7	5.0/8	17/25	$1,462	P
E500 4MATIC	A-5	5.0/8	16/20	$1,626.	P Tax
E55 AMG	A-S5	5.4/8	14/21	$1,720... P S Tax	
MITSUBISHI					
Diamante Sedan	A-4	3.5/6	17/25	$1,462... P	
Galant	A-4	2.4/4	23/30	$1,080	
	A-S4	3.8/6	19/27	$1,392... P	
NISSAN					
Altima	A-4	2.5/4	23/29	$1,040	
	M-5	2.5/4	24/31	$999	
	M-5	3.5/6	21/27	$1,126	
	M-6	3.5/6	20/28	$1,174	
	A-S5	3.5/6	20/30	$1,126	
Maxima	M-6	3.5/6	20/29	$1,126	
	A-S5	3.5/6	20/28	$1,174	
PONTIAC					
Grand Prix	A-4	3.8/6	19/28	$1,331... P S	
	A-4	3.8/6	20/30	$1,174	
	A-S4	3.8/6	18/27	$1,392... P S	
	A-S4	5.3/8	18/27	$1,285	
ROLLS-ROYCE					
Phantom	A-S6	6.7/12	..12/19	$1,951... P Tax	
SAAB					
9-5	M-5	2.3/4	20/30	$1,272... P T	
	A-S5	2.3/4	19/28	$1,331... P T	
SATURN					
L300	A-4	3.0/6	21/28	$1,174	
SUZUKI					
Verona	A-4	2.5/6	20/28	$1,174	
TOYOTA					
Camry	A-5	2.4/4	24/34	$964	

	Trans Type / Speeds	Eng Size / Cylinders	MPG City / Hwy	Annual Fuel Cost	Notes / Abbreviations
Camry	M-5	2.4/4	24/33	$999	
	A-5	3.0/6	20/28	$1,174	
	A-5	3.3/6	21/29	$1,126	
_Prius	A V	1.5/4	60/51	$491...	HEV
VOLKSWAGEN					
Passat	M-5	1.8/4	22/31	$1,170...	P T
	A-S5	1.8/4	21/30	$1,170...	P T
	A-S5	2.0/4	27/38	$751...	D T
	M-5	2.8/6	20/28	$1,272...	P
	A-S5	2.8/6	19/27	$1,331...	P
VOLVO					
S80 AWD	A-5	2.5/5	19/26	$1,331...	P T
S80 FWD	A-5	2.5/5	21/30	$1,220...	P T
	A-S4	2.9/6	18/26	$1,392...	P T

LARGE CARS

	Trans Type / Speeds	Eng Size / Cylinders	MPG City / Hwy	Annual Fuel Cost	Notes / Abbreviations
AUDI					
A8 L	A-S6	4.2/8	18/24	$1,462...	P
	A-S6	6.0/12	.. 15/21	$1,720...	P Tax
BENTLEY					
Arnage LWB	A-4	6.8/8	10/14	$2,437...	P T Tax
BMW					
745I	A-S6	4.4/8	18/26	$1,392...	P
745LI	A-S6	4.4/8	18/26	$1,392...	P
760I	A-S6	6.0/12	.. 15/23	$1,720...	P Tax
760LI	A-S6	6.0/12	.. 15/23	$1,720...	P Tax
BUICK					
LeSabre	A-4	3.8/6	20/29	$1,174	
Park Avenue	A-4	3.8/6	19/28	$1,331...	P S
	A-4	3.8/6	20/29	$1,174	
CADILLAC					
Armored DeVille	A-4	4.6/8	14/20	$1,688...	Tax
DeVille	A-4	4.6/8	17/24	$1,420...	275 HP
	A-4	4.6/8	18/26	$1,285...	300 HP
Funeral Coach/Hearse	A-4	4.6/8	14/20	$1,688...	Tax
Limousine	A-4	4.6/8	15/21	$1,588...	Tax
CHEVROLET					
Impala	A-4	3.4/6	21/32	$1,080	
	A-4	3.8/6	19/28	$1,331...	P S

	Trans Type / Speeds	Eng Size / Cylinders	MPG City / Hwy	Annual Fuel Cost	Notes / Abbreviations
Impala	A-4	3.8/6	20/30	$1,174	
Malibu MAXX	A-4	3.5/6	22/30	$1,080	

CHRYSLER

300C AWD	A-5	3.5/6	17/24	$1,350	
	A-5	5.7/8	17/24	$1,350	
300C/SRT-8	A-4	2.7/6	21/28	$1,126	
	A-4	3.5/6	19/27	$1,228	
	A-5	5.7/8	17/25	$1,350	
	A-5	6.1/8	14/20	$1,828...	P Tax

FORD

Crown Victoria	A-4	4.6/8	18/25	$1,285	
Five Hundred AWD	A V	3.0/6	19/26	$1,285	
Five Hundred FWD	A V	3.0/6	20/27	$1,174	
	A-6	3.0/6	21/29	$1,126	
Taurus (2-Valve)	A-4	3.0/6	20/27	$1,174	
Taurus (4-Valve)	A-4	3.0/6	20/27	$1,174	
Taurus FFV	A-4	3.0/6	15/20	$1,455...	E85
	A-4	3.0/6	19/27	$1,228...	Gas

JAGUAR

Super V8	A-6	4.2/8	17/24	$1,462...	P S
VDP LWB	A-6	4.2/8	18/27	$1,392...	P
XJ8 4.2 Litre	A-6	4.2/8	18/28	$1,331...	P
XJ8L	A-6	4.2/8	18/28	$1,331...	P
XJR 4.2 Litre	A-6	4.2/8	17/24	$1,462...	P S

KIA

Amanti	A-5	3.5/6	17/25	$1,350	

LEXUS

LS 430	A-S6	4.3/8	18/25	$1,462...	P

LINCOLN

Town Car	A-4	4.6/8	18/25	$1,285	

MASERATI

Quattroporte	A-6	4.2/8	12/15	$2,088...	P Tax

MAYBACH

57	A-5	5.5/12..	12/17	$2,088...	P T
62	A-5	5.5/12..	12/17	$2,088...	P T

MERCEDES-BENZ

S430	A-7	4.3/8	17/26	$1,392...	P
S430 4MATIC	A-5	4.3/8	17/22	$1,539...	P Tax
S500	A-7	5.0/8	16/24	$1,539...	P Tax
S500 4MATIC	A-5	5.0/8	16/22	$1,626...	P Tax
S55 AMG	A-S5	5.4/8	14/22	$1,720...	P S Tax

	Trans Type / Speeds	Eng Size / Cylinders	MPG City / Hwy	Annual Fuel Cost	Notes / Abbreviations
S600	A-5	5.5/12..	12/19	$1,951...	P T Tax

MERCURY

Grand Marquis	A-4	4.6/8	18/25	$1,285	
Montego AWD	A V	3.0/6	19/26	$1,285	
Montego FWD	A V	3.0/6	20/27	$1,174	
	A-6	3.0/6	21/29	$1,126	

PONTIAC

| Bonneville | A-4 | 3.8/6 | 20/29 | $1,174 | |
| | A-4 | 4.6/8 | 17/24 | $1,285 | |

TOYOTA

| **Avalon** | **A-S5** | **3.5/6** | **22/31** | **$1,080** | |

VOLKSWAGEN

| Phaeton | A-S6 | 4.2/8 | 16/22 | $1,626... | P Tax |
| | A-S5 | 6.0/12.. | 12/19 | $2,088... | P Tax |

SMALL STATION WAGONS

AUDI

A4 Avant Quattro	M-6	1.8/4	21/30	$1,170...	P T
	A-S5	1.8/4	20/29	$1,272...	P T
	M-6	2.0/4	22/31	$1,170...	P T
	A-S6	2.0/4	22/30	$1,170...	P T
	M-6	3.0/6	18/26	$1,392...	P
	A-S5	3.0/6	18/26	$1,392...	P
	A-S6	3.1/6	19/26	$1,392...	P
S4 Avant	M-6	4.2/8	15/21	$1,720...	P Tax
	A-S6	4.2/8	15/23	$1,626...	P

BMW

325I Sport Wagon	M-5	2.5/6	20/29	$1,220...	P
	A-S5	2.5/6	19/27	$1,331...	P
325XI Sport Wagon	M-5	2.5/6	19/26	$1,331...	P
	A-S5	2.5/6	19/26	$1,331...	P

CHEVROLET

| Optra Wagon | A-4 | 2.0/4 | 20/28 | $1,174 | |
| | M-5 | 2.0/4 | 20/30 | $1,126 | |

MERCEDES-BENZ

C240 4MATIC Wagon	A-5	2.6/6	19/24	$1,392...	P
C240 Wagon FFV	A-5	2.6/6	14/19	$1,547...	E85
	A-5	2.6/6	20/25	$1,331...	P

	Trans Type / Speeds	Eng Size / Cylinders	MPG City / Hwy	Annual Fuel Cost	Notes / Abbreviations
MITSUBISHI Lancer Sportback	A-4	2.4/4	22/29	$1,080	
PONTIAC Vibe	A-4	1.8/4	29/34	$872	
	M-5	1.8/4	30/36	$818	
	M-6	1.8/4	25/32	$1,044...	P
Vibe AWD	A-4	1.8/4	26/31	$964	
SAAB 9-2X Wagon AWD	A-4	2.0/4	19/25	$1,392...	P T
	M-5	2.0/4	20/26	$1,331...	P T
	A-4	2.5/4	23/29	$1,080	
	M-5	2.5/4	22/29	$1,080	
SCION xB	A-4	1.5/4	31/35	$818	
	M-5	1.5/4	31/34	$842	
SUBARU Impreza Wagon/Outback SPT AWD	.. A-4	2.0/4	19/26	$1,331...	P T
	M-5	2.0/4	20/27	$1,331...	P T
	A-4	2.5/4	22/28	$1,080	
	M-5	2.5/4	23/30	$1,080	
SUZUKI Aerio SX	A-4	2.3/4	25/30	$999	
	M-5	2.3/4	25/31	$999	
Aerio SX AWD	A-4	2.3/4	24/29	$1,040	
Forenza Wagon	A-4	2.0/4	20/28	$1,174	
	M-5	2.0/4	20/30	$1,126	
TOYOTA Matrix	A-4	1.8/4	28/34	$872	
	M-5	1.8/4	30/36	$818	
	M-6	1.8/4	25/32	$1,044...	P
Matrix 4WD	A-4	1.8/4	26/31	$964	
VOLKSWAGEN Jetta Wagon	M-5	1.8/4	24/31	$1,082...	P T
	A-S5	1.8/4	22/29	$1,170...	P T
	M-5	1.9/4	36/43	$595...	D T
—	A-S5	1.9/4	32/43	$646...	D T

	Trans Type / Speeds	Eng Size / Cylinders	MPG City / Hwy	Annual Fuel Cost	Notes / Abbreviations
	A-4	2.0/4	23/29	$1,080	
	M-5	2.0/4	24/30	$1,040	

VOLVO

V50 AWD	M-6	2.5/5	19/27	$1,331...	P T
	A-S5	2.5/5	19/26	$1,331...	P T
V50 FWD	M-5	2.4/5	22/29	$1,220...	P
	A-S5	2.4/5	22/30	$1,170...	P
	M-6	2.5/5	·22/31	$1,170...	P T
	A-S5	2.5/5	21/30	$1,220...	P T

MIDSIZE STATION WAGONS

FORD

Focus Station Wagon	A-4	2.0/4	26/32	$964	
	M-5	**2.0/4**	**26/35**	**$932**	
Taurus Wagon (2-Valve)	A-4	3.0/6	19/25	$1,285	
Taurus Wagon (4-Valve)	A-4	3.0/6	19/27	$1,228	
Taurus Wagon FFV	A-4	3.0/6	14/19	$1,547...	E85
	A-4	3.0/6	19/26	$1,285...	Gas

MERCURY

Sable Wagon (2-Valve)	A-4	3.0/6	19/25	$1,285	
Sable Wagon (4-Valve)	A-4	3.0/6	19/27	$1,228	
Sable Wagon FFV	A-4	3.0/6	14/19	$1,547...	E85
	A-4	3.0/6	19/26	$1,285...	Gas

MAZDA

6 Sport Wagon	M-5	3.0/6	19/26	$1,228	
	A-S6	3.0/6	20/27	$1,228	

MERCEDES-BENZ

E320 Wagon	A-5	3.2/6	20/28	$1,272...	P
E320 4MATIC Wagon	A-5	3.2/6	18/24	$1,392...	P
E500 4MATIC Wagon	A-5	5.0/8	16/20	$1,720...	P Tax
E55 AMG Wagon	A-S5	5.4/8	14/21	$1,720...	P S Tax

SAAB

9-5 Wagon	M-5	2.3/4	20/30	$1,272...	P T
	A-S5	2.3/4	19/28	$1,331...	P T

SATURN

LW300	A-4	3.0/6	21/28	$1,174	

SUBARU

Legacy Wagon AWD	M-5	2.5/4	19/25	$1,392...	P T '
	M-5	2.5/4	23/30	$1,080	
	A-S4	2.5/4	22/30	$1,080	

	Trans Type / Speeds	Eng Size / Cylinders	MPG City / Hwy	Annual Fuel Cost	Notes / Abbreviations
Legacy Wagon AWD	A-S5	2.5/4	19/25	$1,392...	P T
VOLKSWAGEN					
Passat Wagon	M-5	1.8/4	22/31	$1,170...	P T
	A-S5	1.8/4	21/30	$1,170...	P T
	A-S5	**2.0/4**	**27/38**	**$751...**	**D T**
—	M-5	2.8/6	20/28	$1,272...	P
	A-S5	2.8/6	19/27	$1,331...	P
Passat Wagon 4MOTION	M-5	1.8/4	21/30	$1,170...	P T
	A-S5	1.8/4	20/29	$1,272...	P T
.	A-S5	2.8/6	19/26	$1,392...	P
VOLVO					
V70 AWD	A-S5	2.5/5	19/26	$1,331...	P T
V70 FWD	A-5	2.4/5	21/28	$1,220...	P
	M-5	2.4/5	22/29	$1,220...	P
	M-6	2.4/5	20/26	$1,331...	P T
	A-S5	2.4/5	19/26	$1,331...	P T
	A-S5	2.5/5	21/30	$1,220...	P T
V70 R AWD	M-6	2.5/5	18/24	$1,392...	P T
	A-S5	2.5/5	18/24	$1,462...	P T

STANDARD PICKUP TRUCKS 2WD

	Trans Type / Speeds	Eng Size / Cylinders	MPG City / Hwy	Annual Fuel Cost	Notes / Abbreviations
CHEVROLET					
C15 Silverado Hybrid 2WD	A-4	5.3/8	18/21	$1,420...	HEV
C1500 Silverado 2WD	A-4	4.3/6	16/21	$1,501	
	M-5	4.3/6	16/22	$1,501	
	A-4	4.8/8	16/21	$1,501	
	M-5	4.8/8	16/21	$1,501	
	A-4	5.3/8	16/20	$1,501	
	A-4	6.0/8	14/19	$1,828...	P
C1500 Silverado 2WD FFV	A-4	5.3/8	12/16	$1,767...	E85
	A-4	5.3/8	16/20	$1,501...	Gas
C2500 HD Silverado 2WD	A-4	6.0/8	9/12	$1,575...	CNG
	A-4	6.0/8	11/13	$2,249...	
Colorado 2WD	A-4	2.8/4	18/25	$1,350	
	M-5	2.8/4	21/27	$1,174	
	A-4	3.5/5	18/23	$1,350	
	M-5	3.5/5	19/25	$1,285	
Colorado Crew 2WD	A-4	2.8/4	18/25	$1,350	
	M-5	2.8/4	21/26	$1,174	
	A-4	3.5/5	18/23	$1,350	
SSR Pickup 2WD	A-4	6.0/8	15/19	$1,720...	P

	Trans Type / Speeds	Eng Size / Cylinders	MPG City / Hwy	Annual Fuel Cost	Notes / Abbreviations
SSR Pickup 2WD	M-6	6.0/8	13/20	$1,828...	P
DODGE					
Dakota Pickup 2WD	A-4	3.7/6	16/22	$1,501	
	M-6	3.7/6	16/22	$1,420	
	A-5	4.7/8	15/20	$1,588	
	M-6	4.7/8	15/20	$1,588	
Ram 1500 Pickup 2WD	A-4	3.7/6	16/21	$1,501	
	M-6	3.7/6	16/21	$1,420	
	A-5	4.7/8	14/19	$1,688	
	M-6	4.7/8	14/19	$1,688	
	A-5	5.7/8	14/18	$1,688	
	A-4	8.3/10..	9/12	$2,925...	P
	M-6	8.3/10..	9/15	$2,659...	P
Ram 1500 Pickup 2WD FFV	A-5	4.7/8	9/11	$2,475...	E85
	A-5	4.7/8	12/15	$2,076...	Gas
FORD					
Explorer Sport Trac 2WD FFV	A-5	4.0/6	11/15	$1,903...	E85
	A-5	4.0/6	15/20	$1,588...	Gas
F150 Pickup 2WD	A-4	4.2/6	15/20	$1,588	
	M-5	4.2/6	15/20	$1,588	
	A-4	4.6/8	15/19	$1,688	
	A-4	5.4/8	14/19	$1,688	
Ranger Pickup 2WD	**A-5**	**2.3/4**	**22/26**	**$1,126**	
—	**M-5**	**2.3/4**	**24/29**	**$1,040**	
	A-5	3.0/6	18/22	$1,350	
	M-5	3.0/6	18/23	$1,350	
	A-5	4.0/6	17/22	$1,420	
	M-5	4.0/6	18/23	$1,350	
GMC					
C15 Sierra Hybrid 2WD	A-4	5.3/8	18/21	$1,420...	HEV
C1500 Sierra 2WD	A-4	4.3/6	16/21	$1,501	
	M-5	4.3/6	16/22	$1,501	
	A-4	4.8/8	16/21	$1,501	
	M-5	4.8/8	16/21	$1,501	
	A-4	5.3/8	16/20	$1,501	
	A-4	6.0/8	14/19	$1,828...	P
C1500 Sierra 2WD FFV	A-4	5.3/8	12/16	$1,767...	E85
	A-4	5.3/8	16/20	$1,501...	Gas
C2500 HD Sierra 2WD	A-4	6.0/8	9/12	$1,575...	CNG

	Trans Type / Speeds	Eng Size / Cylinders	MPG City / Hwy	Annual Fuel Cost	Notes / Abbreviations
	A-4	6.0/8	11/13	$2,249	
Canyon 2WD	A-4	2.8/4	18/25	$1,350	
	M-5	2.8/4	21/27	$1,174	
	A-4	3.5/5	18/23	$1,350	
	M-5	3.5/5	19/25	$1,285	
Canyon Crew 2WD	A-4	2.8/4	18/25	$1,350	
	M-5	2.8/4	21/26	$1,174	
	A-4	3.5/5	18/23	$1,350	

MAZDA

B2300 2WD	**A-5**	**2.3/4**	**22/26**	**$1,126**	
	M-5	**2.3/4**	**24/29**	**$1,040**	
— B3000	A-5	3.0/6	18/22	$1,350	
	M-5	3.0/6	18/23	$1,350	
B4000 2WD	A-5	4.0/6	17/22	$1,420	
	M-5	4.0/6	18/23	$1,350	

NISSAN

Frontier 2WD	A-5	2.5/4	19/24	$1,285	
	M-5	2.5/4	22/25	$1,174	
Frontier V6-2WD	A-5	4.0/6	16/20	$1,501	
	M-6	4.0/6	17/21	$1,420	
Titan 2WD	A-5	5.6/8	14/19	$1,688	
Titan 2WD FFV	A-5	5.6/8	10/14	$2,062...	E85
	A-5	5.6/8	14/19	$1,688...	Gas

TOYOTA

Tacoma 2WD	A-4	2.7/4	21/26	$1,174	
	M-5	2.7/4	20/27	$1,174	
	A-5	4.0/6	18/22	$1,350	
	M-6	4.0/6	16/21	$1,501	
Tundra 2WD	A-5	4.0/6	18/22	$1,350	
	M-6	4.0/6	16/20	$1,588	
	A-5	4.7/8	16/18	$1,588	

STANDARD PICKUP TRUCKS 4WD

CHEVROLET

Colorado 4WD	A-4	2.8/4	17/23	$1,420	
	M-5	2.8/4	19/23	$1,285	
	A-4	3.5/5	18/22	$1,350	
	M-5	3.5/5	19/24	$1,285	
Colorado Crew 4WD	A-4	2.8/4	17/23	$1,420	
	M-5	2.8/4	19/23	$1,285	

	Trans Type / Speeds	Eng Size / Cylinders	MPG City / Hwy	Annual Fuel Cost	Notes / Abbreviations
K15 Silverado Hybrid 4WD	A-4	3.5/5	17/22	$1,420	
K1500 Silverado 4WD	A-4	5.3/8	17/19	$1,501...	HEV
	A-4	4.3/6	14/18	$1,688	
	M-5	4.3/6	15/20	$1,588	
	A-4	4.8/8	16/19	$1,588	
	M-5	4.8/8	15/19	$1,688	
	A-4	5.3/8	15/19	$1,688	
K1500 Silverado 4WD FFV	A-4	5.3/8	11/14	$2,062...	E85
	A-4	5.3/8	15/18	$1,688...	Gas
K1500 Silverado AWD	A-4	6.0/8	14/16	$1,801	
K2500 HD Silverado 4WD	A-4	6.0/8	9/12	$1,575...	CNG
DODGE					
Dakota Pickup 4WD	A-4	3.7/6	15/19	$1,588	
	M-6	3.7/6	16/20	$1,501	
	A-5	4.7/8	15/20	$1,588	
	M-6	4.7/8	15/19	$1,588	
Ram 1500 Pickup 4WD	A-5	4.7/8	14/18	$1,801	
	A-5	5.7/8	13/17	$1,801	
Ram 1500 Pickup 4WD FFV	A-5	4.7/8	9/11	$2,475...	E85
	A-5	4.7/8	12/15	$2,076...	Gas
FORD					
Explorer Sport Trac 4WD FFV	A-5	4.0/6	11/15	$2,062...	E85
	A-5	4.0/6	14/20	$1,688...	Gas
F150 Pickup 4WD	A-4	4.6/8	14/18	$1,801	
	A-4	5.4/8	14/18	$1,688	
Ranger Pickup 4WD	A-5	3.0/6	16/20	$1,501	
	M-5	3.0/6	17/21	$1,501	
	A-5	4.0/6	16/20	$1,588	
	M-5	4.0/6	16/19	$1,588	
GMC					
Canyon 4WD	A-4	2.8/4	17/23	$1,420	
	M-5	2.8/4	19/23	$1,285	
	A-4	3.5/5	18/22	$1,350	
	M-5	3.5/5	19/24	$1,285	
Canyon Crew 4WD	A-4	2.8/4	17/23	$1,420	
	M-5	2.8/4	19/23	$1,285	
	A-4	3.5/5	17/22	$1,420	
K15 Sierra Hybrid 4WD	A-4	5.3/8	17/19	$1,501...	HEV
K1500 Sierra 4WD	A-4	4.3/6	15/18	$1,688	
	M-5	4.3/6	15/20	$1,588	
	A-4	4.8/8	16/19	$1,588	

	Trans Type / Speeds	Eng Size / Cylinders	MPG City / Hwy	Annual Fuel Cost	Notes / Abbreviations
	M-5	4.8/8	15/19	$1,688	
	A-4	5.3/8	15/19	$1,688	
K1500 Sierra AWD	A-4	6.0/8	14/16	$1,801	
K1500 Sierra 4WD FFV	A-4	5.3/8	11/14	$2,062...	E85
	A-4	5.3/8	15/18	$1,688...	Gas
K2500 HD Sierra 4WD	A-4	6.0/8	9/12	$1,575...	CNG

MAZDA

B4000 4WD	A-5	4.0/6	16/20	$1,588	
	M-5	4.0/6	16/19	$1,588	

NISSAN

Frontier V6-4WD	A-5	4.0/6	15/20	$1,588	
	M-6	4.0/6	17/21	$1,501	
Titan 4WD	A-5	5.6/8	14/18	$1,801	
Titan 4WD FFV	A-5	5.6/8	10/13	$2,250...	E85
	A-5	5.6/8	14/18	$1,801...	Gas

TOYOTA

Tacoma 4WD	M-5	2.7/4	19/23	$1,350	
	A-5	4.0/6	17/21	$1,420	
	M-6	4.0/6	16/20	$1,588	
Tundra 4WD	A-5	4.7/8	15/18	$1,688	

VANS, CARGO TYPE

CHEVROLET

Astro 2WD	**A-4**	**4.3/6**	**16/22**	**$1,420**	
Astro 2WD Convsn	A-4	4.3/6	16/21	$1,501	
Astro AWD	A-4	4.3/6	15/19	$1,588	
Astro AWD Convsn	A-4	4.3/6	14/17	$1,801	
G15/25 Chevy Van 2WD Convsn	A-4	4.3/6	14/18	$1,688	
	A-4	5.3/8	14/18	$1,801	
G1500/2500 Chevy Van 2WD	A-4	4.3/6	16/20	$1,501	
	A-4	5.3/8	15/20	$1,588	
H1500 Chevy Van AWD Convsn	A-4	5.3/8	14/18	$1,688	
H1500/2500 Chevy Van AWD	A-4	5.3/8	14/18	$1,688	

FORD

E150 Econoline 2WD	A-4	4.6/8	15/19	$1,588	
	A-4	5.4/8	14/17	$1,801	
E250 Econoline 2WD	A-4	4.6/8	15/19	$1,688	

GMC

G15/25 Savana 2WD Convsn	A-4	4.3/6	14/18	$1,688	
	A-4	5.3/8	14/18	$1,801	

	Trans Type / Speeds	Eng Size / Cylinders	MPG City / Hwy	Annual Fuel Cost	Notes / Abbreviations
G1500/2500 Savana 2WD	A-4	4.3/6	15/20	$1,588	
	A-4	5.3/8	15/20	$1,588	
H15/25 Savana AWD Convsn	A-4	5.3/8	14/18	$1,688	
H1500/2500 Savana AWD	A-4	5.3/8	14/18	$1,688	
_Safari 2WD	A-4	4.3/6	16/22	$1,420	
Safari 2WD Convsn	A-4	4.3/6	16/21	$1,501	
Safari AWD	A-4	4.3/6	15/19	$1,588	
Safari AWD Convsn	A-4	4.3/6	14/17	$1,801	

VANS, PASSENGER TYPE

CHEVROLET

_Astro 2WD	A-4	4.3/6	16/21	$1,501	
Astro AWD	A-4	4.3/6	14/17	$1,801	
G1500/2500 Chevy Express 2WD	A-4	4.3/6	15/19	$1,588	
	A-4	5.3/8	14/18	$1,801	
H1500 Chevy Express AWD	A-4	5.3/8	14/18	$1,688	

FORD

E150 Club Wagon	A-4	4.6/8	15/19	$1,688	
	A-4	5.4/8	13/17	$1,928	

GMC

G1500/2500 Savana 2WD	A-4	4.3/6	15/19	$1,588	
	A-4	5.3/8	14/18	$1,801	
H1500 Savana Van AWD	A-4	5.3/8	14/18	$1,688	
_Safari 2WD	A-4	4.3/6	16/21	$1,501	
Safari AWD	A-4	4.3/6	14/17	$1,801	

MINIVANS 2WD

BUICK

Terraza FWD	A-4	3.5/6	18/24	$1,350	

CHEVROLET

Uplander FWD	A-4	3.5/6	18/24	$1,350	
Venture FWD	A-4	3.4/6	19/26	$1,285	

CHRYSLER

Town & Country 2WD	A-4	3.3/6	19/26	$1,285	
	A-4	3.8/6	18/25	$1,350	
Town & Country 2WD FFV	A-4	3.3/6	13/17	$1,651...	E85
	A-4	3.3/6	18/25	$1,285...	Gas

DODGE

Caravan 2WD	A-4	2.4/4	20/26	$1,228	
	A-4	3.3/6	19/26	$1,285	

	Trans Type / Speeds	Eng Size / Cylinders	MPG City / Hwy	Annual Fuel Cost	Notes / Abbreviations
	A-4	3.8/6	18/25	$1,350	
Caravan 2WD FFV	A-4	3.3/6	13/17	$1,651...	E85
	A-4	3.3/6	18/25	$1,285...	Gas
FORD					
Freestar Cargo Van FWD	A-4	3.9/6	18/23	$1,350	
	A-4	4.2/6	17/23	$1,420	
Freestar Wagon FWD	A-4	3.8/6	18/23	$1,350	
	A-4	4.2/6	17/23	$1,420	
HONDA					
_Odyssey 2WD	**A-5**	**3.5/6**	**20/28**	**$1,174**	
	A-5	3.5/6	19/25	$1,285...	VTEC
KIA					
Sedona	A-5	3.5/6	16/22	$1,501	
MAZDA					
MPV	A-5	3.0/6	18/25	$1,285	
MERCURY					
Monterey Wagon FWD	A-4	4.2/6	17/23	$1,420	
NISSAN					
Quest	A-4	3.5/6	19/26	$1,228	
	A-5	3.5/6	18/25	$1,285	
PONTIAC					
Montana FWD	A-4	3.4/6	19/26	$1,285	
Montana SVX FWD	A-4	3.5/6	18/24	$1,350	
SATURN					
Relay FWD	A-4	3.5/6	18/24	$1,350	
TOYOTA					
Sienna 2WD	A-5	3.3/6	19/26	$1,285	

MINIVANS 4WD

	Trans Type / Speeds	Eng Size / Cylinders	MPG City / Hwy	Annual Fuel Cost	Notes / Abbreviations
BUICK					
Terraza AWD	A-4	3.5/6	17/23	$1,420	
CHEVROLET					
Uplander AWD	A-4	3.5/6	17/23	$1,420	
PONTIAC					
Montana SVX AWD	A-4	3.5/6	17/23	$1,420	

	Trans Type / Speeds	Eng Size / Cylinders	MPG City / Hwy	Annual Fuel Cost	Notes / Abbreviations
SATURN					
Relay AWD	A-4	3.5/6	17/23	$1,420	
TOYOTA					
Sienna 4WD	A-5	3.3/6	18/24	$1,350	

SPORT UTILITY VEHICLES 2WD

	Trans Type / Speeds	Eng Size / Cylinders	MPG City / Hwy	Annual Fuel Cost	Notes / Abbreviations
BUICK					
Ranier 2WD	A-4	4.2/6	16/21	$1,501	
	A-4	5.3/8	16/20	$1,501	
Rendezvous FWD	A-4	3.4/6	19/26	$1,285	
	A-4	3.6/6	18/27	$1,285	
CADILLAC					
Escalade 2WD	A-4	5.3/8	15/20	$1,588	
	A-4	6.0/8	14/18	$1,828...	P
SRX 2WD	A-S5	3.6/6	16/23	$1,420	
	A-S5	4.6/8	15/21	$1,720...	P
CHEVROLET					
Blazer 2WD	A-4	4.3/6	16/22	$1,420	
	M-5	4.3/6	16/22	$1,501	
C1500 Avalanche 2WD FFV	A-4	5.3/8	11/14	$2,062...	E85
	A-4	5.3/8	14/19	$1,688...	Gas
C1500 Suburban 2WD FFV	A-4	5.3/8	11/15	$1,903...	E85
	A-4	5.3/8	15/19	$1,588...	Gas
C1500 Tahoe 2WD	A-4	4.8/8	16/20	$1,588	
	A-4	5.3/8	15/20	$1,588	
C1500Tahoe 2WD FFV	A-4	5.3/8	11/15	$1,903...	E85
	A-4	5.3/8	15/19	$1,588...	Gas
Equinox FWD	A-5	3.4/6	19/25	$1,285	
Trailblazer 2WD	A-4	4.2/6	16/21	$1,501	
Trailblazer EXT 2WD	A-4	4.2/6	15/19	$1,688	
	A-4	5.3/8	15/20	$1,588	
CHRYSLER					
Pacifica 2WD	A-4	3.5/6	17/23	$1,420	
	A-4	3.8/6	18/25	$1,350	
PT Cruiser	A-4	2.4/4	19/26	$1,272...	P T
	A-4	2.4/4	21/26	$1,174	
	M-5	2.4/4	21/27	$1,272...	P T
	M-5	2.4/4	22/29	$1,080	
PT Cruiser Conv/Cabrio	A-4	2.4/4	19/26	$1,272...	P T
	A-4	2.4/4	21/26	$1,174	
	M-5	2.4/4	21/27	$1,272...	P T
	M-5	2.4/4	22/29	$1,080	

	Trans Type / Speeds	Eng Size / Cylinders	MPG City / Hwy	Annual Fuel Cost	Notes / Abbreviations
DODGE					
Durango 2WD	A-4	3.7/6	16/21	$1,501	
	A-5	4.7/8	14/19	$1,688	
	A-5	5.7/8	14/19	$1,688	
Magnum	A-4	2.7/6	21/28	$1,126	
	A-4	3.5/6	19/27	$1,228	
	A-5	5.7/8	17/25	$1,350	
FORD					
Escape 2WD	A-4	2.3/4	22/25	$1,174	
	M-5	2.3/4	24/29	$1,040	
	A-4	3.0/6	20/25	$1,228	
_Escape HEV 2WD	**A V**	**2.3/4**	**36/31**	**$818...**	**HEV**
Expedition 2WD	A-4	5.4/8	14/19	$1,688	
Explorer 2WD	A-5	4.0/6	16/21	$1,588	
	A-5	4.6/8	15/20	$1,688	
Explorer 2WD FFV	A-5	4.0/6	11/15	$1,903...	E85
	A-5	4.0/6	15/20	$1,588...	Gas
Freestyle FWD	A V	3.0/6	20/27	$1,174	
GMC					
C1500 Yukon 2WD	A-4	4.8/8	16/20	$1,588	
	A-4	5.3/8	15/20	$1,588	
C1500 Yukon 2WD FFV	A-4	5.3/8	11/15	$1,903...	E85
	A-4	5.3/8	15/19	$1,588...	Gas
C1500 Yukon XL 2WD FFV	A-4	5.3/8	11/14	$2,062...	E85
	A-4	5.3/8	14/19	$1,688...	Gas
Envoy 2WD	A-4	4.2/6	16/21	$1,501	
	A-4	5.3/8	16/20	$1,501	
Envoy XL 2WD	A-4	4.2/6	15/19	$1,688	
	A-4	5.3/8	15/20	$1,588	
Envoy XUV 2WD	A-4	4.2/6	15/19	$1,688	
	A-4	5.3/8	15/21	$1,588	
HONDA					
CR-V 2WD	A-5	2.4/4	23/29	$1,080	
Element 2WD	A-4	2.4/4	22/26	$1,126	
	M-5	2.4/4	21/25	$1,174	
HYUNDAI					
SantaFe 2WD	A-4	2.4/4	20/26	$1,174	
	M-5	2.4/4	20/27	$1,174	
	A-4	2.7/6	19/25	$1,228	
	A-5	3.5/6	17/23	$1,350	
Tucson 2WD	A-4	2.0/4	22/27	$1,126	
	M-5	2.0/4	22/27	$1,126	

	Trans Type / Speeds	Eng Size / Cylinders	MPG City / Hwy	Annual Fuel Cost	Notes / Abbreviations
	A-4	2.7/6	20/26	$1,228	
INFINITI					
FX35 RWD	A-S5	3.5/6	17/23	$1,420	
QX56 2WD	A-5	5.6/8	13/19	$1,801	
ISUZU					
Ascender 5-Passenger 2WD	A-4	4.2/6	16/21	$1,501	
Ascender 7-Passenger 2WD	A-4	4.2/6	15/19	$1,688	
	A-4	5.3/8	15/20	$1,588	
JEEP					
Grand Cherokee 2WD	A-5	3.7/6	17/22	$1,420	
	A-5	4.7/8	15/20	$1,588	
Liberty/Cherokee 2WD	M-6	2.4/4	21/26	$1,174	
	A-4	3.7/6	17/22	$1,420	
	M-6	3.7/6	18/22	$1,420	
KIA					
Sorento 2WD	A-5	3.5/6	16/22	$1,501	
	M-5	3.5/6	16/20	$1,501	
Sportage 2WD	A-4	2.0/4	22/27	$1,126	
	M-5	2.0/4	22/27	$1,126	
	A-4	2.7/6	19/25	$1,228	
LEXUS					
RX 330 2WD	A-5	3.3/6	19/25	$1,228	
	A-S5	3.3/6	19/25	$1,228	
LINCOLN					
Aviator 2WD	A-5	4.6/8	13/18	$1,951...	P
Navigator 2WD	A-6	5.4/8	13/18	$1,951...	P
MAZDA					
Tribute 2WD	A-4	2.3/4	22/25	$1,174	
	M-5	2.3/4	24/29	$1,040	
	A-4	3.0/6	20/25	$1,228	
MERCURY					
Mariner 2WD	A-4	2.3/4	22/26	$1,126	
	A-4	3.0/6	20/25	$1,228	
Mountaineer 2WD	A-5	4.0/6	16/21	$1,588	
	A-5	4.6/8	15/20	$1,688	
Mountaineer 2WD FFV	A-5	4.0/6	11/15	$1,903...	E85
	A-5	4.0/6	15/20	$1,588	Gas

	Trans Type / Speeds	Eng Size / Cylinders	MPG City / Hwy	Annual Fuel Cost	Notes / Abbreviations
MITSUBISHI					
Endeavor 2WD	A-S4	3.8/6	17/23	$1,462	P
Outlander 2WD	M-5	2.4/4	22/28	$1,126	
	A-S4	2.4/4	21/26	$1,174	
NISSAN					
Armada 2WD	A-5	5.6/8	13/19	$1,801	
Murano FWD	A V	3.5/6	20/25	$1,228	
Pathfinder 2WD	A-5	4.0/6	16/23	$1,420	
Xterra 2WD	A-5	4.0/6	16/22	$1,501	
	M-6	4.0/6	17/22	$1,420	
PONTIAC					
Aztek FWD	A-4	3.4/6	19/26	$1,285	
SATURN					
Vue FWD	A V	2.2/4	22/28	$1,126	
	A-4	2.2/4	22/27	$1,126	
	M-5	2.2/4	23/29	$1,080	
	A-5	3.5/6	20/28	$1,174	
SUZUKI					
Grand Vitara	A-4	2.5/6	19/22	$1,350	
	M-5	2.5/6	19/22	$1,350	
Grand Vitara XL7	A-5	2.7/6	18/22	$1,350	
	M-5	2.7/6	17/22	$1,420	
TOYOTA					
4Runner 2WD	A-5	4.0/6	18/22	$1,350	
	A-5	4.7/8	17/20	$1,501	
Highlander 2WD	A-4	2.4/4	22/27	$1,126	
	A-5	3.3/6	19/25	$1,285	
Rav4 2WD	A-4	2.4/4	24/29	$1,040	
	M-5	**2.4/4**	**24/30**	**$1,040**	
Sequoia 2WD	A-5	4.7/8	15/18	$1,688	
VOLVO					
XC 90 FWD	A-S5	2.5/5	18/23	$1,462	P T

SPORT UTILITY VEHICLES 4WD

	Trans Type / Speeds	Eng Size / Cylinders	MPG City / Hwy	Annual Fuel Cost	Notes / Abbreviations
ACURA					
MDX 4WD	A-5	3.5/6	17/23	$1,539... P VTEC	
AUDI					
Allroad Quattro	M-6	2.7/6	16/23	$1,626...	P T

	Trans Type / Speeds	Eng Size / Cylinders	MPG City / Hwy	Annual Fuel Cost	Notes / Abbreviations
	A-S5	2.7/6	16/22	$1,539...	P T
	A-S5	4.2/8	16/21	$1,626...	P
BMW					
X3					
	M-6	2.5/6	17/24	$1,462...	P
	A-S5	2.5/6	17/23	$1,539...	P
	M-6	3.0/6	17/25	$1,462...	P
	A-S5	3.0/6	16/23	$1,539...	P
X5	M-6	3.0/6	15/21	$1,720...	P
	A-S5	3.0/6	16/21	$1,626...	P
	A-S6	4.4/8	16/22	$1,626...	P
X5 4.8IS	A-S6	4.8/8	16/21	$1,626...	P
BUICK					
Ranier AWD					
	A-4	4.2/6	15/20	$1,588	
	A-4	5.3/8	15/19	$1,688	
Rendezvous AWD	A-4	3.4/6	18/24	$1,350	
	A-4	3.6/6	18/25	$1,350	
CADILLAC					
Escalade AWD	A-4	6.0/8	13/17	$1,951...	P
Escalade ESV AWD	A-4	6.0/8	13/17	$1,951...	P
Escalade EXT AWD	A-4	6.0/8	13/17	$1,951...	P
SRX AWD	A-S5	3.6/6	16/22	$1,501	
	A-S5	4.6/8	15/20	$1,720...	P
CHEVROLET					
Blazer 4WD	A-4	4.3/6	15/19	$1,588	
	M-5	4.3/6	15/19	$1,688	
Equinox AWD	A-5	3.4/6	19/25	$1,285	
K1500 Avalanche 4WD FFV	A-4	5.3/8	11/14	$2,062...	E85
	A-4	5.3/8	14/18	$1,688...	Gas
K1500 Suburban 4WD	A-4	5.3/8	15/19	$1,688	
K1500 Suburban 4WD FFV	A-4	5.3/8	11/14	$2,062...	E85
	A-4	5.3/8	14/18	$1,688...	Gas
K1500 Suburban AWD FFV	A-4	5.3/8	11/14	$2,062...	E85
	A-4	5.3/8	14/18	$1,688...	Gas
K1500 Tahoe 4WD	A-4	4.8/8	16/20	$1,588	
	A-4	5.3/8	15/19	$1,688	
K1500 Tahoe 4WD FFV	A-4	5.3/8	11/14	$2,062	E85
	A-4	5.3/8	14/18	$1,688	Gas
K1500 Tahoe AWD	A-4	5.3/8	15/19	$1,688	
K1500 Tahoe AWD FFV	A-4	5.3/8	11/14	$2,062...	E85
	A-4	5.3/8	14/18	$1,688...	Gas
Trailblazer 4WD	A-4	4.2/6	15/20	$1,588	
Trailblazer EXT 4WD	A-4	4.2/6	14/18	$1,801	
	A-4	5.3/8	14/19	$1,688	

	Trans Type / Speeds	Eng Size / Cylinders	MPG City / Hwy	Annual Fuel Cost	Notes / Abbreviations
CHRYSLER					
Pacifica AWD	A-4	3.5/6	17/22	$1,420	
DODGE					
Durango 4WD	A-5	4.7/8	14/18	$1,801	
	A-5	5.7/8	13/18	$1,801	
Magnum AWD	A-5	3.5/6	17/24	$1,350	
	A-5	5.7/8	17/24	$1,350	
FORD					
Escape 4WD	A-4	2.3/4	19/22	$1,350	
	M-5	2.3/4	22/26	$1,126	
	A-4	3.0/6	18/22	$1,420	
Escape HEV 4WD	A V	2.3/4	33/29	$872...	HEV
Expedition 4WD	A-4	5.4/8	14/18	$1,688	
Explorer 4WD	A-5	4.0/6	14/20	$1,688	
	A-5	4.6/8	14/18	$1,688	
Explorer 4WD FFV	A-5	4.0/6	11/15	$2,062...	E85
	A-5	4.0/6	14/20	$1,688...	Gas
Freestyle AWD	A V	3.0/6	19/24	$1,285	
GMC					
Envoy 4WD	A-4	4.2/6	15/20	$1,588	
	A-4	5.3/8	15/19	$1,688	
Envoy XL 4WD	A-4	4.2/6	14/18	$1,801	
	A-4	5.3/8	14/19	$1,688	
Envoy XUV 4WD	A-4	4.2/6	14/18	$1,801	
	A-4	5.3/8	14/19	$1,688	
K1500 Yukon 4WD	A-4	4.8/8	16/20	$1,588	
	A-4	5.3/8	15/19	$1,688	
K1500 Yukon 4WD FFV	A-4	5.3/8	11/14	$2,062...	E85
	A-4	5.3/8	14/18	$1,688...	Gas
K1500 Yukon AWD	A-4	5.3/8	15/19	$1,688	
	A-4	6.0/8	13/17	$1,951	... P
K1500 Yukon AWD FFV	A-4	5.3/8	11/14	$2,062...	E85
	A-4	5.3/8	14/18	$1,688...	Gas
K1500 Yukon XL AWD	A-4	6.0/8	13/17	$1,951...	P
K1500 Yukon XL 4WD FFV	A-4	5.3/8	11/14	$2,062...	E85
	A-4	5.3/8	14/18	$1,688...	Gas
K1500 Yukon XL AWD FFV	A-4	5.3/8	11/14	$2,062...	E85
	A-4	5.3/8	14/18	$1,688...	Gas
HONDA					
CR-V 4WD	A-5	2.4/4	22/27	$1,126	
	M-5	2.4/4	21/26	$1,174	
Element 4WD	A-4	2.4/4	21/24	$1,228	
	M-5	2.4/4	21/24	$1,228	

	Trans Type / Speeds	Eng Size / Cylinders	MPG City / Hwy	Annual Fuel Cost	Notes / Abbreviations
Pilot 4WD	A-5	3.5/6	17/22	$1,420...	VTEC
HYUNDAI					
SantaFe 4WD	A-4	2.7/6	18/23	$1,350	
	A-5	3.5/6	17/23	$1,420	
Tucson 4WD	M-5	2.0/4	21/26	$1,174	
	A-4	2.7/6	19/24	$1,285	
INFINITI					
FX35 AWD	A-S5	3.5/6	16/22	$1,501	
FX45 AWD	A-S5	4.5/8	15/19	$1,720...	
QX56 4WD	A-5	5.6/8	13/18	$1,801	P
ISUZU					
Ascender 5-Passenger 4WD	A-4	4.2/6	15/20	$1,588	
Ascender 7-Passenger 4WD	A-4	4.2/6	15/20	$1,588	
	A-4	5.3/8	14/19	$1,688	
JEEP					
Grand Cherokee 4WD	A-5	3.7/6	17/21	$1,501	
	A-5	4.7/8	15/20	$1,588	
	A-5	5.7/8	14/19	$1,688	
Liberty	A-4	2.8/4	NA	NA	D T
Liberty/Cherokee 4WD	M-6	2.4/4	20/24	$1,228	
	A-5	2.8/4	21/26	$1,011...	D
	A-4	3.7/6	17/22	$1,420	
	M-6	3.7/6	18/22	$1,420	
Wrangler/TJ 4WD	M-6	2.4/4	18/21	$1,350	
	A-4	4.0/6	14/18	$1,688	
	M-6	4.0/6	15/19	$1.688	
KIA					
Sorento 4WD	A-5	3.5/6	15/20	$1,688	
	M-5	3.5/6	16/20	$1,588	
Sportage 4WD	M-5	2.0/4	21/26	$1,174	
	A-4	2.7/6	19/23	$1,285	
LAND ROVER					
Freelander	A-S5	2.5/6	18/21	$1,420	
LR3	A-S6	4.0/6	14/19	$1,688	
	A-S6	4.4/8	14/18	$1,688	
Range Rover	A-S5	4.4/8	12/16	$2,249...	P
LEXUS					
GX470	A-5	4.7/8	15/19	$1,588	
LX 470	A-5	4.7/8	13/17	$1,928	
RX 330 4WD	A-5	3.3/6	18/24	$1,285	
	A-S5	3.3/6	18/24	$1,350	

	Trans Type / Speeds	Eng Size / Cylinders	MPG City / Hwy	Annual Fuel Cost	Notes / Abbreviations
LINCOLN					
Aviator 4WD	A-5	4.6/8	13/18	$1,951...	P
MAZDA					
Tribute 4WD	A-4	2.3/4	19/22	$1,350	
	M-5	2.3/4	22/26	$1,126	
	A-4	3.0/6	18/22	$1,420	
MERCEDES-BENZ					
G500	A-5	5.0/8	13/14	$2,249...	P
G55 AMG	A-5	5.4/8	12/14	$2,249...	P S
ML350	A-5	3.7/6	15/18	$1,828...	P
ML500	A-5	5.0/8	14/17	$1,951...	P
MERCURY					
Mariner 4WD	A-4	2.3/4	20/23	$1,285	
	A-4	3.0/6	18/23	$1,350	
Mountaineer 4WD	A-5	4.0/6	14/19	$1,688	
	A-5	4.6/8	14/18	$1,688	
Mountaineer 4WD FFV	A-5	4.0/6	10/14	$2,062...	E85
	A-5	4.0/6	14/19	$1,688...	Gas
MITSUBISHI					
Endeavor 4WD	A-S4	3.8/6	17/22	$1,539...	P
Montero	A-S5	3.8/6	15/19	$1,828...	P
Outlander 4WD	M-5	2.4/4	21/27	$1,174	
	A-S4	2.4/4	21/25	$1,228	
NISSAN					
Armada 4WD	A-5	5.6/8	13/18	$1,801	
Murano AWD	A V	3.5/6	20/24	$1,228	
Pathfinder 4WD	A-5	4.0/6	15/21	$1,588	
Xterra 4WD	A-5	4.0/6	16/21	$1,501	
	M-6	4.0/6	17/21	$1,501	
PONTIAC					
Aztek AWD	A-4	3.4/6	18/24	$1,350	
PORSCHE					
Cayenne	A-5	3.2/6	15/19	$1,720...	P
	M-6	3.2/6	15/20	$1,720...	P
Cayenne S	A-5	4.5/8	14/18	$1,828...	P
Cayenne Turbo	A-5	4.5/8	13/18	$1,951...	P T
SAAB					
9-7X AWD	A-4	4.2/6	15/21	$1,588	
	A-4	5.3/8	15/19	$1,688	
SATURN					
Vue AWD	A V	2.2/4	21/26	$1,174	

	Trans Type / Speeds	Eng Size / Cylinders	MPG City / Hwy	Annual Fuel Cost	Notes / Abbreviations
	A-5	3.5/6	19/25	$1,285	
SUBARU					
Baja AWD	A-4	2.5/4	21/28	$1,126	
	M-5	2.5/4	19/25	$1,392...	P T
	M-5	2.5/4	21/27	$1,174	
Forester AWD	A-S4	2.5/4	18/23	$1,462...	P T
	A-4	2.5/4	20/23	$1,392...	P T
	A-4	2.5/4	22/28	$1,080	
	M-5	2.5/4	19/24	$1,392...	P T
Outback AWD	M-5	2.5/4	23/30	$1,080	
Outback Wagon AWD	A-S5	3.0/6	19/25	$1,331...	P
	M-5	2.5/4	19/25	$1,392...	P T
	M-5	2.5/4	23/28	$1,080	
	A-S4	2.5/4	22/28	$1,080	
	A-S5	2.5/4	19/24	$1,392...	P T
	A-S5	3.0/6	19/25	$1,331...	P
SUZUKI					
Grand Vitara 4WD	A-4	2.5/6	19/22	$1,350	
	M-5	2.5/6	19/22	$1,350	
Grand Vitara XL7 4WD	A-5	2.7/6	17/22	$1,420	
	M-5	2.7/6	17/22	$1,420	
TOYOTA					
4Runner 4WD	A-5	4.0/6	17/21	$1,501	
	A-5	4.7/8	16/19	$1,588	
Highlander 4WD	A-4	2.4/4	21/25	$1,174	
	A-5	3.3/6	18/24	$1,285	
Land Cruiser Wagon 4WD	A-5	4.7/8	13/17	$1,928	
Rav4 4WD	A-4	2.4/4	22/27	$1,126	
	M-5	2.4/4	22/27	$1,126	
Sequoia 4WD	A-5	4.7/8	15/18	$1,688	
VOLKSWAGEN					
Touareg	A-S6	3.2/6	16/21	$1,626	... P
	A-S6	4.2/8	14/18	$1,951...	P
VOLVO					
XC 70 AWD	A-S5	2.5/5	18/24	$1,392...	P T
XC 90 AWD	A-S5	2.5/5	17/22	$1,539...	P T
	A-S4	2.9/6	15/20	$1,720...	P T
	A-S6	4.4/8	15/20	$1,720...	P

ABBREVIATIONS:

‾	Highest MPG in class
2WD	Two-Wheel Drive
4WD	Four-Wheel Drive
A	Automatic Transmission
A-S	Automatic Transmission-Select Shift
AV	Continuously Variable Transmission
AWD	All Wheel Drive
City	MPG on City Test Procedure
CNG	Compressed Natural Gas
Conv	Convertible
Convsn	Conversion
D	Diesel
DVVT	Dual Variable Valve Timing
E85	85% Ethanol/15% Gasoline
Eng Size	Engine Volume in Liters
FFV	Flexible-Fuel Vehicle
FWD	Front-Wheel Drive
HEV	Hybrid-Electric Vehicle
Hwy	MPG on Highway Test Procedure
LB	Lean Burn Fuel System
M	Manual Transmission
Mode	Multimode Transmission
NA	Not Available at Press Time
P	Premium Gasoline
S	Supercharger
T	Turbocharger
Tax	Subject to Gas Guzzler Tax
Trans	Transmission
VIS	Variable Induction System
VTEC	Variable Valve Timing and Lift Electronic Control

APPENDIX 2
HYBRID-ELECTRIC VEHICLES

It's no accident the most fuel-efficient vehicles in some classes for the 2005 model year are hybrid-electric vehicles (HEVs). Hybrids can be configured in many different ways to achieve a variety of different objectives. They combine the best features of the internal combustion engine with an electric motor and can significantly improve fuel economy without sacrificing performance or driving range. HEVs may also be configured to provide electrical power to auxiliary loads such as power tools.

HEVs are primarily propelled by an internal combustion engine, just like conventional vehicles. However, they also convert energy normally wasted during coasting and braking into electricity, which is stored in a battery until needed by the electric motor. The electric motor is used to assist the engine when accelerating or hill climbing and in low-speed driving conditions where internal combustion engines are least efficient. Unlike all-electric vehicles, HEVs now being offered do not need to be plugged into an external source of electricity to be recharged; conventional gasoline and regenerative braking provide all the energy the vehicle needs.

Potential buyers should also be aware that the federal government is currently offering tax incentives for HEVs and other alternative fuel vehicles. Some states also offer incentives.

Additional information on HEVs, including tax incentives, can be found at www.fueleconomy.gov/feg/hybrid_sbs.shtml. Annual fuel cost is estimated assuming 15,000 miles of travel each year (55% city and 45% highway) and a gasoline fuel cost of $1.80 per gallon (regular unleaded).

	Trans Type / Speeds	Eng Size / Cylinders	MPG City / Hwy	Annual Fuel Cost	Battery Size / Type
		TWO SEATERS			
HONDA					
Insight	AV	1.0/3	..57/56	$483	... 144 V, Ni-MH
	M5	1.0/3	..61/66	$429	... 144 V, Ni-MH
		COMPACT CARS			
HONDA					
Civic Hybrid (LB)	AV	1.3/4	..48/47	$562	... 144 V, Ni-MH
Civic Hybrid	AV	1.3/4	..47/48	$575	... 144 V, Ni-MH
Civic Hybrid (LB)	M5	1.3/4	..46/51	$562	... 144 V, Ni-MH
Civic Hybrid	M5	1.3/4	..45/51	$575	... 144 V, Ni-MH

	Trans Type / Speeds	Eng Size / Cylinders	MPG City / Hwy	Annual Fuel Cost	Battery Size / Type
MIDSIZE CARS					
HONDA Accord Hybrid	A5	3.0/6	..29/37	$842	...
TOYOTA Prius	AV	1.5/4	..60/51	$491	... 202 V, Ni-MH
STANDARD PICKUP TRUCKS 2WD					
CHEVROLET C15 Silverado Hybrid 2WD	A4	5.3/8	..18/21	$1,420	... Lead Acid
GMC C15 Sierra Hybrid 2WD	A4	5.3/8	..18/21	$1,420	... Lead Acid
	Trans Type / Speeds	Eng Size / Cylinders	MPG City / Hwy	Annual Fuel Cost	Battery Size / Type
STANDARD PICKUP TRUCKS 4WD					
CHEVROLET K15 Silverado Hybrid 4WD	A4	5.3/8	.. 17/19	$1,501	... Lead Acid
GMC K15 Sierra Hybrid 4WD	A4	5.3/8	.. 17/19	$1,501	... Lead Acid
SPORT UTILITY VEHICLES 2WD					
FORD Escape HEV 2WD	AV	2.3/4	.. 36/31	$818	... 330 V, Ni-MH
SPORT UTILITY VEHICLES 4WD					
FORD Escape HEV 4WD	AV	2.3/4	.. 33/29	$872	... 330 V, Ni-MH

ABBREVIATIONS:

A	Automatic Transmission
A-S	Automatic Transmission-Select Shift
AV	Continuously Variable Transmission
City	MPG on City Test Procedure
CNG	Compressed Natural Gas
Conv	Convertible
E85	85% Ethanol/15% Gasoline
Eng Size	Engine Volume in Liters

FFV	Flexible Fuel Vehicle
Hwy	MPG on Highway Test Procedure
LB	Lean Burn Fuel System
M	Manual Transmission
NA	Not Available at Press Time
Ni-MH	Nickel-metal hydride
T	Turbocharger
Trans	Transmission
V	Volts

ETHANOL FLEXIBLE-FUEL VEHICLES

This section contains the driving range and fuel economy values for ethanol flexible-fuel passenger cars and light trucks. Ethanol flexible-fuel vehicles are designed to operate on gasoline, E85 (a mixture of 85% ethanol and 15% gasoline), or any mixture of the two fuels. Annual fuel cost is estimated assuming 15,000 miles of travel each year (55% city and 45% highway) and an average fuel cost of $1.65 per gallon of E85, $1.80 per gallon of regular unleaded gasoline, and $1.95 per gallon of premium unleaded gasoline.

The driving range and fuel economy values are shown for both gasoline and E85. When operating your FFV on mixtures of gasoline and E85, such as when alternating between using these fuels, your driving range and fuel economy values will be somewhere between those listed for the two fuels, depending on the actual percentage of gasoline and E85 in the tank.

	Trans Type / Speeds	Eng Size / Cylinders	MPG City / Hwy	Annual Fuel Cost Fuel	Range (miles)
COMPACT CARS					
CHRYSLER					
Sebring Conv	A-4	2.7/6	.. 15/20	$1,455 ...E85	270
			21/28	$1,174 ...Gas	390
Sebring Conv (2-Mode)	A-4	2.7/6	.. 15/20	$1,455 ...E85	270
			21/28	$1,174 ...Gas	390
MERCEDES-BENZ					
C240 FFV	A-5	2.6/6	.. 14/19	$1,547 ...E85	310
			20/25	$1,331 ...P	420
C320 FFV	A-5	3.2/6	.. 14/19	$1,547 ...E85	310
			20/26	$1,331 ...P	430
C320 Sports Coupe FFV	A-5	3.2/6	.. 14/18	$1,651 ...E85	300
			19/24	$1,392 ...P	400

	Trans Type / Speeds	Eng Size / Cylinders	MPG City / Hwy	Annual Fuel Cost Fuel	Range (miles)
MIDSIZE CARS					
CHRYSLER					
Sebring 4-dr	A-4	2.7/6	.. 15/20 21/28	$1,455 ...E85 $1,174 ...Gas	270 390
Sebring 4-dr (2-Mode)	A-4	2.7/6	.. 15/20 21/28	$1,455 ...E85 $1,174 ...Gas	270 390
DODGE					
Stratus 4-dr	A-4	2.7/6	.. 15/20 21/28	$1,455 ...E85 $1,174 ...Gas	270 390
Stratus 4-dr (2-Mode)	A-4	2.7/6	.. 15/20 21/28	$1,455 ...E85 $1,174 ...Gas	270 390
MERCURY					
Sable	A-4	3.0/6	.. 15/20 19/27	$1,455 ...E85 $1,228 ...Gas	310 390
LARGE CARS					
FORD					
Taurus	A-4	3.0/6	.. 15/20 19/27	$1,455 ...E85 $1,228 ...Gas	310 390
MIDSIZE STATION WAGONS					
FORD					
Taurus Wagon	A-4	3.0/6	.. 14/19 19/26	$1,547 ...E85 $1,285 ...Gas	290 380
MERCURY					
Sable Wagon	A-4	3.0/6	.. 14/19 19/26	$1,547 ...E85 $1,285 ...Gas	290 380
SMALL STATION WAGONS					
MERCEDES-BENZ					
C240 Wagon FFV	A-5	2.6/6	.. 14/19 20/25	$1,547 ...E85 $1,331 ...P	310 420
SPORT UTILITY VEHICLES 2WD					
CHEVROLET					
C1500 Avalanche 2WD	A-4	5.3/8	..11/14 14/19	$2,062 ...E85 $1,688 ...Gas	310/540* 410/690*
C1500 Suburban 2WD	A-4	5.3/8	..11/15 15/19	$1,903 ...E85 $1,588 ...Gas	310/540* 410/690*
C1500 Tahoe 2WD	A-4	5.3/8	..11/15 15/19	$1,903 ...E85 $1,588 ...Gas	310/540* 410/690*
FORD					
Explorer 2WD FFV	A-5	4.0/6	..11/15 15/20	$1,903 ...E85 $1,588 ...Gas	290 380

	Trans Type / Speeds	Eng Size / Cylinders	MPG City / Hwy	Annual Fuel Cost Fuel	Range (miles)
GMC					
C1500 Yukon 2WD	A-4	5.3/8	..11/15	$1,903	...E85 310/540*
			15/19	$1,588	...Gas 410/690*
C1500 Yukon XL 2WD	A-4	5.3/8	..11/14	$2,062	...E85 310/540*
			14/19	$1,688	...Gas 410/690*
MERCURY					
Mountaineer 2WD	A-5	4.0/6	..11/15	$1,903	...E85 290
			15/20	$1,588	...Gas 380
MINIVANS 2WD					
CHRYSLER					
Town & Country 2WD	A-4	3.3/6	.. 13/17	$1,651	...E85 300
			18/25	$1,285	...Gas 420
DODGE					
Caravan	A-4	3.3/6	.. 13/17	$1,651	...E85 300
			18/25	$1,285	...Gas 420
SPORT UTILITY VEHICLES 4WD					
CHEVROLET					
K1500 Avalanche 4WD	A-4	5.3/8	..11/14	$2,062	...E85 310/460*
			14/18	$1,688	...Gas 410/620*
K1500 Suburban 4WD	A-4	5.3/8	..11/14	$2,062	...E85 310/460*
			14/18	$1,688	...Gas 410/620*
K1500 Suburban AWD	A-4	5.3/8	..11/14	$2,062	...E85 310/460*
			14/18	$1,688	...Gas 410/620*
K1500 Tahoe 4WD	A-4	5.3/8	..11/14	$2,062	...E85 310/460*
			14/18	$1,688	...Gas 410/620*
K1500 Tahoe AWD	A-4	5.3/8	..11/14	$2,062	...E85 310/460*
			14/18	$1,688	...Gas 410/620*
FORD					
Explorer 4WD FFV	A-5	4.0/6	..11/15	$2,062	...E85 290
			14/20	$1,688	...Gas 380
GMC					
K1500 Yukon 4WD	A-4	5.3/8	..11/14	$2,062	...E85 310/460*
			14/18	$1,688	...Gas 410/620*
K1500 Yukon AWD	A-4	5.3/8	..11/14	$2,062	...E85 310/460*
			14/18	$1,688	...Gas 410/620*
K1500 Yukon XL 4WD	A-4	5.3/8	..11/14	$2,062	...E85 310/460*
			14/18	$1,688	...Gas 410/620*
K1500 Yukon XL AWD	A-4	5.3/8	..11/14	$2,062	...E85 310/460*
			14/18	$1,688	...Gas 410/620*
MERCURY					
Mountaineer 4WD FFV	A-5	4.0/6	.. 10/14	$2,062	...E85 270
			14/19	$1,688	...Gas 360

	Trans Type / Speeds	Eng Size / Cylinders	MPG City / Hwy	Annual Fuel Cost Fuel	Range (miles)
STANDARD PICKUP TRUCKS 2WD					
CHEVROLET C1500 Silverado 2WD	A-4	5.3/8	.. 12/16 16/20	$1,767 ...E85 $1,501 ...Gas	310/540* 410/690*
DODGE Ram 1500 2WD	A-5	4.7/8	.9/11 12/15	$2,475 ...E85 $2,076 ...Gas	260 340
FORD Explorer Sport Trac 2WD FFV	A-5	4.0/6	..11/15 15/20	$1,903 ...E85 $1,588 ...Gas	290 380
GMC C1500 Sierra 2WD	A-4	5.3/8	..12/16 16/20	$1,767 ...E85 $1,501 ...Gas	310/540* 410/690*
NISSAN Titan 2WD	A-5 A-5	5.6/8 5.6/8	..10/14 14/19	$2,062 ...E85 $1,688 ...Gas	310/330 420/450
STANDARD PICKUP TRUCKS 4WD					
CHEVROLET K1500 Silverado 4WD	A-4	5.3/8	..11/14 15/18	$2,062 ...E85 $1,688 ...Gas	310/460* 410/620*
DODGE Ram 1500 4WD	A-5	4.7/8	.9/11 12/15	$2,475 ...E85 $2,076 ...Gas	260 340
FORD Explorer Sport Trac 4WD FFV	A-5	4.0/6	..11/15 14/20	$2,062 ...E85 $1,688 ...Gas	290 380
GMC K1500 Sierra 4WD	A-4	5.3/8	..11/14 15/18	$2,062 ...E85 $1,688 ...Gas	310/460* 410/620*
NISSAN Titan 4WD	A-5 A-5	5.6/8 5.6/8	..10/13 14/18	$2,250 ...E85 $1,801 ...Gas	310/330* 420/450*

* Vehicle is available with various tank sizes. Driving ranges are shown for the smallest and largest available fuel tanks.

DIESEL VEHICLES

This section contains fuel economy values for diesel-fueled vehicles. Diesel fuel contains approximately 10% more energy per gallon than gasoline. In addition, diesel engines have higher compression ratios, run "lean," and are unthrottled, giving them a substantial fuel economy advantage over gasoline engines. Annual fuel cost is estimated assuming 15,000 miles of travel each year (55% city and 45% highway) and a diesel fuel cost of $1.55 per gallon.

	Trans Type / Speeds	Eng Size Cylinders	MPG City / Hwy	Annual Fuel Cost	Notes / Abbreviations
SUBCOMPACT CARS					
VOLKSWAGEN					
New Beetle	M-5	1.9/4	38/46	$567...	T
	A-S6	1.9/4	35/42	$611...	T
COMPACT CARS					
VOLKSWAGEN					
Golf	M-5	1.9/4	38/46	$567...	T
	A-S5	1.9/4	32/43	$646...	T
Jetta	M-5	1.9/4	38/46	$567...	T
	A-S5	1.9/4	32/43	$646...	T
	A-S6	1.9/4	35/42	$611...	T
MIDSIZE CARS					
MERCEDES-BENZ					
E320 CDI	A-5	3.2/6	27/37	$774...	T
VOLKSWAGEN					
Passat	A-S5	2.0/4	27/38	$751... T	
SMALL STATION WAGONS					
VOLKSWAGEN					
Jetta Wagon	M-5	1.9/4	36/43	$595... T	
	A-S5	1.9/4	32/43	$646... T	
MIDSIZE STATION WAGONS					
VOLKSWAGEN					
Passat Wagon	A-S5	2.0/4	27/38	$751... T	
SPORT UTILITY VEHICLES 4WD					
JEEP					
Liberty	A-4	2.8/4	NA	NA... T	
Liberty/Cherokee 4WD	A-5	2.8/4	21/26	$1,011	

ABBREVIATIONS:

A	Automatic Transmission
A-S	Automatic Transmission-Select Shift
AV	Continuously Variable Transmission
City	MPG on City Test Procedure
CNG	Compressed Natural Gas
Conv	Convertible
E85	85% Ethanol/15% Gasoline
Eng Size	Engine Volume in Liters
FFV	Flexible Fuel Vehicle
Hwy	MPG on Highway Test Procedure
LB	Lean Burn Fuel System
M	Manual Transmission
NA	Not Available at Press Time
Ni-MH	Nickel-metal hydride
T	Turbocharger
Trans	Transmission
V	Volts

COMPRESSED NATURAL GAS VEHICLES

This section supplies the driving range and fuel economy values for vehicles that operate on compressed natural gas (CNG). CNG fuel is normally dispensed in "equivalent gallons," where one equivalent gallon is equal to 121.5 cubic feet of CNG. Therefore, the fuel economy values are shown in miles per gallon-equivalent. Annual fuel cost estimates are based on an average fuel price of $1.05 per gasoline equivalent gallon of CNG.

The driving range is shown in miles and represents the distance the vehicle can travel on a full tank (or tanks) of fuel during combined city and highway driving (55% city and 45% highway).

Trans Type / Speeds	Engine Size / Cylinders	MPG City/Hwy	Annual Fuel Cost	Fuel	Range
COMPACT CARS					

HONDA

Civic	A V	1.7/4..	30/34	$491	...CNG	200

	Trans Type / Speeds	Engine Size / Cylinders	MPG City/Hwy	Annual Fuel Cost	Fuel	Range
STANDARD PICKUP TRUCKS 2WD						

CHEVROLET

C2500 HD Silverado 2WD	A-4	6.0/8.. /	9/12	$1,575	...CNG	180

	Trans Type / Speeds	Engine Size Cylinders	MPG City/Hwy	Annual Fuel Cost	Fuel	Range

GMC

C2500 HD Sierra 2WD	A-4	6.0/8 ..	9/12	$1,575	...CNG	180

STANDARD PICKUP TRUCKS 4WD						

CHEVROLET

K2500 HD Silverado 4WD	.. A-4	6.0/8 ..	9/12	$1,575	...CNG	180

GMC

K2500 HD Sierra 4WD	A-4	6.0/8 ..	9/12	$1,575	...CNG	180

ABBREVIATIONS:

A	Automatic Transmission
A-S	Automatic Transmission-Select Shift
AV	Continuously Variable Transmission
City	MPG on City Test Procedure
CNG	Compressed Natural Gas
Conv	Convertible
E85	85% Ethanol/15% Gasoline
Eng Size	Engine Volume in Liters
FFV	Flexible Fuel Vehicle
Hwy	MPG on Highway Test Procedure
LB	Lean Burn Fuel System
M	Manual Transmission
NA	Not Available at Press Time
Ni-MH	Nickel-metal hydride
T	Turbocharger
Trans	Transmission
V	Volts

Fuel Cell Vehicles

Advanced Transportation Technology

Although fuel cell vehicles (FCVs) are not expected to reach the mass market for at least a decade, a limited number will be available for sale or lease in 2004-2005 to demonstration fleets in parts of the country with a readily accessible hydrogen supply.

FCVs represent a radical departure from conventional vehicles with internal combustion engines. They use emerging technology with the potential to reduce harmful emissions substantially, as well as energy use and our dependence on foreign oil.

FCVs are propelled by electric motors powered by fuel cells, which produce electricity from the chemical energy of hydrogen. They are more efficient than conventional vehicles, and the only by-product of a hydrogen fuel cell is water. FCVs may also incorporate other advanced automotive technologies to increase efficiency.

The Challenges Ahead

Much work remains before FCVs can be mass-marketed and sold at local dealerships. Significant research and development is required to reduce costs and improve performance in areas such as driving range, cold-weather operation, and durability. A new refueling infrastructure may also be required to make hydrogen fuel widely available to consumers.

Automakers, fuel cell and component developers, government agencies, and others are working hard to accelerate the introduction of FCVs. In fact, partnerships such as the DOE-led FreedomCAR Initiative and the California Fuel Cell Partnership have been formed to encourage private companies and government agencies to work together to prove this technology's viability and move FCVs toward widespread commercialization. For more information about FCVs and links to fuel cell websites, please visit www.fueleconomy.gov/feg/ fuelcell.shtml.

SAMPLE FUEL ECONOMY LABEL
(Attached to New Vehicle Window)

Use these two estimates to
compare to other models.

Compare this vehicle to others by using the FREE FUEL ECONOMY GUIDE available in the dealer showroom

This is the
average
estimate for
city driving.

CITY MPG
24

Fuel Economy
Information

HIGHWAY MPG
31

This is the
average
estimate for
highway
driving.

These
numbers
represent a
range of fuel
economy that
most drivers
achieve with
this particular
model.

Actual Mileage will vary with
options, driving conditions, driving
habits and vehicle's conditions.
Results reported to EPA indicate
that the majority f vehicles with
these estimates will achieve
between

20 and 28 mpg in the city

and between

26 and 36 on the highway.

2005 GREEN CAR 2WD, 4CYL,
2.0 LITER, MULTIPOINT FUEL
INJECTION, 4-SPEED AUTO
TRANS, CATALYST.

Estimated Annual
Fuel Cost: $999

For Comparison Shopping
All vehicles classified as
COMPACT CARS have been
issued mileage ratings ranging
from

13 to 48 mpg city

and

19 to 51 mpg highway.

These
numbers
represent the
range of fuel
economy for
other models of
this size class.

This fuel cost is
based on 15,000
miles/yr at $1.80
per gallon for
regular unleaded
and $1.95 for
premium.

See www.fueleconomy.gov

Check the fuel economy label on the vehicle at the dealers showroom for its specific
fuel economy (mpg) ratings. The ratings may vary slightly from the values in this
guide because of engine anf fuel system differences not listed here.

In: Automobile Industry: Current Issues   ISBN: 1-59454-686-X
Editor: L. R. Domansky, pp. 77-94   © 2006 Nova Science Publishers, Inc.

Chapter 3

AUTOMOBILE AND LIGHT TRUCK FUEL ECONOMY: THE CAFE STANDARDS [*]

Robert Bamberger

SUMMARY

The Energy Policy and Conservation Act of 1975 (P.L. 94-163, EPCA) established new car fuel economy standards for passenger automobiles and light-duty trucks. The current corporate average fuel economy standard (CAFE) is 27.5 miles per gallon (mpg) for passenger automobiles. Light truck standards, set for many years at 20.7 mpg, are required to reach 22.2 for model year (MY) 2007. It was the first increase in CAFE since MY1996. The light-duty truck category includes sport utility vehicles (SUVs). The standards are determined by the National Highway Traffic Safety Administration (NHTSA) within the Department of Transportation.

The House passed H.R. 6, the Energy Policy Act of 2005, on April 21, 2005 (249-183). It includes provisions strongly similar to language that appeared in the omnibus energy legislation reported from conference during the 108th Congress. The legislation would authorize $2 million annually during FY2006-FY2010 for NHTSA to carry out fuel economy rulemakings. It also would expand the criteria that the agency takes into account in setting maximum feasible fuel economy for cars and light trucks. An amendment to

---

[*] Excerpted from CRS Report IB90122. Updated June 7, 2005.

the House bill to raise the CAFE standard to 33 miles per gallon by MY2015 was rejected (177-254).

An omnibus energy bill reported from the Senate Committee on Energy and Natural Resources on May 26, 2005, also would provide NHTSA with $2 million annually to conduct CAFE activities, but does not add to the criteria weighted by NHTSA in setting standards.

One issue over the years has been the test procedures that measure vehicle fuel economy. Consumers have noted that in-use fuel economy rarely meets rated fuel economy. One bill introduced in the 109th Congress, the Fuel Efficiency Truth in Advertising Act of 2005 (H.R. 1103), would direct the Environmental Protection Agency (EPA) to revise its test procedures, taking into account a number of changes in vehicle characteristics and use since the procedures were last changed.

During House debate on H.R. 6, an amendment that would require the fuel economy stickers on new cars to better reflect in-use fuel economy was passed (259-172). No such language is included in the comprehensive legislation that was approved by the Senate Committee on Energy and Natural Resources.

The Committee on Energy and Natural Resources bill includes language to require the Administration to develop a plan to reduce U.S. oil consumption by 1 million barrels daily by 2015 from projected consumption levels. The amendment would not create any new authorities. Rather, it would give the Administration the latitude to use currently existing authorities, including CAFE. A similar provision was rejected as an amendment to the committee print marked up by the House Energy and Commerce Committee in mid-April 2005, and is not in H.R. 6 as passed by the House.

Interest has continued in studying whether the CAFE standards and program should be restructured. One bill introduced in the House (H.R. 70) would require that standards gradually apply to vehicles of up to 10,000 pounds gross vehicle weight (GVR).

MOST RECENT DEVELOPMENTS

The House passed H.R. 6, the Energy Policy Act of 2005, on April 21, 2005 (249-183). It includes provisions strongly similar to language that appeared in the omnibus energy legislation reported from conference during the 108th Congress. The new legislation would authorize $2 million annually during FY2006-FY2010 for the National Highway Traffic Safety

Administration (NHTSA) to carry out fuel economy rulemakings. It also would expand the criteria that the agency takes into account in setting maximum feasible fuel economy for cars and light trucks. An amendment to raise the Corporate Average Fuel Economy (CAFE) standard to 33 miles per gallon by model year (MY) 2015 was rejected (177-254).

One issue over the years has been the test procedures that measure vehicle fuel economy. During House debate on H.R. 6, an amendment that would require the fuel economy stickers on new cars to better reflect in-use fuel economy was passed (259-172). No such language is included in the legislation ordered to be reported from the Senate Committee on Energy and Natural Resources on May 26, 2005.

Some policymakers also argue that the CAFE standards and program should be restructured. Among the issues here are the definitions and regulations for passenger cars and light duty trucks, and whether CAFE requirements should apply to a larger universe of vehicles. One bill introduced in the House (H.R. 705) would require that CAFE standards gradually apply to vehicles of up to 10,000 pounds gross vehicle weight (GVW).

BACKGROUND AND ANALYSIS

Origins of CAFE

The Arab oil embargo of 1973-1974 and the tripling in the price of crude oil brought into sharp focus the fuel inefficiency of U.S. automobiles. New car fleet fuel economy had declined from 14.8 miles per gallon (mpg) in model year (MY)1967 to 12.9 mpg in 1974. In the search for ways to reduce dependence on imported oil, automobiles were an obvious target. The Energy Policy and Conservation Act (P.L. 94-163) established corporate average fuel economy (CAFE) standards for passenger cars for MY1978-MY1980 and 1985 and thereafter. The CAFE standards called for a doubling in new car fleet fuel economy, establishing a standard of 18 mpg in MY1978 and rising to 27.5 by MY1985. (Interim standards for model years 1981-1984 were announced by the Secretary of Transportation in June of 1977.) EPCA also established fuel economy standards for light duty trucks, beginning at 17.2 mpg in MY1979 and currently 20.7 mpg. However, on April 1, 2003, NHTSA issued a final rule that will boost light truck fuel economy to 22.2 mpg in MY2007 — an increase of 1.5 mpg. (The CAFE standards to FY2003 are summarized in **Table 1**.)

Compliance with the standards is measured by calculating a sales-weighted mean of the fuel economies of a given manufacturer's product line, with domestically produced and imported vehicles measured separately. The penalty for non-compliance is $5.50 for every 0.1 mpg below the standard, multiplied by the number of cars in the manufacturer's new car fleet for that year. Civil penalties collected from 1983 to 2002 totaled slightly more than $600 million.

When oil prices rose sharply in the early 1980s, smaller cars were selling well, and it was expected that manufacturers would have no difficulty complying with the standards. However, oil prices had declined by 1985. Sales of smaller cars tapered off as consumers began to place less value on fuel economy and gasoline cost as an input in the overall costs of vehicle ownership. In response to petitions from manufacturers facing stiff civil penalties for noncompliance, the National Highway Traffic Safety Administration (NHTSA) relaxed the standard for model years 1986-1989, but it was restored to 27.5 in MY1990. The Persian Gulf War in 1990 caused a brief spike in oil prices, but it also demonstrated that it was unlikely that the United States or many of the producing nations would tolerate a prolonged disruption in international petroleum commerce. As a consequence, U.S. dependence upon imported petroleum, from a policy perspective, was considered less of a vulnerability.

It was also becoming apparent that reducing U.S. dependence on imported oil would be extremely difficult without imposing a large price increase on gasoline, or restricting consumer choice in passenger vehicles. Many argued that the impacts of such actions upon the economy or the automotive industry would be unacceptable. Meanwhile, gasoline consumption, which fell to 6.5 million barrels per day (mbd) in 1982, averaged nearly 8.4 mbd in 1999, and in April 2005, had reached roughly 9.0 mbd despite prices exceeding year-earlier levels by more than $.40/gallon.

Past Role of CAFE Standards. The effectiveness of the CAFE standards themselves has been controversial. Since 1974, domestic new car fuel economy has roughly doubled; the fuel economy of imports has increased by roughly one-third. Some argue that these improvements would have happened as a consequence of rising oil prices during the 1970s and 1980s. Some studies suggest that the majority of the gains in passenger car fuel economy during the 1970s and 1980s were technical achievements, rather than the consequence of consumers' favoring smaller cars. Between 1976 and 1989, roughly 70% of the improvement in fuel economy was the result of weight reduction, improvements in transmissions and aerodynamics, wider use of front-wheel drive, and use of fuel-injection. The fact that overall passenger car fleet fuel economy remained comparatively flat during a period of declining real prices for gasoline also suggested that the CAFE regulations have contributed to placing some sort of floor under new-car fuel economy.

General criticisms of raising the CAFE standards have been that, owing to the significant lead times manufacturers need to change model lines and because of the time needed for the vehicle fleet to turn over, increasing CAFE is a slow and inefficient means of achieving reductions in fuel consumption. Further, it is argued that the standards risk interfering with consumer choice and jeopardize the economic well-being of the automotive industry. Opponents of raising CAFE usually cite fears that higher efficiency will likely be obtained by downsizing vehicle size and weight, raising concerns about safety.

Table 1. Fuel Economy Standards for Passenger Cars and Light Trucks: Model Years 1978 Through 2007 (miles per gallon)

Model year	Passenger cars	Light trucks[a]		
		Two-wheel drive	Four-wheel drive	Combined[b,c]
1978	[d]18.0	—	—	—
1979	[d]19.0	17.2	15.8	—
1980	[d]20.0	16.0	14.0	([e])
1981	2.0	[f]16.7	15.0	([e])
1982	24.0	18.0	16.0	17.5
1983	26.0	19.5	17.5	19.0
1984	27.0	20.3	18.5	20.0
1985	[d]27.5	[g]19.7	[g]18.9	[g]19.5
1986	[h]26.0	20.5	19.5	20.0
1987	[i]26.0	21.5	19.5	20.5
1988	26.0	21.0	19.5	20.5
1989	[j]26.5	21.5	19.0	20.0
1990	[d]27.5	20.5	19.0	20.2
1991	[d]27.5	20.7	19.1	20.2
1992	[d]27.5	—	—	20.2
1993	[d]27.5	—	—	20.4
1994	[d]27.5	—	—	20.5
1995	[d]27.5	—	—	20.6
1996	[d]27.5	—	—	20.7
1997	[d]27.5	—	—	20.7
1998	[d]27.5	—	—	20.7

Table 1 Continued

Model year	Passenger cars	Light trucks[a]		
		Two-wheel drive	Four-wheel drive	Combined[b,c]
1999	[d]27.5	—	—	20.7
2000	[d]27.5	—	—	20.7
2001	[d]27.5	—	—	20.7
2002	[d]27.5	—	—	20.7
2003	[d]27.5	—	—	20.7
2004	[d]27.5	—	—	20.7
2005	[d]27.5	—	—	21.0
2006	[d]27.5	—	—	21.6
2007	[d]27.5	—	—	22.2

Source: Automotive Fuel Economy Program, Annual Update, Calendar Year 2001, appearing in full at [http://www.nhtsa.dot.gov/cars/problems/studies/fuelecon/ index.html#TOC]; and U.S. Department of Transportation. National Highway Traffic Safety Administration. *Light Truck Average Fuel Economy Standard, Model Year 2004*. Final Rule. [http://www.nhtsa.dot.gov/cars/rules/rulings/Cafe/LightTruck/ NPRM-final.htm].

a. Standards for MY1979 light trucks were established for vehicles with a gross vehicle weight rating (GVWR) of 6,000
pounds or less. Standards for MY1980 and beyond are for light trucks with a GVWR of 8,500 pounds or less.
b. For MY1979, light truck manufacturers could comply separately with standards for four-wheel drive, general utility
vehicles and all other light trucks, or combine their trucks into a single fleet and comply with the standard of 17.2
mpg.
c. For MYs 1982-1991, manufacturers could comply with the two-wheel and four-wheel drive standards or could combine
all light trucks and comply with the combined standard.
d. Established by Congress in Title V of the act.
e. A manufacturer whose light truck fleet was powered exclusively by basic engines which were not also used in passenger
cars could meet standards of 14 mpg and 14.5 mpg in MYs 1980 and 1981, respectively.
f. Revised in June 1979 from 18.0 mpg.
g. Revised in October 1984 from 21.6 mpg for two-wheel drive, 19.0 mpg for four-wheel drive, and 21.0 mpg for
combined.
h. Revised in October 1985 from 27.5 mpg.
i. Revised in October 1986 from 27.5 mpg.
j. Revised in September 1988 from 27.5 mpg.

Proponents of CAFE increases have argued that boosting the standards might bring about the introduction of technological improvements that do not compromise features that consumers value, but which would otherwise not be added because these improvements do add to the cost of a new vehicle.

Table 2. Domestic and Import Passenger Car and Light Truck Fuel Economy Averages for Model Years 1978-2002 (in MPG)

Model Year	Domestic			Import			All cars	All light trucks	Total fleet
	Car	Light Truck	Com-bined	Car	Light[a] truck	Com-bined			
1978	18.7	—	—	27.3	—	—	19.9	—	—
1979	19.3	17.7	19.1	26.1	20.8	25.5	20.3	18.2	20.1
1980	22.6	16.8	21.4	29.6	24.3	28.6	24.3	18.5	23.1
1981	24.2	18.3	22.9	31.5	27.4	30.7	25.9	20.1	24.6
1982	25.0	19.2	23.5	31.1	27.0	30.4	26.6	20.5	25.1
1983	24.4	19.6	23.0	32.4	27.1	31.5	26.4	20.7	24.8
1984	25.5	19.3	23.6	32.0	26.7	30.6	26.9	20.6	25.0
1985	26.3	19.6	24.0	31.5	26.5	30.3	27.6	20.7	25.4
1986	26.9	20.0	24.4	31.6	25.9	29.8	28.2	21.5	25.9
1987	27.0	20.5	24.6	31.2	25.2	29.6	28.5	21.7	26.2
1988	27.4	20.6	24.5	31.5	24.6	30.0	28.8	21.3	26.0
1989	27.2	20.4	24.2	30.8	23.5	29.2	28.4	20.9	25.6
1990	26.9	20.3	23.9	29.9	23.0	28.5	28.0	20.8	25.4
1991	27.3	20.9	24.4	30.1	23.0	28.4	28.4	21.3	25.6
1992	27.0	20.5	23.8	29.2	22.7	27.9	27.9	20.8	25.1
1993	27.8	20.7	24.2	29.6	22.8	28.1	28.4	21.0	25.2
1994	27.5	20.5	23.5	29.6	22.0	27.8	28.3	20.7	24.7
1995	27.7	20.3	23.8	30.3	21.5	27.9	28.6	20.5	24.9
1996	28.1	20.5	24.1	29.6	22.2	27.7	28.5	20.8	24.9
1997	27.8	20.2	23.3	30.1	22.1	27.5	28.7	20.6	24.6
1998	28.6	20.5	23.3	29.2	22.9	27.6	28.8	21.1	24.7
1999	28.0	—	—	29.0	—	—	28.3	20.9	24.5
2000	28.7	—	—	28.3	—	—	28.5	21.2	24.8
2001	28.7	—	—	29.0	—	—	28.8	20.9	24.6
2002	29.0	—	—	28.7	—	—	28.9	21.3	24.6

Note: Beginning with MY1999, the agency ceased categorizing the total light truck fleet by either domestic or import fleets.

a. Light trucks from foreign-based manufacturers.

There were highly controversial attempts to significantly raise the CAFE standards on passenger cars in the early 1990s. One proposal included in omnibus energy legislation was so controversial that it contributed to the Senate's inability in 1991 to bring the bill up for debate on the floor.

Current fleet fuel economy averages are shown in the preceding table.

NHTSA typically established truck CAFE standards 18 months prior to the beginning of each model year, as EPCA allows. However, such a narrow window permitted NHTSA to do little more than ratify manufacturers' projections for the model year in question. In April 1994, the agency proposed to abandon this practice and issued an Advance Notice of Proposed Rulemaking inviting comment on what level that standards might be established for trucks for MY1998-MY2006. The following year, however, after a change in congressional leadership, Congress included language in the FY1996 Department of Transportation (DOT) Appropriations to prohibit expenditures for any rulemaking that would make any adjustment to the CAFE standards. Identical language was included in the appropriations and spending bills for FY1997-FY2000. An effort to pass a sense of the Senate amendment that conferees on the FY2000 DOT Appropriations should not agree to the House-passed rider for FY2000 was defeated in the Senate on September 15, 1999 (55-40). The rider also appeared in the FY2001 DOT Appropriations (H.R. 4475) approved by the House Committee on Appropriations May 16, 2000, and approved by the House May 19, 2000. However, the Senate insisted that the language be dropped in conference, opening the way for NHTSA to initiate rulemakings once again.

The conferees also agreed to authorize a study of CAFE by the National Academy of Sciences (NAS) in conjunction with DOT. That study, released on July 30, 2001, concluded that it was possible to achieve more than a 40% improvement in light truck and SUV fuel economy over a 10-15 year period at costs that would be recoverable over the lifetime of ownership. A study released in December 2004 by a National Commission on Energy Policy established by foundation money recommended that Congress instruct NHTSA to raise CAFE standards over a five-year period beginning not later than 2010. The commission recommended that manufacturers be able to trade the fuel economy credits earned by exceeding the standards. Additionally, should technologies not advance as quickly as anticipated, the government should also sell credits at some pre-specified price for the purpose of placing a cap on compliance costs. Lastly, the commission suggested an aggressive tax incentive program to encourage production and purchase of hybrid and advanced diesel vehicles. The commission report, *Ending the Energy Stalemate: A Bipartisan Strategy to Meet America's Energy Challenges*, is available online at [http://64.70.252.93/O82F4682.pdf].

NHTSA Rulemaking for MY2005-MY2007: Light Truck Fuel Economy

Today, light trucks are a larger portion of the total vehicle population, and travel more annual vehicle miles, than in the past. For example, in 1980, light trucks composed 19.9% of the U.S. new automobile market. By 2001, this figure had increased to 50.8%; SUVs alone accounted for 23.1% of the new vehicle market in 1999, while mini-vans accounted for 5.8%. However, a comparison of market share underestimates this growth and its consequences. While the number of passenger cars sold each year in the United States has decreased somewhat since 1980, the number of light trucks sold has more than tripled, from 2.2 million in 1980 to 8.7 million in 2001. In 2001, SUV sales alone (4.0 million) nearly doubled total light truck sales for 1980. As a result, the total fuel usage attributable to these vehicles has increased.

On December 16, 2002, NHTSA issued a proposed rule calling for an increase in light-duty truck CAFE to 21.0 mpg in MY2005, 21.6 mpg in MY2006, and 22.2 mpg in MY2007. Noting the target of a 5 billion gallon savings between MY2006 and MY2012 called for in the conference energy bill, NHTSA indicated that the proposed increases for MY2006-MY2007 would save more than 3 billion gallons and, if the standard remained at 22.2 mpg through MY2012, approximately 8 billion gallons of gasoline would be saved during the period of MY2006-MY2012. On April 1, 2003, NHTSA announced its adoption of the proposed rule.

In the December 2002 proposal, NHTSA expressed its belief that "some manufacturers may be able to achieve CAFE performance better than they currently project." The agency's analysis assumed that compliance would be achieved by improvements in technology, and not by lightening vehicles and jeopardizing vehicle safety. NHTSA also indicates that it has "tentatively concluded that it is unnecessary for any manufacturer to restrict the utility of their products to meet our proposed CAFE standards."

NHTSA's calculation of the net benefits of the proposed boost to SUV CAFE is shown below. The estimate of the net benefits is significantly higher in the second and third years because the first increment of improvement is only 0.3 mpg, while it is 0.6 mpg in the second and third years. The "societal benefits" are calculated on an assumption of $0.083 per gallon over the lifetime of the vehicle. This assumes a benefit of $0.048 for the effect on the world market price for gasoline owing to lower U.S. demand, and $0.035 for the reduction in threat from oil supply disruption.

	Total Costs (million)	Total Societal Benefits (million)	Net Benefits (million)
MY2005	$108	$219	$111
MY2006	221	513	292
MY2007	373	794	421

Though NHTSA announced a boost of 1.5 mpg in light truck fuel economy in its final rule issued April 1, 2003, some argue that more steps should be taken. Some policymakers believe an increase in passenger automobile CAFE is also in order. Another idea has been to require efficiency improvements in the operation of heavy trucks. In the 108th Congress, Senator Feinstein introduced legislation (S. 255) that, among other provisions, would have expanded the applicability of fuel economy standards to vehicles up to 10,000 pounds GVW. Others argue that the automotive industry should not be further burdened at this time by higher CAFE requirements.

Advance Notice of Proposed Rulemaking: December 2003

On December 22, 2003, NHTSA issued an Advance Notice of Proposed Rulemaking inviting comments not on the appropriate stringency of CAFE standards but on the structure of the program. The agency noted four broad criticisms of the program, and areas in which it invited comment:

- *Vehicle classifications.* Some argue that the considerable difference in passenger car and light truck fuel economy standards presents an incentive for manufacturers to produce vehicles that can be classified in the light truck category. Similarly, the applicability of CAFE standards to vehicles less than 8,500 pounds Gross Vehicle Weight (GVW) encourages manufacturers to offer vehicles that exceed this weight. Among many issues, the agency invited comment on whether or not the CAFE program should be extended to encompass vehicles of less than 10,000 pounds GVW. Legislation to make vehicles rated at this weight subject to CAFE standards has been introduced in the 109th Congress (H.R. 705).
- *Safety.* The trade-off between vehicle weight and safety continues to be controversial. Some argue that the increase in light truck fleet fuel economy to 22.2 mpg by 2007 will be achieved, in part, by reducing the weight of vehicles and

possibly raising the risk to passengers and drivers. However, it is also noted that weight reduction of the heaviest vehicles in this category might achieve some savings without penalty to safety. Complicating any analysis is the fact that reductions in vehicle weight raise the odds of survival for occupants of other vehicles involved in an accident. There are a number of other factors governing safety; it is a complex issue.

- *Economic impacts.* Increases in mandated fuel economy have economic consequences. Analysis by the Energy Information Administration suggests that a "sustained gradual increase" in light truck fuel economy of 0.6 mpg from 2007 to 2025 would incur a loss of $84 billion in real GDP over the period. Additionally, the structure of the light truck standards favors manufacturers who produce a line of models that includes some of the smaller vehicles in the light truck class. For example, two manufacturers could produce a vehicle of similar weight. However, the manufacturer of the less efficient of these two vehicles could still have a lower overall truck fleet fuel economy average if its product mix includes more smaller trucks than the other manufacturer.

- *Vehicle attributes.* The agency invited comment on whether or not the definitions and classifications of light trucks need to be amended in light of the considerable change in the vehicle feet and consumer demand since the CAFE program went into effect in 1977. Options that have been proposed include keying vehicle CAFE to vehicle "attributes," which could include vehicle weight or vehicle size, and the establishment of multiple classifications. Some argue that this will still encourage "upsizing," or "vehicle creep," to place a vehicle in a less stringent CAFE category. Classification of vehicles with "flat floors" as light trucks — that is, the capability of removing seats to create a flat load floor — has enabled manufacturers to incorporate flat floor design into vehicles that might have otherwise been classified as passenger automobiles. The PT Cruiser is cited as an example of this. Inclusion of cargo beds of any size may also allow classification of a vehicle as a light truck.

Legislation introduced in the 109th Congress would also address the test cycle used by the Environmental Protection Agency (EPA) to measure vehicle fuel economy for determining whether a manufacturer's fleet of new cars is in compliance with the CAFE standard. Consumers have found that in-use fuel economy falls short of the published measurements that also appear posted on the windows of new cars for sale. Advocates of changes argue that the current test cycle is not consistent with current vehicle characteristics and the way light-duty vehicles are used. For example, the estimated average length of vehicle trips is shorter than the length assumed in the test cycle and would not reflect the typical number of engine cold starts. The test cycle does not include the operation of air conditioning.

The fuel economy of individual vehicles is calculated by running vehicles through a test on a dynamometer intended to simulate a driving cycle that assumes 11 miles driven in an urban setting and 10 miles on open highway. To bring this calculation more into line with in-use fuel economy experienced by drivers, the EPA makes a downward adjustment of 10% for the city portion of the cycle and 22% for the highway portion. However, many argue that this is an insufficient adjustment and that in-use fuel economy is still less than the estimate provided to drivers on a sticker posted to the windows of new cars.

An amendment was brought to the House floor during the debate on H.R. 6 to require EPA to make adjustments to bring the posted information on in-use fuel economy further in conformity with drivers' actual on-road experience. Without specifying a second test for the purpose of providing an estimate of in-use fuel economy, opponents of the amendment were fearful that the effect of the amendment as drafted would be to lower manufacturers' calculated annual CAFE by as much as 10%-20% and make compliance with the CAFE standards significantly more difficult. A "perfecting" amendment was approved (259-172) that would essentially require that EPA make further adjustment in deriving the adjusted, in-use fuel economy that is posted to new vehicle windows in the showroom.

CAFE in the 109th Congress: Omnibus Energy Legislation

The House passed H.R. 6, the Energy Policy Act of 2005, on April 21, 2005 (249-183). With one exception noted above, the bill includes provisions strongly similar to language that appeared in the omnibus energy legislation reported from conference during the 108th Congress. The new legislation would authorize $2 million annually during FY2006-FY2010 for NHTSA to carry out fuel economy rulemakings. It also would expand the criteria that the agency takes into account in setting maximum feasible fuel economy for cars and light trucks, including the effects on automotive industry employment. As noted above, H.R. 6 was amended on the House floor to require that fuel economy information posted on new cars would more closely approximate in-use fuel economy (259-172). An amendment to raise the CAFE standard to 33 miles per gallon by MY2015 was rejected (177-254).

The legislation ordered reported on May 26, 2006, from the Senate Committee on Energy and Natural Resources would also provide $2 million annually to NHTSA for rulemaking, but does not include the language to expand the criteria to be considered in setting standards. It also does not include language that would affect the estimated fuel economy that is posted in the window of new cars.

However, the bill ordered reported from the Committee on Energy and Natural Resources does include language to require the Administration to develop a plan to reduce U.S. oil consumption by 1 million barrels daily by 2015 from projected consumption levels. The amendment would not create any new authorities. Rather, it would give the Administration the latitude to use currently existing authorities, including CAFE. A similar provision was in the comprehensive legislation that came out of conference in the 108th Congress. An attempt to include a comparable provision in the legislation that went to the floor of the House was rejected during markup by the House Energy and Commerce Committee, and is not in H.R. 6 as passed by the House.

IMPROVING FUEL ECONOMY: OTHER POLICY APPROACHES

Two possible approaches to reduce gasoline consumption involve (1) raising the price of gasoline through taxation, or other means, to a level that induces some conservation; and (2) increasing the efficiency of the automobile fleet in use. Of course, a combination of these two broad approaches can be used as well.

The Hydrogen Fuel Initiative, FreedomCAR and the Partnership for a New Generation of Vehicles (PNGV) (1993-2003). Over five years, the Administration is seeking a total funding increase of $720 million. These initiatives would fund research on hydrogen fuel and fuel cells for transportation and stationary applications. The 108th Congress for FY2004 appropriated approximately $50 million for the initiatives ($20 million less than the Administration request) above the FY2003 level, and for FY2005 an additional $25 million above the FY2004 level. The Energy Policy Act of 2005 (H.R. 6) would authorize $4 billion during the period FY2006-FY2010. The comprehensive legislation in the 108th Congress would have set goals for the production of hydrogen-fueled passenger vehicles. No goals are included in H.R. 6.

Critics of the Administration initiative have suggested that the hydrogen program was intended to forestall attempts to significantly raise vehicle CAFE standards, and that it relieves the automotive industry of assuming more initiative in pursuing technological innovations. In addition, critics argue that hydrogen-fueled vehicles may ultimately be infeasible, and that attention and funding should be focused on other research areas. On the other hand, supporters argue that it is appropriate for government to become involved in the development of technologies that are too costly to draw private sector investment. At issue for these policymakers will be whether the federal initiative and level of funding is aggressive enough. (For additional information, see CRS Report RS21442, *Hydrogen and Fuel Cell R&D: FreedomCAR and the President's Hydrogen Fuel Initiative.*)

Price of Gasoline. Owing to higher taxation of gasoline in other nations, Americans enjoy one of the lowest prices for gasoline. The price of gasoline has increased significantly, although, adjusted into real dollars, current prices are still well short of any historic high. Past proposals to raise the price of gasoline to leverage consumers into more efficient vehicles have garnered little support. Owing to the relative price inelasticity of gasoline demand, many believe that the size of the price increase it would take to curb gasoline consumption to any degree would have a damaging effect on the economy of several times greater magnitude. Indeed, analysis of the research (Plotkin, Greene, 1997, cited in References) suggested that an increase in gasoline taxes would be one-third as effective in achieving a reduction in demand as studies of the 1980s once projected. This is a significant reflection of the place that personal transportation and inexpensive gasoline has assumed in our economy and value system.

Some have argued during past episodes of high prices that, when prices softened again, the federal government should step in and capture the difference as a tax, and possibly devote the proceeds to developing public transportation infrastructure and incentives. This tax could be adjusted periodically to see that gasoline would not become less expensive than a certain level in real (inflation adjusted) dollars.

Owing to the unpopularity of raising gasoline prices, raising the CAFE standard is more comfortable for some; however, it is a long-term response. Depending upon the magnitude of an increase in gasoline prices, no matter what the cause, a price-induced conservation response could be nearly immediate, and may grow as consumers initially drive less and eventually seek out more efficient vehicles. However, U.S. gasoline consumption has held relatively steady despite the sharp increase in gasoline prices through the spring of 2005. It is possible that gasoline demand during the summer will be lower than it might otherwise be were prices lower, but this may prove difficult to measure and remains to be seen.

CAFE and Reduction of Carbon Dioxide Emissions. Motor vehicles are a major source of key air pollutants. Vehicles account for one-fifth of U.S. production of CO_2 emissions. There is some debate over whether raising the CAFE standards would be an ineffective or marginal way to reduce emissions of carbon dioxide. On one hand, improvements in fuel economy should enable the same vehicle to burn less fuel to travel a given distance. However, to the extent that technologies to improve fuel economy add cost to new vehicles, it has been argued that consumers will tend to retain older, less efficient cars longer. It has also been suggested that there is a correlation between improved fuel economy and an increase in miles driven and vehicle emissions. Vehicle miles traveled have continued to increase in recent years when fuel economy improved only slightly.

Perhaps the most significant current issue regarding automotive fuel economy is the decision by the state of California to require carbon dioxide emissions standards for passenger cars and light trucks. Enacted in 2002, A.B. 1498 requires the state to promulgate regulations to achieve the maximum feasible and cost-effective reduction of greenhouse gases from cars and trucks. The regulations, adopted by the California Air Resources Board on September 24, 2004, require a reduction of greenhouse gas emissions of 30% by 2016. The regulation covers passenger vehicles, but would not affect heavier vehicles such as commercial trucks or buses.

Under the Clean Air Act, California is permitted to establish its own emissions standards for automobiles, as long as those standards are at least as stringent as the federal standard. However, there is no current federal standard for greenhouse gas emissions; federal standards focus on pollutants with direct effects on air quality and health, including ground-level ozone (smog) and carbon monoxide. Critics challenge that greenhouse gases are not pollutants, and that the greenhouse gas standard is a *de facto* fuel economy standard, since reducing emissions of carbon dioxide — the key greenhouse gas — requires reductions in fuel consumption. Under CAFE, states do not have the authority to set their own standards; authority remains solely with the federal government.

Several auto manufacturers and dealers have challenged the California auto greenhouse gas standard in court. The plaintiffs argue that California lacks the authority to set a fuel economy standard under CAFE, and that greenhouse gases are not a pollutant under the Clean Air Act. California officials maintain that they have the authority under the Clean Air Act to regulate vehicle greenhouse gas emissions.

The outcome of this case will likely have major effects on the U.S. auto industry. If the standards are upheld, New York will adopt California's standards, and other states are likely to follow suit. The state of California estimates that complying with the standard could cost $1,000 per vehicle by 2016, while opponents argue that costs could be as much as $3,000 per vehicle. While reducing greenhouse gas emissions and fuel consumption, the new standards would likely increase purchase costs and potentially diminish the new car market. Further, it is likely that the standards would have varying effects on automakers who sell more or less efficient products. (For additional background, see CRS Report RS20298, *Sport Utility Vehicles, Mini-Vans, and Light Trucks: An Overview of Fuel Economy and Emissions Standards*, and CRS Report RL32764, *Global Warming: The Litigation Heats Up.*)

Other Initiatives. During Senate debate on comprehensive energy legislation in the 108th Congress, the Senate agreed (99-1) on June 9, 2003, to an amendment proposed by Senator Landrieu that would have required the Administration to develop a plan to reduce U.S. oil consumption by 1 million barrels daily by 2013 from projected consumption levels. The amendment would not have created any new authorities. Rather, it would have given the Administration the latitude to use currently existing authorities, including CAFE. Opponents of an increase in CAFE especially embraced the amendment because it would have required a significant reduction in petroleum consumption without necessarily using CAFE as one of the levers. The bill ordered reported to the Senate from the Commitee on Energy and Natural Resources on May 26, 2005, includes similar language. However, a similar provision was rejected as an amendment to the committee print marked up by the House Energy and Commerce Committee in mid-April 2005, and is not in H.R. 6 as passed by the House.

Some policymakers argue that more needs to be done to reduce vehicle fuel consumption. Currently, light truck fuel economy standards do not apply to vehicles above 8,500 pounds gross vehicle weight (GVW). Senator Feinstein has introduced legislation (S. 255) that, among other provisions, would expand the applicability of fuel economy standards to vehicles up to 10,000 pounds GVW. The Tax Incentives for Fuel Efficient Vehicles Act (S.

795), would establish a new tax credit for purchases of vehicles that exceed the current CAFE standards by at least 5 mpg and would modify the gas guzzler tax to include SUVs and some larger vehicles not currently subject to the tax. Opponents of measures like these argue that the automotive industry should not be further burdened at this time by higher CAFE requirements.

LEGISLATION

H.R. 6 (Barton)

Energy Policy Act of 2005. Introduced April 18, 2005. Among other provisions, would authorize $2 million annually during FY2006-FY2010 for the National Highway Traffic and Safety Administration (NHTSA) to carry out fuel economy rulemakings. It also would expand the criteria that the agency takes into account in setting maximum feasible fuel economy for cars and light trucks, and require that EPA make further adjustments in deriving in-use fuel economy predictions that are posted on the window of new cars. Passed by the House on April 21, 2005 (249-183).

H.R. 705 (Gilchrist)

Automobile Fuel Economy Act of 2005. To amend Title 49, United States Code, to require phased increases in the fuel efficiency standards applicable to light trucks; to require fuel economy standards for automobiles of up to 10,000 pounds gross vehicle weight; to increase the fuel economy of the federal fleet of vehicles, and for other purposes. Introduced February 9, 2005, and referred to House Subcommittee on Energy and Air Quality.

H.R. 1103 (Johnson)

Fuel Efficiency Truth in Advertising Act of 2005. Would direct EPA to update its test procedures for light-duty vehicles for the purpose of calculating vehicle fuel economy. Introduced March 3, 2005, and referred to House Committee on Energy and Commerce.

H.R. 6 (Tauzin) (108th Congress)

Enhances energy conservation and research and development, provides for security and diversity in the energy supply for the American people, and for other purposes. Introduced April 7, 2003. Passed House (247-175) April 11, 2003. Senate version passed (84-14) July 31, 2003. Reported from conference, November 17, 2003. Passed House (246-180) November 19, 2003. Motion to invoke cloture failed in the Senate (57-40), November 21, 2003.

CONGRESSIONAL HEARINGS, REPORTS AND DOCUMENTS

National Research Council. Committee on the Effectiveness and Impact of Corporate Average Fuel Economy Standards. *Effectiveness and Impact of Corporate Average Fuel Economy (CAFE) Standards.* Washington, D.C., National Academy Press, 2001. 166 pp.

Plotkin, Steve. Greene, David. "Prospects for Improving the Fuel Economy of Light Duty Vehicles." *Energy Policy*, vol. 25, no. 14-15. December 1997. Pp. 1179-1188.

U.S. Department of Transportation. National Highway Traffic Safety Administration. *Reforming the Fuel Economy Standards Program.* [http://www.nhtsa.dot.gov/cars/rules/ CAFE/Rulemaking/CAFEReformdata.pdf].

U.S. Department of Transportation. National Highway Traffic Safety Administration. Light Truck Average Fuel Economy Standards, Model Years 2005-2007. 68 FR 16867; April 7, 2003.

U.S. Department of Transportation. National Highway Traffic Safety Administration. Automotive Fuel Economy Program. Annual Update, Calendar Year 2002, appearing in full at [http://www.nhtsa.dot.gov/ cars/problems/studies/fuelecon/index.html].

U.S. Federal Register. Department of Transportation. National Highway Traffic Safety Administration. *Light Truck Fuel Economy Standards, Model Years 1998-2006.*

Advance Notice of Proposed Rulemaking (ANPRM). Vol. 59, No. 66. Wednesday, April 6, 1994, p. 16324-16332.

In: Automobile Industry: Current Issues   ISBN: 1-59454-686-X
Editor: L. R. Domansky, pp. 95-114   © 2006 Nova Science Publishers, Inc.

Chapter 4

TAX PREFERENCES FOR SPORT UTILITY VEHICLES (SUVs): CURRENT LAW AND LEGISLATIVE INITIATIVES IN THE 109TH CONGRESS [*]

Gary Guenther

SUMMARY

The growing presence of large sport utility vehicles (SUVs) on U.S. streets, roads, and highways since the early 1990s has fueled a lively debate over what steps the federal government should take, if any, to alter their effects on the environment, highway safety, traffic congestion, and overall gasoline consumption.

Legislative activity in the 108th Congress enlarged the scope of the debate to include the effect of federal tax policy on the demand for heavy-duty SUVs. In passing the Jobs and Growth Tax Relief Reconciliation Act of 2003, Congress raised the maximum expensing allowance under Section 179 of the Internal Revenue Code from $25,000 to $100,000. Heavy-duty SUVs purchased mainly for business use qualified for this allowance. Critics of SUV and their allies in Congress took exception to making large SUVs eligible for the enhanced allowance on the grounds that doing so would encourage their purchase by lowering their after-tax cost relative to smaller, more fuel-efficient vehicles. In an apparent response to this concern, the 108th Congress added a provision to the final tax bill it passed — the American Jobs Creation Act of 2004 (AJCA) — lowering the maximum expensing allowance for SUVs weighing between 6,000 and 14,000 pounds and placed in service after October 22, 2004 from $100,000 to $25,000. While it is substantial, the reduction appears to have done little to curtail the effective tax preference for large SUVs arising from the tax treatment of depreciation.

One important way in which the federal tax code can influence the purchase of heavy-duty SUVs for business use is through important differences in the tax treatment of depreciation for these vehicles and passenger cars. Under current tax law, the depreciation of passenger cars is treated less generously than that of light trucks (including many SUVs). Passenger cars, which are defined as motor vehicles weighing 6,000 pounds or less, are considered so-called "listed property" and thus subject to annual limits on allowable depreciation deductions. By contrast, light trucks, which are defined as motor vehicles weighing more than 6,000 pounds (with some exceptions), are generally depreciated under a different and more favorable set of rules. As a result, a business taxpayer can realize a greater total depreciation allowance (measured in constant dollars) over a vehicle's useful life by purchasing a heavy-duty SUV than a passenger car of comparable value.

The federal tax code also influences the purchase of heavy-duty SUVs by excluding them from the gas guzzler excise tax. The tax is levied on domestic sales of new automobiles that have relatively poor fuel economy ratings. It is paid by manufacturers and importers. Automobiles are defined as motor vehicles weighing 6,000 pounds and less. Vehicles with a gross weight above that limit are exempt from the tax.

There are no current legislative initiatives in the 109th Congress to modify these tax preferences for heavy-duty SUVs. The report will be updated to reflect significant legislative activity addressing them.

Some regard sport utility vehicles (SUVs) as symbols of profligate consumption and a selfish disregard for highway safety, environmental protection, and fuel economy. To others, they are marvels of automotive engineering and design, offering an unrivaled combination of storage space, personal safety, rugged styling, and access to wilderness areas and other rough terrain. In the past decade, SUVs have become both an ubiquitous and conspicuous presence on American roads, streets, and highways, as their

---

* Excerpted from CRS Report RL32173. Updated March 21, 2005.

sales and average size and weight have steadily increased. Although many SUV owners use them as passenger cars, there are some notable differences in design and performance between the typical SUV and the typical passenger car. On the whole, SUVs are taller and boxier. Most are built on the rigid chassis of a pick-up truck, giving them a relatively high clearance between the road surface and the undercarriage. Partly because most SUVs have higher center of gravity than the typical passenger car, their ride typically feels bumpier and more like that of a truck, despite the availability of the same luxury options found in many automobiles. The increasing popularity of so-called crossover vehicles, which blend some of the features of passenger cars and light trucks, and a drop in domestic purchases of heavy-duty SUVs in the past year or so have lessened these differences to some extent.[1]

The effects of large SUVs on air quality, highway safety, and fuel consumption have fueled a vigorous debate over whether the federal government should subject them to more stringent regulatory standards for safety and fuel economy. Recent legislative activity by Congress has expanded the scope of debate to include the ways in which federal tax policy affects the demand for heavy-duty SUVs.

In passing the Jobs and Growth Tax Relief Reconciliation Act of 2003 (JGTRRA, P.L. 108-27), the 108th Congress pursued a variety of policy objectives, including accelerated rates of growth in domestic business investment and job creation. Congressional debate over the measure gave no indication, however, that boosting domestic demand for heavy-duty SUVs was one of these objectives. Yet a provision in JGTRRA to stimulate small business investment in machinery and equipment (including certain motor vehicles) and packaged software appears to have had such an effect. The provision made the expensing allowance under Section 179 of the Internal Revenue Code (IRC) more generous in 2003 through 2005.

Not surprisingly, producers and sellers of heavy-duty SUVs welcomed the stimulus. They tend to earn sizable profit margins on sales of such vehicles.[2]

But not everyone was pleased that the newly enhanced expensing allowance applied to large SUVs. SUV critics denounced it as a "SUV tax loophole." They said that the allowance should be modified so that heavy-duty SUVs no longer would qualify for it. In their view, it was unacceptable for the federal government to offer a tax subsidy for the purchase of motor vehicles mainly intended for business use that from their perspective received poor gas mileage, emitted high concentrations of air pollutants, and posed significant safety hazards to their own occupants and to passengers in other vehicles.[3]

Apparently in response to the objections raised against the SUV tax preference created by JGTRRA, the 108th Congress included a provision to curtail the preference in the final tax bill it passed, the American Jobs Creation Act of 2004 (AJCA, P.L. 108-357). The provision limited the IRC Section 179 expensing allowance for SUVs exempt from the depreciation limitations for passenger cars under IRC Section 280F to $25,000. This limit applied to SUVs placed in service after October 22, 2004. AJCA also extended the changes in the allowance made by JGTRRA through 2007.

This report explains the ways in which the federal tax code might affect the purchase of heavy-duty SUVs and will discuss any proposals in 109th Congress to alter this treatment. Two statutory provisions make up the core of the report: the expensing allowance under IRC Section 179 and the gas guzzler excise tax on domestic sales of new automobiles under IRC Section 4064.

DEPRECIATION OF MOTOR VEHICLES UNDER THE FEDERAL TAX CODE

Perhaps the most important way in which the federal tax code affects the purchase of heavy-duty SUVs is the tax treatment of depreciation for motor vehicles other than passenger cars. In order to understand the connection between the two, it is essential to consider the current rules for writing off the cost of motor vehicles bought mainly for business use and their rationale.

In general, business taxpayers — such as subchapter C corporations, owners of S corporations, and members of partnerships and limited liability corporations — are allowed to deduct all the ordinary and necessary expenses they incur in determining their taxable business income in a particular tax year. One such expense is depreciation, which represents the decline in the economic value of business assets resulting from wear and tear and obsolescence. Under current tax law, the cost of a depreciable asset such as a building, patent, light truck, or machine tool is recovered over a specified period — one that may or may not coincide with its actual useful life — using an allowable method of depreciation, such as the straight-line or double-declining balance methods.[4]

In an effort to bolster the domestic climate for business investment, the federal government sometimes permits taxpayers to recover the cost of certain business assets well before their economic value has been exhausted.

Such an acceleration in the rate of tax depreciation encourages firms to invest more than they otherwise would in these assets in the short run, setting the stage for faster growth in the overall economy. But accelerated depreciation can also distort the allocation of economic resources by encouraging investment in favored assets at the expense of other assets which may offer higher pre-tax rates of return on investment, and into industries that intensively use the tax-favored assets at the expense of other industries whose pre-tax rates of return on investment may be higher. Accelerated depreciation can have these undesirable economic effects mainly because it lowers the user cost of capital for investment in favored assets relative to that for investment in other assets, all other things being equal.

The cost of most tangible depreciable business assets placed in service after 1986 is recovered under what is known as the Modified Accelerated Cost Recovery System (MACRS), which was established by the Tax Reform Act of 1986 (P.L. 99-514). Under this system, new and used automobiles and light trucks (including SUVs, vans, and minivans) used primarily in a trade or business are assigned a recovery period of five years. Their cost may be recovered using the most advantageous depreciation method: the double-declining balance method. Nevertheless, as is explained below, an exception to this treatment is made for passenger cars used primarily in a trade or business that the Internal Revenue Service (IRS) regards as luxurious.

In many cases, the cost of motor vehicles bought mainly for business use may also be expensed under Section 179 of the Internal Revenue Code (IRC). Generally, expensing involves writing off or deducting the cost of a depreciable asset in the year when it is placed into service, regardless of the asset's useful life. As may seem obvious, expensing is the most accelerated form of depreciation. Owing to changes in Section 179 made by JGTRRA and AJCA, business taxpayers may expense in a tax year up to $100,000 of the cost of qualified assets placed in service from 2003 through 2007;[5] before JGTRRA, the maximum expensing allowance in that period was fixed at $25,000.[6] With a few minor exceptions, qualified assets are defined as new and used business machines and equipment (including motor vehicles) and packaged or off-the-shelf software used in the active conduct of a trade or business. The amount that a business taxpayer may expense under Section 179 is subject to two important limitations: a dollar limitation and an income limitation. Under the dollar limitation, the maximum annual expensing allowance of $100,000 is reduced, dollar for dollar, by the amount by which the total cost of qualified property placed in service in a single tax year exceeds a phase-out threshold of $400,000 from 2003 through 2007;[7] that threshold was fixed at $200,000 before the enactment of JGTRRA. Under the income limitation, the expensing allowance cannot exceed the taxable income a taxpayer earns from the active conduct of the trade or business in which the qualified assets are used. Assuming no change in current law, the maximum expensing allowance will revert to $25,000 and the phase-out threshold to $200,000 in 2008 and beyond.

A critical aspect of the expensing allowance is its impact on small business. Because of the phase-out threshold, most of the firms able to take advantage of the allowance are relatively small in asset, employment, or revenue size.

In addition, new (but not used) motor vehicles used primarily in a trade or business were among the business assets that qualified for temporary first-year depreciation deductions of 30% under the Job Creation and Worker Assistance Act of 2002 (JCWAA, P.L. 107-147) and 50% under JGTRRA. The 30% deduction applied to qualified property acquired after September 10, 2001, and before January 1, 2005, and placed in service before January 1, 2005.[8] And the 50% deduction applied to the same set of assets acquired after May 5, 2003, and before January 1, 2005, and placed in service before January 1, 2005. Business taxpayers could claim either deduction, but not both. In effect, they operated as partial expensing allowances, and firms of all asset, employment, or revenue sizes and forms of legal organization were able to benefit from them.

It is possible for a business taxpayer to claim all three depreciation allowances for a new motor vehicle bought and placed in service in 2004. The key considerations are the cost of the vehicle, the total cost of assets eligible for the Section 179 expensing allowance that were placed in service in 2004, and the business share of the vehicle's total use. If the cost of a vehicle is sufficiently large, the total cost of eligible assets sufficiently small, and business use accounted for more than 50% of total use, then all three depreciation allowances may be claimed. In doing so, a prescribed sequence must be followed. First, the taxpayer determines whether an expensing allowance can be claimed. If so, then any allowance that is claimed has to be deducted from the taxpayer's basis in the vehicle.[9] If the adjusted basis is greater than zero, then the taxpayer may claim either the 30% or 50% temporary first-year depreciation deduction. This deduction of course further reduces the taxpayer's basis in the vehicle. If upon further adjustment the basis still is positive, then the taxpayer may claim the depreciation allowances permitted under MACRS in 2004.

DOMESTIC DEMAND FOR SUVS AND THE DEBATE OVER THEIR SOCIAL WELFARE EFFECTS

Sport utility vehicles are classified as light trucks in existing data on domestic motor vehicle sales and production. In 2003, U.S. motor vehicles sales totaled 16.967 million units.[10]   Of that number, light trucks accounted for 53%, followed by passenger cars (45%) and medium and heavy trucks (2%). Sales of light trucks exceeded those of passenger cars for the first time in 2001. In 1992, by contrast, the share of passenger cars was nearly double that of light trucks: 63% to 35%.

A major reason for the rise in the light-truck share of domestic motor vehicle sales since the early 1990s has been the increasing popularity of SUVs. U.S. sales of SUVs jumped from less than a million units in the early 1990s to around 4.5 million units in 2003.[11] Automobile manufacturers have contributed to the growth in domestic ownership of SUVs by spending substantial sums on developing, producing, and marketing these vehicles in the past decade or so.[12]   Fueling this heavy investment has been the prospect of reaping substantial returns. In 1998, the Ford Motor Company reportedly earned about $2.4 billion in after-tax profits from sales of two of its SUV lines, the Expedition and Navigator.[13] And one analyst estimated that an SUV with a 2003 sticker price of $50,000 might yield a profit of $20,000 or more, whereas the profit on a minivan might be one tenth as much.[14]

The steady rise in domestic ownership of light trucks in general and SUVs in particular since the early 1990s has fueled an increasingly lively debate over their impact on highway safety, air quality, and U.S. reliance on foreign sources of crude oil and petroleum products, among other topics.[15] Critics charge that SUVs, especially the heaviest ones, wastefully consume gasoline, contribute more to air pollution and global warming than passenger cars, and pose a significant threat to the safety of their own passengers, as well as other people on the road. Owners of the vehicles, by contrast, retort that SUVs in general and large ones in particular offer greater protection to passengers than smaller vehicles and are much safer than critics contend. They also argue that in a democratic society, consumers should be free to own heavy-duty motor vehicles if they place a high value on personal safety and comfort.

This much seems beyond dispute in the ongoing discussion about the social welfare effects of SUVs. SUVs have accounted for an increasing share of total fuel consumption and emissions by motor vehicles in the past decade. On average, their gas mileage has been lower, their emissions of carbon monoxide and nitrogen oxides higher, and their risk of rolling over in an accident greater than most passenger cars.[16] And relative to passenger cars, SUVs face less stringent federal standards for fuel economy and emissions, and their safety record is thought to receive less scrutiny from federal agencies.[17] But several recent public announcements by federal regulatory agencies and manufacturers of SUVs have raised the possibility that these discrepancies might shrink or disappear in coming years.[18]

TAX TREATMENT OF DEPRECIATION FOR SUVS

The tax treatment of depreciation for an SUV hinges on the vehicle's weight. Depending on its weight, a vehicle may be classified as either a passenger car or a light truck for federal tax purposes. This distinction has important implications for the number of tax years required to recover the cost of an SUV and the present value of total depreciation allowances that may be claimed.

In general, current federal tax law imposes limits on depreciation deductions for passenger cars that do not apply to light trucks. For tax purposes, passenger cars are defined as four-wheeled vehicles made primarily for use on public streets, roads, and highways and having an unloaded gross vehicle weight (i.e., curb weight fully equipped for service but without passengers or cargo) of 6,000 pounds or less. Under this definition, most trucks, vans, minivans, and SUVs built on an automobile chassis with a gross vehicle weight (i.e., maximum total weight of a loaded vehicle as specified by the manufacturer) of 6,000 pounds or less are subject to the same depreciation rules as passenger cars.[19]

As was noted earlier, motor vehicles in general are assigned a class or depreciation life of five years under the MACRS. But the depreciation of passenger cars is subject to annual limits under IRC Section 280F, and these limits may extend the period required to recover their costs beyond five years. This statutory provision, which was added to the federal tax code by the Deficit Reduction Act of 1984 (P.L. 98-369), establishes a new category of tangible depreciable assets known as listed property. In general, listed property covers assets whose nature or functional purpose readily allows for both business and personal use. Under current law, passenger cars and other transportation equipment; property used in entertainment, recreation, or amusement; computers and peripheral equipment; and cellular telephones and similar telecommunications equipment are considered listed property.

This property is subject to specific dollar limits on the amount that may be deducted for depreciation in a single tax year, assuming business use accounts for 50% or more of total use of the property.[20] If business use accounts for all of a listed property's total use, then the maximum depreciation allowance may be claimed for a tax year. But if business use represents less than 100% of the property's total use, then the depreciation allowance that may be claimed is proportional to the business share of total use.[21]

In the case of passenger cars, the limits under IRC Section 280F represent the maximum annual depreciation deductions that may be claimed under a combination of the MACRS, the IRC Section 179 expensing allowance, and the temporary 30% and 50% first-year depreciation deductions established by JCWAA and JGTRRA (if applicable). For passenger cars placed in service in 2004, a business taxpayer may claim a depreciation allowance for that tax year of $10,610 if he or she claims the 50% deduction.[22] The limits began in 1984 and have been adjusted for inflation since 1988. Although their original intent was to discourage the purchase of luxury cars for business use, the limits no longer effectively serve this purpose because they have not kept pace with increases in the cost and improvements in the quality and design of passenger cars.[23] The federal tax code does not define a luxury passenger car, but its dollar value for a new car placed in service in a tax year is determined by the sum of the depreciation limits for each of the first five years of the vehicle's useful life. Thus, for cars placed in service in 2004 and disregarding the temporary depreciation deduction of 50% under JGTRRA, any passenger car costing $13,960 or more was considered luxurious.

Pick-up trucks, vans, and minivans built on a truck chassis with a gross vehicle weight of more than 6,000 pounds are considered light trucks for tax purposes and thus exempt from the depreciation limitations for luxury passenger cars under IRC Section 280F.[24] The exemption originated with the Deficit Reduction Act of 1984 and was intended to exclude heavy-duty working vehicles such as pickup trucks used in farming or construction or heavy vans used by the self-employed. As a result, the cost of excluded vehicles may be recovered under the same statutory provisions governing the depreciation of motor vehicles other than luxury passenger cars. Permissible depreciation deductions for light trucks placed in service in 2004 reflected the application of the IRC Section 179 expensing allowance, the 50% temporary first-year depreciation deduction, and the MACRS. Small business owners, including self-employed individuals, are the taxpayers most likely to claim all three deductions.

Among other things, AJCA carved out a niche in IRC Section 179 for SUVs built on a truck chassis with a gross vehicle weight of more than 6,000 pounds. These vehicles are not subject to the limitations on depreciation deductions mandated under IRC Section 280F. Under the act, these vehicles were defined as any four-wheeled vehicle designed mainly "to carry passengers over public streets, roads, or highways" with a gross vehicle weight of under 14,000 pounds. Because this definition could apply to many heavy pickup trucks, vans, and small buses, as well as SUVs, it is further refined to exclude them from the limitation on depreciation deductions for heavy-duty SUVs.[25] The act limited the cost of SUVs with a gross vehicle weight of more than 6,000 pounds and less than 14,000 pounds that may be expensed to $25,000.[26] This rule applies to vehicles placed in service after October 22, 2004.

ACCELERATED DEPRECIATION AND DEMAND FOR HEAVY-DUTY SUVS

What does the current tax treatment of depreciation for motor vehicles mean for the demand for heavy-duty SUVs? It is difficult to assess the impact of federal tax law on domestic sales of any depreciable asset. Nevertheless, there is reason to believe that current law encourages the purchase of heavy-duty SUVs for business use over lighter SUVs or passenger cars of comparable value. The reason lies in the tax subsidy available to business taxpayers who buy an SUV not subject to the depreciation limitations on luxury passenger cars. This subsidy increased significantly under JGTRRA but was reduced somewhat under AJCA.

This subsidy can be illustrated from the data in the following table. It compares the maximum first-year depreciation deductions a business taxpayer may claim and the present value of the total depreciation allowances (in 2004 dollars) the taxpayer may claim as a result of purchasing and placing in service in 2004, both before and after the enactment of AJCA a new SUV weighing more than 6,000 pounds and a new passenger car of equal value.[27] In computing the depreciation deductions, it is assumed (perhaps implausibly) that each vehicle is driven solely for business purposes, that the taxpayer earns at least $40,000 in 2004 from the trade or business in which the vehicle is used, and that the double-declining balance method of depreciation with the half-year convention is used. And in computing the present value of the total depreciation allowances claimed for each vehicle, it is assumed that the discount rate is 5%.

Table 1. First-Year Depreciation Deductions and Present Value of Total Depreciation Deductions for Two Motor Vehicles Placed in Service in 2004 Before and After the Enactment of the American Jobs Creation Act of 2004

Vehicle	New Heavy-Duty SUV		New Passenger Car
Assumed Curb Weight (pounds)	6,400		3,200
Purchase Price	$40,000		$40,000
Maximum First-Year Depreciation Allowance[a]	**Under the American Jobs Creation Act of 2004**	**Before the American Jobs Creation Act of 2004**	**$10,610**
	$34,000[b]	**$40,000**[c]	
Years Required to Recover the Acquisition Cost[d]	6	1	16
Present Value of Total Depreciation Deductions (2004 dollars)[e]	**$39,387**	**$40,000**	**$32,022**

Source: Congressional Research Service

a. The passenger car is subject to annual limits on depreciation deductions under IRC Section 280F. The SUV is not subject to any such limits and thus is eligible for the maximum expensing allowance allowed under IRC Section 179, along with the 50% temporary depreciation deduction in effect during 2004 and the regular depreciation allowance under the MACRS.

b. The figures in this column reflect the current limit of $25,000 on the maximum expensing allowance in a single tax year for an SUV with a gross vehicle weight of over 6,000 pounds but less than 14,000 pounds. This limit was established by the American Jobs Creation Act of 2004.

c. The figures in this column reflect the limit of $102,000 on the maximum expensing allowance in 2004 for SUVs with a gross vehicle weight of more than 6,000 pounds. This limit was in effect before the enactment of the American Jobs Creation Act of 2004.

d. According to IRS Revenue Procedure 2004-20, the maximum depreciation allowance in 2004 for a passenger car eligible for the 50% temporary depreciation deduction and placed in service that year was $10,610, followed by $4800 in 2004, $2850 in 2005, and $1,675 in each succeeding year. The SUV is depreciated using the double-declining balance method with a half-year convention.

e. In estimating the present value of total depreciation allowances, it is assumed that the discount rate is 5%.

The results indicate that a business taxpayer would realize higher after-tax returns on investment and a greater cash flow in the short run by purchasing the SUV instead of the passenger car. This conclusion is warranted by the differences among the three scenarios in the present value of total depreciation deductions. The greater the present value, the lower the tax burden on the returns to investment in a depreciable business asset. The present value in 2004 dollars of total depreciation allowances for the SUV under an expensing allowance of $102,000 is 20% greater than the present value of those allowances for the passenger car; the difference drops to 19% when the maximum expensing allowance for the SUV is reduced to $25,000.

Perhaps the most surprising finding is that there is little difference (1.5%) between the present value of total depreciation allowances for the SUV under the current version of IRC Section 179 and the one in effect under JGTRRA before the enactment of AJCA. At least in this example, the sharp reduction in the maximum expensing allowance for heavy-duty SUVs under AJCA did little to curtail the tax subsidy for investment in these vehicles offered by current depreciation rules.

Is there any evidence that the faster depreciation of heavy-duty SUVs relative to comparable lighter motor vehicles under current tax law has increased domestic sales of these vehicles? It is not known to what extent this tax preference has affected domestic sales of light trucks weighing over three tons. Available evidence seems mixed. On the one hand, some press reports suggested that the availability of the preference, efforts by dealers to spur sales by making customers aware of it through local advertising campaigns, and initiatives being considered in Congress to eliminate or curtail the stronger preference created by JGTRRA partly explained why domestic sales of full-size and luxury SUVs were surprisingly strong in December 2003 and January 2004.[28] On the other hand, U.S. sales of the heaviest SUVs declined by 6% in 2004 compared to 2003, even though for much of the year the maximum expensing allowance for the vehicles was four times greater than its present value.[29]

Of course, the decision to purchase a motor vehicle primarily for business use hinges on more factors than its depreciation for tax purposes. The income and tastes of the business owner, present and expected future gasoline prices, and the relative prices and average expected gas mileage of alternative vehicles also influence the decision. Owing to the limitations on the use of the IRC Section 179 expensing allowance, small business owners and self-employed individuals are the business buyers of motor vehicles whose decisions would be influenced the most by the tax subsidy for heavy-duty SUVs.

GAS GUZZLER EXCISE TAX

The tax treatment of depreciation for heavy-duty SUVs is not the only way in which the federal tax code might encourages the purchase of these vehicles. IRC Section 4064, which imposes an excise tax on sales by manufacturers or importers of new automobiles failing to meet statutory standards for fuel economy, also offers consumers (including small business owners) an incentive to prefer heavy-duty SUVs to motor vehicles that are more economical in fuel consumption. This tax is known as the gas guzzler tax.

The gas guzzler tax, which originated with the Energy Tax Act of 1978 (P.L. 95-618), applies to domestic sales of automobiles by manufacturers and importers. IRC Section 4064(b) defines an automobile as any "4-wheeled vehicle propelled by fuel which is manufactured primarily for use on public streets, roads, and highways, and which is rated at 6,000 pounds unloaded gross vehicle weight or less." Certain vehicles matching this description are exempt from the tax, including emergency vehicles such as ambulances and police cars. The amount of the tax levied on each make and model of automobile depends on its combined city and highway fuel economy rating, which is defined as the average number of miles traveled by an automobile per gallon of gasoline as determined by the Environmental Protection Agency. Presently, the tax ranges from $1,000 for cars with a fuel economy rating of at least 21.5 miles per gallon but less than 22.5 miles per gallon to $7,700 for cars that have a rating of less than 12.5 miles per gallon; cars with a rating of 22.5 miles per gallon and above avoid the tax. These amounts have been in effect since the enactment of the Omnibus Budget Reconciliation Act of 1990 (P.L. 101-508). The Internal Revenue Service, which administers the tax, issued the initial regulations implementing it in 1980. In FY2003, the tax raised $126.685 million in revenue, up from $70.788 million in FY2000 and $52.641 million in FY1996.

The tax appears to serve two related policy goals. It clearly seeks to promote the development, manufacture, and sale of fuel-efficient cars by raising the average cost of producing cars with relatively low gas mileage (and thus subject to the tax) relative to that of cars with relatively high gas mileage (and thus exempt from the tax). At the same time, the tax can be seen as an effort to mitigate the negative social costs or deleterious effects of driving relatively fuel-inefficient cars. Prominent among these effects is the added air pollution these vehicles cause. To the extent that the excise tax raises the unit production cost for low-mileage cars, it causes manufacturers to bear at least some of the social cost of this pollution.

THE GAS GUZZLER TAX AND THE DEMAND FOR HEAVY-DUTY SUVS

The gas guzzler tax does not apply to motor vehicles weighing in excess of 6,000 pounds. Therefore, heavy-duty SUVs are exempt from it. As a result, demand for these SUVs is no doubt greater than it would be if they were subject to the tax. Since many of these vehicles get relatively low gas mileage, it is conceivable that retail prices could be as much as $2,000 to $7,700 higher for many models if current law were changed to subject sales of heavy-duty SUVs to the tax and manufacturers and dealers passed the full amount of the tax on to buyers. According to one estimate, the U.S. Treasury loses billions of dollars in revenue each year because of the exemption of light trucks (including SUVs) from the tax.[30]

How would domestic sales of heavy-duty SUVs respond to the imposition of the gas guzzler tax? The answer of course hinges on how much of the tax would be passed on to consumers and the sensitivity of demand for heavy-duty SUVs to increases in retail prices. While manufacturers and importers would be legally obligated to pay the tax, it is far from certain that they would also end up bearing its entire economic burden through declines in the revenue they receive from domestic SUV sales. They could attempt to shift some or all of the tax to their employees through lower compensation; or to suppliers of needed materials, parts, and components through lower prices; or to buyers of heavy-duty SUVs through higher retail prices. The distribution of the economic burden of the tax between manufacturers and consumers ultimately hinges on the price sensitivity (or elasticity) of demand for and supply of heavy-duty SUVs. To maintain their sizable profit margins on sales of heavy-duty SUVs, manufacturers presumably would want to pass the entire amount of the tax onto buyers, but they would be constrained by the prospect of potential buyers losing interest in the vehicles if retail prices were to rise because of the tax. In general, producers are likely to bear much of the burden of a tax like the gas guzzler excise tax if demand is more sensitive to price changes than supply in the short run; however, consumers are likely to bear much of the burden if demand is less sensitive to price changes than supply in the short run. Unfortunately, the data needed to estimate these sensitivities for heavy-duty SUVs are not publicly available.

LEGISLATIVE INITIATIVES IN THE 109TH CONGRESS TO REDUCE OR ELIMINATE SUV TAX PREFERENCES

No legislation to curtail or enhance current tax preferences for heavy-duty SUVs has been introduced in the 109th Congress. It is uncertain whether the issue will receive attention in coming months. Efforts to curtail the preferences would run into opposition from the automotive industry and its allies in Congress. But efforts to enhance them would arouse opposition from environmentalists and their allies in Congress.

The issue did surface in some legislation considered in the previous Congress. Identical bills to subject SUVs weighing more than 6,000 pounds to the same annual depreciation limits that apply to passenger cars under IRC Section 280F was introduced in the House (H.R. 727/Representative Eshoo) and the Senate (S. 265/Senator Boxer). The measures defined a sports utility vehicle as any motor vehicle that has the "primary load-carrying device or container attached" and a seating capacity of 12 or fewer individuals and is designed to seat nine or fewer individuals behind the driver's seat, irrespective of the vehicle's weight. In addition, the bills specified that vehicles equipped with an "open cargo area or a covered box not readily accessible for the passenger compartment" of a minimum interior length of 72 inches, an integral enclosure that fully surrounded the driver compartment and load-carrying device, or a body section that extended "more than 30 inches ahead of the leading edge of the windshield" would be excluded from the depreciation limits. No action was taken on either bill.

Nonetheless, there was enough support in the 108th Congress for a reduction in the subsidy for purchases of heavy-duty SUVs for business use available through the tax treatment of depreciation for motor vehicles that such a reduction was included in the conference agreement on H.R. 4520 (the American Jobs Creation Act of 2004, P.L. 108-357) approved by the House and Senate in October 2004. More specifically, the agreement contained a provision limiting the IRC Section 179 expensing allowance to $25,000 for heavy-duty SUVs, instead of the maximum allowance of $100,000 allowed under previous law. Such an SUV was defined as "any four-wheeled vehicle which is primarily designed or which can be used to carry passengers over public streets, roads, or highways, which is not subject to IRC Section 280F, and which is rated at not more than 14,000 pounds gross vehicle weight." The provision was originally included in a tax bill (S. 1637) passed by the Senate on May 11, 2004. In its consideration of H.R. 4520 as passed by the House, the Senate substituted the text of S. 1637 as an amendment and passed it. According to estimates by the Joint Committee on Taxation, the limited expensing allowance for SUVs could yield a revenue gain of $223 million from FY2005 to FY2009. President Bush signed H.R. 4520 into law on October 20, 2004.

There was less interest in the 108th Congress in modifying the gas guzzler tax to make it applicable to heavy-duty SUVs. Senator Durbin introduced a bill (S. 795) that would have done so. But it attracted no co-sponsors, and the Finance Committee took no action on it. The measure would have altered the definition of an automobile so that the gas guzzler tax would apply to motor vehicles with an unloaded gross vehicle weight of 12,000 pounds or less. Such a limit would have covered every heavy-duty SUV presently sold in the United States. Under the proposal, light trucks used primarily for business such as vans and pick-up trucks would have been exempt from the tax

REFERENCES

[1]   See Brett Clanton, "Large SUVs Lose Luster; Cost Big 3," *Detroit News*, Jan. 16, 2005, p. 1A.

[2]   See Robert Schoenberger, "Excursion May Get Stay of Execution; High Profit Margin Offsets Low Unit Sales," *The Courier-Journal*, Oct. 29, 2003, p. 1F.

[3]   See Aileen Roder and Lucas Moinester, "A Hummer of a Tax Break," *Taxpayers for Common Sense* (Washington: Jan. 23, 2003); Pamela Najor, "Tax Cut Bill 'Bad Policy', Group Says, Creating Perverse Incentives for SUVs," *Daily Report for Executives* (Washington: Bureau of National Affairs, May 28, 2003), p. G-7; and "Make Fuel-Efficient SUVs a Go, But Stop Tax Break," editorial, *Atlanta Journal-Constitution*, Oct. 27, 2003, p. 10A.

[4]   Generally, most depreciable tangible assets placed in service after 1986 are depreciated under a system known as the Modified Accelerated Cost Recovery System (MACRS). Under MACRS, the cost of an asset is recovered by applying the proper depreciation method, the proper recovery period, and the proper convention. A taxpayer may choose to use the straight-line method, which involves writing off the same amount of the asset's acquisition cost in each year of its recovery period; its basic rate is equal to one divided by the number of years in the recovery period. Otherwise, the cost of assets in the 3-, 5-, 7-, and 10-year classes is recovered using the 200% or double-declining

balance method. Under this method, the basic rate of depreciation is simply twice that of the straight-line method. The cost of assets in the 15- and 20-year classes is recovered using the 150% declining balance method, whose basic rate is 1.5 times larger than that of the straight-line method.   Longer-lived assets must be depreciated using the straight-line method.

[5]   This amount is indexed for inflation in 2004 through 2007. As a result, the maximum expensing allowance in 2004 was $102,000.

[6]   For more details on the expensing allowance and how it was altered by JGTRRA, see CRS Report RL31852, *Small Business Expensing Allowance Under the Jobs and Growth Tax Relief Reconciliation Act of 2003: Changes and Likely Economic Effects*, by Gary Guenther.

[7]   This amount is also indexed for inflation in 2004 through 2007. As a result, the phase-out threshold in 2004 was $410,000.

[8]   The 30% and 50% temporary depreciation allowances were available for new assets that were depreciable under the MACRS and had recovery periods of 20 or fewer years.   They also applied to water utility property, computer software that was depreciable over three years under IRC Code 167, and qualified leasehold improvements. Some property can be placed in service in 2005 still qualify for the allowances. Specifically, the property must be produced by a business taxpayer and subject to the uniform capitalization rules under IRC Section 263A, have a production period of more than two years or more than one year and a cost exceeding $1 million, and have a recovery period under the MACRS of at least 10 years or be used in the business of transporting people for hire.

[9]   Generally, a taxpayer's basis in an asset is the value of the original capital investment. In most situations, it is the cost of the asset to the taxpayer.

[10] Standard & Poor's, *Industry Surveys: Autos & Auto Parts* (New York: June 24, 2004), p. 13.

[11] Brett Clanton, "SUV Glut Signals Dip in Interest," *Detroit News*, Aug. 13, 2004, p. A1.

[12] Spending on SUV advertising in the United States rose from $172.5 million in 1990 to $1.51 billion in 2000. See Keith Bradsher, *High and Mighty* (New York: Public Affairs, 2002), p. 112.

[13] Ibid., p. 89.

[14] Jonathan Weisman, "Businesses Jump on an SUV Loophole; Suddenly $100,000 Tax Deduction Proves a Marketing Bonanza," *Washington Post*, Nov. 7, 2003.

[15] For an overview of the principal arguments made by proponents on both sides of this debate, see Cooper, "SUV Debate," pp. 451-461; Gregg Easterbrook, "America's Twisted Love Affair With Sociopathic Cars," *New Republic*, vol. 228, Jan. 20, 2003, pp. 27-34; and Sam Kazman, "Is Big Bad?: SUV Critics Hold Consumers in Contempt," *Reason*, Aug./Sept. 2003, available at [http://www.cei.org].

[16] Cooper, "SUV Debate," pp. 453-458.

[17] See Cooper, "SUV Debate," p. 454; and CRS Report RS20298, *Sport Utility Vehicles, Mini-Vans, and Light Trucks: An Overview of Fuel Economy and Emissions Standards*, by Brent D. Yacobucci.

[18] The Environmental Protection Agency issued a final rule in February 2000 that beginning with the 2009 model year (MY), all light trucks, including SUVs, will be held to the same emissions standards as passenger cars (see 65 Federal Register 6698, Feb. 10, 2000). In addition, in December 2002, the Department of Transportation proposed that starting with MY2005, all light trucks, including SUVs, will be subject to higher fuel economy standards. Under the rule, their average fuel economy would rise from the current requirement 20.7 miles per gallon (mpg) to 21.0 mpg in MY2005, 21.6 mpg in MY2006, and 22.2 mpg in MY2007 (see 67 Federal Register 77015-77029, Dec. 16, 2002). Finally, in early December 2003, 15 automobile makers from four nations voluntarily agreed to redesign the SUVs and pick-up trucks they sell in the United States to make them less dangerous to the occupants of passenger cars. The announced design changes are to be phased in so that all MY2010 light trucks will incorporate them. Many of the largest SUVs and pick-up trucks sold domestically will need to be redesigned. Because the action is being taken voluntarily, it is unclear what role federal regulatory agencies will play in the redesign effort. (See Danny Hakim, "Automakers to Redesign S.U.V.'s to Reduce Risks," *New York Times*, Dec. 4, 2003, p. A1; and Lorrie Gilbert, "Automakers Announce Plans to Improve Designs for Vehicle Occupant Protection," *Daily Report for Executives*, Bureau of National Affairs, Dec. 5, 2003, p. A-37.)

[19] Under temporary rules (T.D. 9069) issued by the Internal Revenue Service on July 7, 2003, certain vans and light trucks weighing 6,000 pounds or less have not been treated as passenger cars for tax purposes since the 2003 tax year. More specifically, the exclusion applies to vans and light trucks that are modified for business use in a way that precludes any personal use. The rules were issued in response to swelling complaints from small business owners that current dollar

limits on depreciation deductions for passenger cars were making it impossible to write off the cost of a basic model van or light truck in the five years permitted under MACRS.

[20] If business use of listed property drops below 50% of total use, the property must be depreciated under the MACRS alternative depreciation system (ADS), which tends to be much less generous than the regular MACRS. Property whose cost is recovered under the ADS is not eligible for the 30% or 50% temporary first-year depreciation allowances under JCWAA and JGTRRA, respectively.

[21] For example, if the business share of total use for a passenger car is 75%, then the depreciation deduction that may be claimed in a particular tax year is 75% of the maximum allowed under IRC Section 280F.

[22] See IRS Revenue Procedure 2004-20. For passenger cars subject to the temporary 50% first-year depreciation allowance, a business taxpayer may claim depreciation deductions of $4,800 in 2005, $2,850 in 2006, and $1,675 in each succeeding tax year.

[23] See U.S. Congress, Joint Committee on Taxation, *General Explanation of the Revenue Provisions of the Deficit Reduction Act of 1984*, JCS-41-84 (Washington: GPO, 1985), pp. 559-560.

[24] SUVs belonged to this category of vehicles before the enactment of the American Jobs Creation Act of 2004.

[25] The following vehicles are excluded from the definition of SUVs under IRC Section 179(b)(6)(B)(i): (1) those designed to have a seating capacity of more than nine persons behind the driver's seat; (2) those equipped with a cargo area of at least six feet in length that is an open area and is not readily accessible from the passenger compartment; (3) those equipped with a cargo area of at least six feet in interior length that is designed for use as an open area but is enclosed by a cap and is not readily accessible directly from the passenger compartment; and (4) those with an integral enclosure spanning the driver compartment and load-carrying device, no seating behind the driver's seat, and no body section protruding more than 30 inches ahead of the leading edge of the windshield.

[26] Under JGTRRA, the maximum expensing allowance for SUVs weighing more than 6,000 pounds was $100,000. So any such SUV bought and placed in service from January 1 2004 through October 22, 2004 was eligible for that allowance. AJCA reduced it to the amount that was in effect in 2003 before the enactment of JGTRRA.

[27] Examining first-year depreciation allowances offers a useful and illuminating frame of reference because the tax benefits linked to accelerated depreciation depend on the proportion of an asset's acquisition cost recovered in the first year or two of its tax life. These benefits increase as the proportion expands and a depreciable asset's tax life lengthens. The fundamental reason lies in the time value of money and its relation to the tax deferral made possible by accelerated depreciation: tax savings realized today are more valuable than the same amount of tax savings realized over five or 10 years.

[28] See Jim Hopkins, "SUV Sales Climb on Tax Loophole; Small Businesses Discover Benefit," *USA Today*, Feb. 11, 2004, p. B3.

[29] Brett Clanton, "Large SUVs Lose Luster, Cost Big 3," *Detroit News*, Jan. 16, 2005, available at [http://www.detnews.com].

[30] A 2000 study issued by the environmental advocacy group Friends of the Earth concluded that domestic and foreign automobile manufacturers avoided paying $10.2 billion in gas guzzler excise taxes in 1999 and $43.1 billion from 1995 through 1999 because of the exemption of light trucks from the tax. It is not clear from the study what assumptions were made in arriving at this estimate. See Friends of the Earth, *Gas-Guzzler Loophole: SUVs and Light Trucks Drive Off with Billions* (Washington: 2000), available at [http://www.foe.org].

In: Automobile Industry: Current Issues　　　　ISBN: 1-59454-686-X
Editor: L. R. Domansky, pp. 115-193　　© 2006 Nova Science Publishers, Inc.

Chapter 5

DATA COLLECTION STUDY: DEATHS AND INJURIES RESULTING FROM CERTAIN NON-TRAFFIC AND NON-CRASH EVENTS[*]

U.S. Department of Transportation National Highway Traffic Safety Administration

- Vehicle-Generated Carbon Monoxide
- Vehicle Backing
- Vehicle Heat (Weather Induced)
- Power Windows

A Continuation of the Study of Non-Traffic and Non-Crash Motor Vehicle-Related Safety Issues Focusing on 1998 Death Certificates and Other Sources Containing Relevant Data and Information

---

[*] Excerpted from U.S. Department of Transportation National Highway Traffic Safety Administration Report dated May 2004.

I. EXECUTIVE SUMMARY

This report presents results of a study to determine the extent of certain selected non-traffic or non-crash motor vehicle-related hazards, and the relative value of various sources for providing the National Highway Traffic Safety Administration (NHTSA) with information on those hazards. This investigation was conducted as a result of safety issues that have been raised concerning potential non-traffic and non-crash safety problems. NHTSA's Office of Rulemaking, with assistance from the National Center for Health Statistics (NCHS), conducted a study of selected death certificates. Although NHTSA has an extensive database of statistical information on motor vehicle crashes that occur on the public traffic way, the agency does not have a database or other means to adequately determine the number of motor vehicle-related deaths that involve a motor vehicle in certain non-traffic or non-crash situations. The data included in this report continues work begun following the deaths of 11 children from heat exposure in three incidents of accidental trunk entrapment in a one-month period of the summer of 1998. That study of 1997 death certificates found that death certificates represent a good source for identifying non-traffic and non-crash motor vehicle-related deaths. A final report of that study was published on May 6, 2002 and is in NHTSA Docket No. 1999-5063. The data in this report examines 1998 death certificates and other sources of information relating to the following four hazards:

1. Persons left in a vehicle's passenger compartment or who lock themselves in the trunk of a vehicle in hot weather,
2. Children strangled by a vehicle's power window or sunroof,
3. Persons killed or injured as a result of a vehicle backing up, and
4. Persons killed or injured as a result of vehicle-generated carbon monoxide.

Only issues #1 and #2 above were examined in the study of 1997 death certificates referenced above. This report is based on 4,046 death certificates from 1998, received from 35 states and the District of Columbia, out of an identified sample of an estimated 5,500 cases. The cases were derived from the most recent NCHS death certificate data that was available when this study was conducted. National estimates were extrapolated from this sample based on a simple ratio of identified cases to cases for which death certificates were received. This study also examined a number of databases and other data sources, both within NHTSA and outside the agency, as well as peer reviewed research articles. The results of the study are summarized below.

- *Carbon monoxide* - Unintentional deaths from vehicle-generated carbon monoxide found in 1998 death certificates project to a national total of slightly less than 200 such deaths a year. This is consistent with other sources examined. These deaths often involve adults who are in or around running vehicles in closed garages or in their homes having forgotten to turn off a vehicle in an attached garage. Victims in some of the cases identified were under the influence of alcohol at the time of their death.
- *Vehicles backing up* - Deaths found in 1998 death certificates project to a national total of about 120 deaths annually of persons struck by a vehicle backing up. Most of the victims are either very young (less than five years old) or elderly (60 and above), with most of the elderly victims over age 70. As many as 6,000 injuries occur each year as a result of vehicles backing into a person, but these injuries are almost all very minor.
- *Excessive heat inside a vehicle passenger compartment* - Deaths found in 1998 death certificates project to a national total of 29 deaths annually of persons exposed to excessive heat inside a vehicle passenger compartment. A similar level of annual deaths (27) from this cause was found in the agency's study of 1997 death certificates when a national projection was made.
- *Vehicle window* - Four deaths resulting from interaction with a vehicle window were found in 1998 death certificates. The study of 1997 death certificates also found four deaths involving interaction with a vehicle window.

II. BACKGROUND

NHTSA is responsible for reducing deaths and injuries associated with motor vehicles. The agency, in its Fatality Analysis Reporting System (FARS), collects detailed data from states that produce an actual count of fatalities resulting from traffic crashes. The agency also gathers a national sample of police reported traffic crashes through the National Automotive Sampling System (NASS) General Estimates System (GES). NHTSA is also responsible for motor vehicle safety when there is not a crash or the event occurs off the public traffic way. When the agency tries to quantify safety problems associated with non-traffic or non-crash situations it often finds that it has little or no data and must rely on the data gathering efforts of others. While providing interesting and useful information, the data available from others usually provide insufficient detail to guide NHTSA as to whether or not a regulatory or some other response is needed and, if so, what that response should be. Issues arising in this area therefore sometimes require ad hoc information-gathering efforts.

Such was the case in the summer of 1998 when in three separate incidents 11 children died from excessive heat after accidentally locking themselves in vehicle trunks. In January 1999, the agency assembled a panel of experts composed of industry, safety advocates, medical experts, law enforcement, and other relevant groups to address the non-traffic non-crash safety issue of trunks that cannot be opened from the inside should someone accidentally or through criminal intent become trapped inside. In June 1999, this panel recommended that NHTSA "should establish a national data system designed to measure the frequency and consequences of trunk entrapment." On October 20, 2000, NHTSA published a Final Rule in the Federal Register establishing a new Federal Motor Vehicle Safety Standard, (FMVSS) No. 401: Internal Trunk Release, that requires all new passenger cars with trunks to be equipped with a release latch inside the trunk compartment beginning September 1, 2001. In March 2000, the agency also initiated a study of selected 1997 death certificates to determine the utility of death certificates in identifying deaths resulting from certain non-traffic or non-crash motor vehicle-related situations. That study focused on the following three issues:

1. children who die as a result of being left unattended in a motor vehicle's passenger compartment in hot weather or who die after locking themselves in the trunk of a vehicle,
2. kidnap victims who die as a result of being locked in the trunk of a vehicle, and
3. children strangled by motor vehicle power window.

A report on this study of 1997 death certificates was published on May 6, 2002 and is in NHTSA Docket No. 1999-5063-286. NHTSA's Office of Rulemaking conducted additional research to expand the work begun in the study of 1997 death certificates. The research involved an examination of selected 1998 death certificates. Other sources, including several databases and a number of academic research articles, were also examined. Invaluable assistance and guidance concerning the death certificate research involved was provided by the National Center for Health Statistics (NCHS).

The hazards examined in this report include two from the study of 1997 death certificates – death from excessive heat in the passenger compartment or trunk of a vehicle and death resulting from a power window or sunroof – and two other hazards - death from vehicle-generated carbon monoxide and death as a result of being struck by a vehicle backing up. In addition, this report examines the extent to which these non-traffic or non-crash hazards result in injuries. The criteria used to identify deaths from excessive heat inside the passenger compartment of a vehicle are essentially the same as those used to identify heat related deaths inside a vehicle trunk. The research methodology and results are reported on in the sections of the report that follow.

III. METHODOLOGY

NHTSA's study of 1997 death certificates was successful in locating a small number of certain types of non-traffic or non-crash motor vehicle-related deaths. That study also confirmed death certificates' value as a source for identifying non-traffic and non-crash motor vehicle-related deaths. There were inherent limitations of the data in the study 1997 death certificates, however. Although the criteria for selecting death certificates for review were carefully chosen, there was no way of knowing for certain whether or not all of the death certificates reflecting non-traffic or non-crash deaths had been identified and if not, what percentage of the total was represented by those found. Even among death certificates received, there were some that suggested that a non-traffic or non-crash incident was involved, but this could not be confirmed based on the information in the death certificate, and in some cases even after the appropriate coroner or other official was contacted. Finally, there was no way of knowing whether or not the number of incidents found for just one year was indicative of the ongoing magnitude and scope of a hazard or whether the snapshot of data from one year might be contradicted by data derived from another year or years, or from another source or sources. In the broadest and simplest sense then, the methodology for the research reflected in this report was to collect whatever data was available on the non-traffic and non-crash motor vehicle-related hazards of interest from whatever sources were available. The sources in which relevant information was found for each of the issues are indicated below.

<u>Carbon Monoxide</u>:	death certificates, LexisNexis™, literature review
<u>Backing</u>:	death certificates, LexisNexis™, FARS, literature review, injury databases (NEISS and GES)
<u>Vehicle Heat</u>:	death certificates, LexisNexis™, literature review
<u>Vehicle Window</u>:	death certificates, LexisNexis™, literature review

The totals of non-traffic and non-crash motor vehicle-related incidents located in death certificates, LexisNexis™ and some of the other sources reviewed for this study represent simple counts of relevant incidents. While there were no hard and fast rules that applied to identifying relevant cases, incidents involving particularly unusual events were excluded from the counts. As an example, if a person were backed over by a vehicle that was left running, in reverse, and unattended, this case was excluded from the count of backing incidents. The specific methodology that applied to each of the types of sources investigated is described below.

A. 1998 Death Certificates

State laws require death certificates to be completed for all deaths. Furthermore, federal law mandates national collection and publication of death and other vital statistics data. As a result, and as confirmed by the study of 1997 death certificates conducted by NHTSA, death certificates represent a reliable and comprehensive source of information regarding non-traffic and non-crash motor vehicle-related deaths, particularly if information is entered for all of the key elements of a death certificate and if the certificate includes at least some description of how the injury that resulted in death occurred.

As it did in researching 1997 death certificates, NHTSA's Office of Crash Avoidance Standards contacted and met with representatives of the NCHS to solicit their help in researching 1998 death certificates. NCHS publishes annual reports of all deaths in the United States using information derived from death certificates. Among other information, each death is assigned various codes that identify the disease or condition directly leading to death, antecedent causes, and other significant medical conditions involved.

For the year 1998, the underlying cause of death, and the other specific injuries, diseases, and conditions related to a death are classified and coded using the International Classification of Diseases, 9th Revision (ICD-9). ICD-9 is designed for the classification of morbidity and mortality information for statistical purposes, for the indexing of hospital records by disease and operations, and for data storage and retrieval. ICD-9 also contains a supplementary classification of external causes of injury (E-Codes) that permits the classification of environmental events, circumstances, and conditions as the cause of injury and other adverse effects. NHTSA identified what it considered to be the ICD-9 codes, primarily E-Codes, most likely to be indicated on death certificates reflecting one of the non-traffic or non-crash motor vehicle issues included in this study. Clearly, not all deaths assigned ICD-9 codes suggestive of these conditions involve non-traffic or non-crash motor vehicle-related events. In addition, deaths of interest may have been coded, for various reasons, with codes other than those on which this research focused. However, deaths associated with the ICD-9 codes identified for this research represented a universe of deaths that would most likely contain deaths resulting from the non-traffic or non-crash injuries being studied. In June of 2002, NHTSA met with NCHS officials to discuss NHTSA's review of the public use Multiple Cause of Death (MCOD) data, the annual data file containing information derived from all U.S. death certificates, and how to proceed with the study of 1998 death certificates. It was agreed that the same protocol followed for the study of 1997 death certificates would be followed for purposes of obtaining 1998 death certificates. The seven steps of the protocol are:

(1) Submission of materials by NHTSA to NCHS reflecting the purpose of the study and how information on the death certificates would be used.

(2) Submission of NHTSA's materials to the National Association for Public Health Statistics and Information Systems' Executive Committee for review and approval.

(3) Assistance to NHTSA from NCHS in identifying the selection criteria from the information available in the electronic files with special attention paid to the injury codes.

(4) The submission by NCHS of a request to each state for permission to release the death certificate numbers to NHTSA in support of this study.

(5) Release of death certificate numbers to NHTSA by NCHS as states agreed to this.

(6) NHTSA's submission of a request to each state asking for copies of death certificates (by identifying number), including any applicable fee for the service. In the request, NHTSA stated that it would under no circumstances attempt to contact family members of the

decedents. In some cases additional paperwork and state level approvals were required for research of this sort.

(7) NHTSA's review of death certificates, taking precautions to protect all information obtained from them. States consider both the death certificate numbers and the identifying information on the certificates to be confidential, and are sensitive to the risk of "identity theft."

Research involving death certificates necessarily creates a substantial gap between the year in which the deaths involved occurred and the time when the research is completed. This gap is largely the product of the time it takes for NCHS to receive and assemble data from the states and finalize its annual MCOD file. Typically, the most recently completed MCOD file is two years or more older than the year in which it becomes publicly available. In addition, considerable time is required to complete the process described above. Some states add another step to this process by requiring detailed paperwork and state review board approvals, which are above and beyond the initial approvals required to obtain death certificate numbers.

NHTSA initiated and followed the recommended protocol. NCHS staff reviewed a NHTSA suggested list of selection criteria for the non-traffic and non-crash motor vehicle issues to be studied and proposed some additional selection criteria. Table I provides the E-Codes, code descriptions, associated issues and any other data filters that were used in identifying the more than 15,000 death certificates of initial interest to the study.

Table I: E-Codes Used in Locating Death Certificates For Use in National Highway Traffic Safety Administration Research of Non-Traffic and Non-Crash Deaths in 1998

Issues:

1.   Children left in a vehicle's passenger compartment in hot weather or who lock themselves in the trunk of a vehicle, **(Vehicle heat/trunk)**

2.   Children strangled by a vehicle's power window or sunroof, **(Vehicle window)**

3.   Persons killed or injured as a result of a vehicle backing up, **(Backing)** and

4.   Persons killed or injured as a result of vehicle-generated carbon monoxide. **(CO)**

E-code	Description	Issue	Ncode Limits	Age Limits (if any)
814	Motor vehicle traffic accident involving collision with pedestrian	Backing		
817	Noncollision motor vehicle traffic accident while boarding or alighting	↓ ↓		
818	Other noncollision motor vehicle traffic accident	↓		
819	Motor vehicle traffic accident of unspecified nature			
822.7	Other motor vehicle nontraffic accident involving collision with moving object(pedestrian)	↓		
823.7	Other motor vehicle nontraffic accident involving collision with stationary object	↓		
824	Other motor vehicle nontraffic accident while boarding and alighting	↓		
825.0 825.1 825.6 825.7 825.8 825.9	Other motor vehicle nontraffic accident of other and unspecified nature	↓ ↓ ↓ ↓		
868.2	Accidental poisoning by other utility gas and other carbon monoxide – motor vehicle exhaust gas	CO		
900	Excessive heat – due to weather conditions	Vehicle heat/ trunk		
913.2	Due to lack of air (in closed place)	Vehicle heat/ trunk		
913.8	Accidental mechanical suffocation – Other specified means	Vehicle window		Less than 9 years old

E-code	Description	Issue	Ncode Limits	Age Limits (if any)
913.9	Accidental mechanical suffocation – unspecified means	↓ ↓ ↓		Less than 9 years old
918	Caught accidentally in or between objects	↓		Less than 9 years old
962.2	Assault by poisoning – other gases and vapors	CO	Only records also with N986	
968.4	Criminal neglect	Vehicle heat/ trunk& CO	Only if N986 or N992 is also present	
982.0	Poisoning by other gases, undetermined whether accidentally or purposely inflicted – motor vehicle exhaust gas	CO		
983.0	Hanging, strangulation, or suffocation, undetermined whether accidentally or purposely inflicted	Vehicle window ↓		
983.8	Hanging, strangulation, or suffocation, undetermined whether accidentally or purposely inflicted – Other specified means	↓ ↓ ↓		
983.9	Hanging, strangulation, or suffocation, undetermined whether accidentally or purposely inflicted – Unspecified means	↓ ↓ ↓		
988.8	Injury by other specified means, undetermined intent	All		
N-codes for use with selected E-codes as additional filters				

N-code	Description	Comments
986	Toxic effect of carbon monoxide	For use in selected circumstances (noted above) in combination with an E-Code
992	Effects of heat and light	For use in selected circumstances (noted above) in combination with an E-Code

The MCOD file includes a variable for the "Underlying Cause of Death" and variables for up to 20 injuries or diseases that may have contributed to the death. In the language of the MCOD file, these are called "Record Axis Conditions." NHTSA expected that deaths caused by non-traffic and non-crash motor vehicle-related injuries would be a subset of those with codes for the underlying cause of death, but records were also examined according to the 20 record axis conditions. In addition to searching the underlying cause of death and other conditions using the ICD-9 codes in Table I, certain data filters, also reflected in Table I, were imposed. A search of 1998 death certificate data was limited to children less than 9 years of age for E-Code 913.8, 913.9 and 918. These E-Codes were intended to identify victims of strangulation by power window. The search using E-Code 962.2 was limited to those records also containing an N-Code (nature of injury code) of 986. Finally, for E-Code 968.4, the search was limited to those records also containing an N code of either 986 or 992. Using the public use version of the MCOD file, NHTSA made some preliminary calculations as to the number of death certificates that might include people who died in a non-traffic or non-crash motor vehicle-related event. Depending on the E-Codes and other criteria used, it was determined that the number of death certificates that might reflect incidents of the type under study exceeded 15,000. In contrast, only 1,792 death certificates were identified as being of interest for the study of 1997 death certificates. The bulk of the increase in the 1998 death certificates resulted from the inclusion of backing incidents as an area of study. The E-Codes that were likely to reflect backing incidents were sufficiently broadly defined that it was clear they included a wide range of other, more common motor vehicle crashes as well. At an average price per death certificate on the order of $8 to $9, it was strongly felt, and budgetary constraints required, that every effort be made to minimize the number of death certificates that ultimately would be requested from the 50 states, the District of Columbia and New York City. A large percentage of the deaths included in this number were likely from conventional traffic crashes because the E-Codes 814-825 are used in death certificates for a wide spectrum of motor vehicle crashes. For example, "E-Code 822.7 – Other motor vehicle non-traffic accident involving collision with moving object (pedestrian)" – would apply to non-traffic vehicle and pedestrian accidents in which a vehicle was moving either forward or backward. Those involving the forward motion of a vehicle were not part of this study. NHTSA representatives on several occasions discussed with NCHS representatives possible ways of reducing the number of death certificates to be obtained. The focus of those discussions was on how to eliminate from the death certificates that would be requested from the states those that would clearly not be of interest to this study because they resulted from traffic crashes that did not involve backing. In most cases, motor vehicle-related deaths from the MCOD file that were initially identified as being of possible interest to the study would actually not be of interest if they were also contained in FARS because the vast majority of deaths in FARS do not involve backing. Combining the electronic version of the MCOD file with other data is not permitted by NCHS. So that NHTSA could eliminate deaths identified in the NCHS MCOD file that were clearly the result of crashes that did not involve backing, the Office of Rulemaking printed out some basic data from this death certificate file. Death certificate numbers were not in the file used and therefore were not included in the data printout. The Office of Rulemaking also printed out some basic data from the more than 40,000 deaths contained in FARS for 1998. Using these printouts, data were manually compared and, as a result, a large number of deaths from the list of death certificates of interest were eliminated. Most deaths in the MCOD file that also appeared to be in FARS were eliminated from further consideration. However, if FARS data indicated that the crash involved a pedestrian and the first point of impact was the rear of the vehicle, these deaths were included in those for which death certificates were requested since a backing incident relevant to the study was strongly suggested. Some deaths were retained among those of interest, particularly if a pedestrian was involved, even though there was no data to suggest a backing incident was involved. The researchers wanted to eliminate those deaths that clearly were not of interest, but also wanted to be sure to leave in those with even a remote possibility of being relevant. Some states (a small number) were delayed in granting NCHS permission to allow NHTSA to receive death certificate numbers. As a result, some death certificates were not requested from some of the states in time for those certificates to be included in the data presented in this report. The exact number of death certificates that would have been requested from those states is not known. However, it was estimated that if all certificates of interest had been received from all of the jurisdictions, the total number of certificates would have been approximately 5,500. As of the date of this report, 4,729 death certificates have been requested from 44 states and the District of Columbia.

Counts of incidents of any type from death certificates represent a floor as to the number of incidents that actually occurred. Deaths of interest may not have been coded according to the selection criteria chosen. Also, death certificates are often very sketchy in the descriptive information they provide. Limited follow up with medical examiner's and other offices thus far has uncovered backing incidents, for example, that were not clearly identifiable from death certificates alone. In some cases, information on a death certificate strongly suggests it is an incident of interest, but the medical examiner's office and even the police agency involved were unable to clarify the situation. Not all death certificates requested have been received, nor is it anticipated that death certificates from every jurisdiction will be received. As of the writing of this report, NHTSA has received and reviewed 4,046 death certificates from 36 jurisdictions, 35 states and the District of Columbia. Data from these death certificates, excluding personal identifiers and certificate numbers, has been entered into a database.

The 36 jurisdictions that provided death certificates for this study represent a good cross section of states. They reflect a balanced mix of characteristics, such as urban and rural, cold climate and warm climate, and geographic regions of the country.

Straight-line projections of anticipated national totals are made in this report using the number of deaths found in 1998 death certificates. A simple ratio was used to account for the missing death certificates. The ratio was determined from the number of certificates selected and received (5,500/4,046=1.36). The researchers believe that projections from the available data are reasonable estimates and reflect the magnitude and scope of the hazards studied because of the balanced mix of the states that provided death certificates. Had those states been skewed toward warmer climates, for example, this might have had an effect on the projected national totals of vehicle-related carbon monoxide deaths since these incidents tend to happen in colder climates during the winter months.

B. LexisNexis™

To support this research, NHTSA subscribed to LexisNexis™ so that it could search for news articles related to the four types of motor vehicle-related hazards under study. A variety of words and phrases likely to be associated with these hazards were used to conduct searches of LexisNexis™.

LexisNexis™ served several purposes. When a death certificate was suggestive of a type of incident under study, but not conclusive, an article in LexisNexis sometimes confirmed the nature of the incident so that it could be included or excluded from this study. Sometimes, articles in LexisNexis identified incidents from 1998 that were not located in 1998 death certificates. Also, LexisNexis™ identified incidents from years beyond 1998.

References to LexisNexis™ derived data or information appear in various contexts in the data and information presented in this report. In the case of some death certificates, an article found in LexisNexis™ either confirmed the nature of the incident or provided additional information concerning that incident. In such cases, this is indicated. A count of the incidents that have occurred in the five completed calendar years, 1998-2002, and that were located in LexisNexis™ is presented in this report. For the year 1998, the number of LexisNexis™ identified deaths that were also found in death certificates is indicated. For the years 1999-2002, data presented are derived solely from LexisNexis™.

It should be emphasized again here that the cases identified through LexisNexis only represent a count of cases. It is very clear from experience with LexisNexis that many cases of interest to this research are either not reported in news outlets or not included in LexisNexis because the news outlets in which such cases might be reported are not included in the universe of outlets from which LexisNexis™ draws. Unlike either death certificates or FARS, as described immediately following, articles found in LexisNexis™ report on both deaths and injuries. Therefore, LexisNexis™ derived data presented in this report include injuries.

C. Fatality Analysis Reporting System

NHTSA's Fatality Analysis Reporting System (FARS) focuses on fatalities from vehicle crashes that occur on public roads. FARS is a count of the annual national total of fatalities resulting from vehicle crashes on public roadways. FARS represented a potential source of backing incidents since backing incidents may occur off-road or on a public road.

Among the various bits of data noted and entered into the FARS database is the point on the vehicle at which the first impact relating to the incident occurred. An examination of FARS data relating to pedestrian fatalities that occurred in 1998 identified a number of incidents in which a pedestrian was first struck by the rear of the vehicle involved. In other words, cases were identified in FARS with a high probability of being backing incidents of the sort of interest to this research. As described previously, this was helpful in being sure to select for review certain 1998 death certificates whose data matched a FARS record in which the rear of the vehicle was the first point of impact. It also demonstrated that FARS contains backing incidents of the sort under study. Since backing incidents were found in FARS for 1998, FARS data was examined to identify potentially relevant backing incidents that occurred in years later than 1998. FARS is created from data that are derived from Police Accident Reports (PARs) that are reviewed to identify deaths from vehicle crashes that are appropriate to include in FARS. The rules governing FARS require that PARs from the two most recently completed calendar years plus the current year be retained. Older PARs are typically destroyed. FARS data was examined for possible backing incidents in late 2002. At that time, the years for which PARs were still available were 2000 and 2001. A search of FARS data for the years 2000 and 2001 located 91 apparent backing fatalities in 2000 and 67 in 2001. States were requested to provide the PARs for these incidents. A total of 138 for the two years were received. Thirty-six of the incidents reflected in the PARs received and reviewed were not entered into the NHTSA database of non-traffic and non-crash cases because they involved situations outside the scope of the research, such as an incident involving an unusual vehicle like a small front end loader. A few of the 36 were not entered because either the quality of the photocopy or the limited information provided was such that what exactly happened could not be determined.

Fourteen (14) backing deaths identified in FARS had been previously identified through other sources, usually LexisNexis™ The remaining 88 deaths had not been found in other sources. Even though FARS focuses on deaths from vehicle crashes that occur on public roads, many of the backing incidents in FARS occurred in driveways or other off-road locations similar to those found in 1998 death certificates and in other sources. These incidents may have been included in FARS because the circumstances were ambiguous as to exactly where the incident took place or they ultimately involved a public roadway in that the vehicle and/or the victim ended up in a public roadway.

D. Peer-Reviewed Scientific, Medical and Public Health Journals

A review of scientific, medical and public health research literature dealing with the issues being investigated was begun using PubMed, an on-line service of the National Library of Medicine that provides access to the library's MEDLINE. MEDLINE contains more than 12 million life science and public health article citations dating back to the mid-1960's. In most cases, only abstracts are provided so several trips to the National Library of Medicine in Bethesda, MD were made to examine and, when necessary and appropriate, make copies of full articles relevant to the issues covered in this report.

E. The National Electronic Injury Surveillance System (NEISS)

For nearly 30 years, the U.S. Consumer Product Safety Commission (CPSC) has operated this statistically valid injury surveillance and follow-back system. The primary purpose of NEISS has been to provide timely data on consumer product-related injuries occurring in the U.S. Beginning in 2000, NEISS was expanded to collect data on all injuries, including those involving a motor vehicle. Collection of information on this more broadly defined universe of injuries began as of July 1, 2000. NEISS provided valuable information on backing injuries.

NEISS injury data are gathered from the emergency departments of 100 hospitals. These hospitals are selected as a probability sample of all 5,300+ U.S. hospitals with emergency departments. A "trauma weight" is determined for each case in NEISS. According to the CPSC, when there are 20 or more cases of a particular type of incident, one may add the trauma weights for those incidents to come up with a projection as to the number of such incidents that occur nationally in a given year. When there are fewer than 20 incidents of a given type, the CPSC indicates that the national projections that one derives from these trauma weights are less reliable statistically.

As part of this round of research, NHTSA obtained finalized NEISS data for the last six months of 2000 and preliminary, although close to finalized data for the first six months of 2001. This was the most recent data available when this research was conducted.

This year's worth of NEISS data was searched for young children who were left in a hot vehicle, trapped in a trunk, or caught by a power window. It was also searched for backing incidents. Backing was the only area in which multiple cases of injuries were found. A total of 265 possible backing incidents were located in NEISS. The text fields in each record were reviewed to determine which of the incidents actually involved incidents of the type under study.

F. NHTSA's General Estimates System (GES)

Data for the General Estimates Systems (GES) come from a nationally representative sample of police reported motor vehicle crashes of all types, from minor to fatal. The system began operation in 1988. It was created to identify traffic safety problem areas, provide a basis for regulatory and consumer initiatives, and support cost benefit analyses of traffic safety programs. The information is used to estimate how many motor vehicle crashes of different kinds take place, and what happens when they occur. Although various sources suggest that about half the motor vehicle crashes in the country are not reported to the police, the majority of these unreported crashes involve only minor property damage and no significant personal injury. By restricting attention to police-reported crashes, GES concentrates on those crashes of greatest concern to the highway safety community and the general public. A search of GES data for the years 1996 to 2000, the most recent data available when the search was done, was conducted to identify GES records for which non-occupant impact was the first harmful event in the crash, with damage to the rear of the vehicle as the initial impact and with vehicle role and maneuver consistent with backing. Incidents were identified that allowed for national projections of backing incidents. There was no language describing what occurred in the incidents that could be reviewed. So the national projections may include backing incidents of a type, such as vehicle rollaways, that are outside the scope of this study.

G. Health Care Utilization Databases of the Centers for Disease Control and Prevention

Several databases related to health care utilization maintained by the National Center for Health Statistics (NCHS) of the Centers for Disease Control and Prevention seemed like strong candidates for providing good information on the issues under study. They were not. Information derived from these databases applicable to the non-traffic and non-crash injuries considered for this report was extremely limited. The CDC databases exist to measure large indicators of how health care resources in the United States are utilized, such as the extent to which health care resources are used by various age groups, the payers involved in obtaining health care, or the types of treatments, therapies and drugs that are employed nationally. In short, the databases are aimed at big picture issues, not more narrow subjects such as non-traffic and non-crash motor vehicle-related safety issues that involve small numbers of occurrences annually. The databases do offer a limited opportunity to identify incidents involving non-traffic and non-crash motor vehicle-related safety concerns and for getting a very generalized (nonstatistical) sense of the relative magnitude of certain non-traffic and non-crash motor vehicle-related hazards. That opportunity exists in the text fields for each record in the databases. Unfortunately, information is not always entered in these text fields and the information that is entered is not always descriptive enough to determine exactly what happened to cause an injury. For example "MVA," referring to a motor vehicle accident, sometimes appears as the only thing entered in the text field of a record.

Unintentional injuries, which are how each of the types of incidents in this study would be characterized, are a subset of the data contained in each of the CDC databases. By searching the text fields of unintentional injuries in the databases for certain words likely to be used in describing an injury resulting from the issues under study, several relevant incidents were located. However, because the number of incidents found was so few, reliable national projections of the numbers of these types of incidents could not be made. The CDC databases generally require at least 30 incidents of a given type before statistically reliable national projections about the incident type can be made. Each of the CDC databases examined is briefly described below.

1. National Ambulatory Medical Care Survey

The National Ambulatory Medical Care Survey (NMACS) is a national sample of patient visits to office-based physicians who are not employed through the federal government and who are primarily engaged in direct patient care. The survey, which includes specialists, is conducted annually. The opportunity to gain some insights into how an injury occurred is in a small text field on the survey form called "cause of injury." The NAMCS determines a "patient visit weight" for each record in this database. This represents the projected total number of office visits that occurred across the country and that are similar to the particular record involved. The patient-visit weights for all of the records in the NAMCS sample indicate that there were a total of 823,541,999 physician office visits in the year 2000 involving physicians of the type included in the NAMCS. National projections for subcategories of office visits, by age group for example, may also be tallied with varying degrees of statistical confidence. If there are less than 30 records in any subgroup, national projections are considered less reliable statistically. NHTSA examined the NAMCS data file for the calendar year 2000, the latest year for which survey results were available when research for this report was conducted. That file contains 27,369 records, of which 3,042 relate to an unintentional injury. Of the 3,042 unintentional injury records, 994 contained no text in the "cause of injury" field. A review of the 2,148 records with entries in the "cause of injury" field located one record of interest to this study. That was an incident in which the "cause of injury" was given as "mother backed car over child," in this case a three year old.

With only one record of a backing incident identified, the "patient visit weight" of 3,983 for that incident was of little or no predictive value.

2. National Hospital Ambulatory Medical Care Survey

The National Hospital Ambulatory Medical Care Survey (NHAMCS) collects data on the utilization and provision of ambulatory care services in hospital emergency and outpatient departments. Findings are based on a national sample of visits to the emergency and outpatient departments of non-institutional general and short-stay hospitals, exclusive of federal, military, and Veterans Administration hospitals, located in the 50 States and the District of Columbia. Annual data collection began in 1992. As with the other CDC databases, the text fields of each record were searched to locate incidents of interest that are included in the database.

Emergency Departments

The 2000 NHAMCS file for emergency department visits contains 25,622 records, 8,791 of which are for unintentional injuries. The text fields of the unintentional injury records were searched for certain words that would likely be used in describing one of the types of non-traffic or non-crash motor vehicle-related incidents under study. A total of five incidents involving a vehicle backing up were found in the NHAMCS emergency department file. Details of those incidents are provided elsewhere in this report.

Outpatient Departments

The outpatient portion of the NHAMCS for the calendar year 2000 file has 27,510 records, 3,002 of which relate to an unintentional injury. As with the emergency department records, the text fields of the outpatient department unintentional injury records were searched for certain words that would likely be used in describing one of the types of non-traffic or non-crash motor vehicle-related incidents under study. No records of injuries reflecting the types of hazards under study were found in the search of this file.

3. National Hospital Discharge Survey

The National Hospital Discharge Survey (NHDS) has been conducted annually since 1965. It is a national probability survey designed to meet the need for information on characteristics of inpatients discharged from non-Federal short-stay hospitals in the United States. The NHDS collects data from a sample of approximately 270,000 inpatient records acquired from a national sample of about 500 hospitals. Only hospitals with an average length of stay of fewer than 30 days for all patients, general hospitals, or children's general hospitals are included in the survey. Federal, military, and Department of Veterans Affairs hospitals, as well as hospital units of institutions (such as prison hospitals), and hospitals with fewer than six beds staffed for patient use, are excluded. This database proved to be of no use since it does not contain a text field for describing the circumstances that led to the patient being hospitalized in the first place.

IV. DISCUSSION OF RESEARCH RESULTS

A. Carbon Monoxide

Information found through the research for this report indicates that somewhere between 200 and 250 deaths a year that are not known to be suicides result from vehicle-generated carbon monoxide. These types of deaths occur more frequently than deaths from any of the other issues researched.

1. 1998 Death Certificates

As of the writing of this report, 122 incidents involving 140 deaths have been located in 1998 death certificates. The 1998 deaths found in death certificates project to 190 deaths in all of the 1998 death certificates that have been identified for this study, including those that have not yet been received. Victims of this hazard are predominantly adults. Only five of the 140 deaths located in death certificates were children less than 10 years of age. Among the scenarios encountered multiple times are someone working on or sitting in a running vehicle with the garage door closed, an intoxicated person who passes out in a car in a garage with a vehicle running, and persons who are killed in a residence when someone unintentionally leaves a vehicle running in a garage attached to a home. Both the numbers and types of incidents found in death certificates were supported by information found in other sources. Details beyond what is contained in death certificates were found for some of the cases in news articles located in LexisNexis™ as were incidents for years more recent than 1998.

Summary data relating to vehicle-generated carbon monoxide deaths found in 1998 death certificates appear in Table II below. Basic information about each of the incidents, including an indication of whether or not the death was located in LexisNexis™ as well, may be found in the Appendix I to this report.

Table II: Summary Data: Vehicle-Generated Carbon Monoxide Deaths From 1998 Death Certificates

Age	# of Deaths	In Garage, Home or Residence		Other Locations
		In vehicle	Not in vehicle or unclear	
90 +	5	1	4	
80-89	20	1	19	
70-79	15	1	14	
60-69	8	1	7	
50-59	10	3	6	1
40-49	16	4	12	
30-39	32	15	13	4
20-29	23	10	8	5
10-19	6	3	2	1
0-10	5	2	3	
Subtotal	140	41	88	11
Total	140	140		

2. LexisNexis ™

The table below reflects the vehicle-generated carbon monoxide deaths and injuries that were located in LexisNexis™ for the period 1998-2002. The figures for 1998 include 26 deaths for which both death certificates and articles in LexisNexis™ were found. Four of the deaths that were found only in LexisNexis™ occurred in states from which death certificates had not been received. The remaining deaths found in LexisNexis™ were not found in the death certificates selected for review according to the criteria described previously in this report.

Table III: Carbon Monoxide Deaths and Injuries Found In LexisNexis™ (1998-2002)

Year	Total Incidents	Deaths	Ijuries
1998	22	42	1
1999	17	27	15
2000	13	18	8
2001	12	22	0
2002	11	14	9+
			(number of victims in one incident was not specified)

3. Literature Review

Numerous articles, including several from sources other than those at the National Library of Medicine, relating to carbon monoxide poisoning from vehicle-generated carbon monoxide were found. The findings of these articles are for the most part consistent with what was found in death certificates regarding vehicle-generated carbon monoxide incidents. In general, these articles reported on the number of such incidents nationally or in prescribed geographic areas or they reported on the kinds of circumstances that led to carbon monoxide poisonings. The articles reviewed are in the list of references at the back of this report. Unintentional poisonings from vehicle-generated carbon monoxide diminished toward the close of the 20th century, with a particular decline in these types of incidents noted in the years following 1975 when catalytic converters were introduced into automobiles. [1], [2] The steady decline from 4.0 to 0.9 deaths per 1 million person-years since 1975 represents a 76.3 percent decrease. The total number of 1998 unintentional motor vehicle-related deaths from carbon monoxide has been reported at 238. Most of these deaths involved adults. [1]. Vehicle-generated carbon monoxide deaths tend to occur more often in colder climates and colder months of the year. [3], [4] Significant snow accumulation has also been associated with spikes in incidents of motor vehicle-related carbon monoxide poisonings and deaths when people sit in operating vehicles with tailpipes obstructed by snow. [5] Alcohol intoxication is frequently involved in motor vehicle-related carbon monoxide deaths when intoxicated persons pass out in circumstances that expose them to this hazard. [4], [6], [7] Death certificate research and other sources indicate that vehicle-related carbon monoxide poisonings and deaths tend to occur when the vehicle is not moving and particularly when the vehicle is operating in an enclosed space. However, a consistent level of accidental vehicle-related carbon monoxide deaths, between 60 and 75 per year, while the vehicle is moving has also been reported. [8] A report on a group of 68 cases, including one death, over a five-year period identified a specific danger to children riding in the backs of pickup trucks. [9]

Older vehicles have been associated with an increased risk of carbon monoxide poisonings. [7]

Data from the various articles reviewed dealing with vehicle-related carbon monoxide deaths is presented in Appendix II.

B. Backing

1. 1998 Death Certificates

As of the writing of this report, 91 backing deaths have been identified in the 4,046 death certificates that have been received. A straight-line projection based on these figures suggests that 123 backing deaths would be located in the approximately 5,500 death certificates from 1998 that have been identified for review. The situations in which these deaths occurred included both those that would be considered non-traffic and some that would be considered as traffic. The charts that follow present breakdowns of the 91 deaths.

Table IV: Backing Deaths Identified in 1998 Death Certificates By Age*

Age	# of Victims
1<	1
1-4	40
5-9	4
10-19	2
20-29	0
30-39	3
40-49	3
50-59	6
60-69	5
70+	27
Total	91

*Deaths involved occurred in both non-traffic and traffic situations

Table V: Backing Deaths Identified in 1998 Death Certificates By Vehicle Type

Vehicle Type	# of Victims
SUV	3
Van/minivan	5
Pickup truck	11
Passenger Car	25
Truck - Delivery	3
Truck - Dump	8
Truck - Garbage/Recycling	4
Truck Other	13
Unclear	19
Total	91

Vehicle type is an example of information that is included in death certificates that may not get much attention from or may not be readily available to people who prepare final death certificates. This is best demonstrated by the high percentage (21%) of instances in which it was unclear as to the type of vehicle involved in a backing incident. It is not uncommon for the simple word "vehicle" or "automobile" to be used, which leaves no clear indication as to exactly the type of vehicle that was involved in the incident.

Table VI: Backing Deaths Identified in 1998 Death Certificates By Location

Location	# of Victims
Driveway	21
Home	21
Parking Lot	21
Road/Street	13
Sidewalk	2
Other off road	13
Total	91

A complete list of all of the backing incidents located in death certificates along with certain information relating to each may be found in Appendix III.

2.   LexisNexis™

Table VII contains summary data reflecting the backing deaths and injuries that were found in LexisNexis™ for the years 1998-2002. Twenty-six (26) of the 1998 deaths were also located in death certificates. LexisNexis™ identified a number of 1998 backing deaths (19) that occurred in states from which death certificates were not received. The remaining 1998 backing deaths found in LexisNexis™ were not found in the death certificates selected for review according to the criteria previously described in this report.

Table VII: Backing Incidents (1998 – 2002) Found in LexisNexis

Year	Total Events	Multiples (more than one victim involved)	Deaths	Injs.	Car	Pickup	Van, Minibus or SUV	Gbge./ Dump Truck	Truck-Other	Other/ Unspecified
'98	68	1	56*	13	15	10	10	2/6	13	12
'99	52	1	42	11	16	7	7	4/4	12	2
'00	56	4	47	13	16	10	9	1/6	11	3
'01	58	1	50	9	11	10	8	9/6	10	4
'02	63	2	55	10	8	15	11	8/5	11	5
Total	297	9	250	56	66	52	45	24/27	57	26

*Includes 26 deaths that were also found in death certificates.

3. Fatality Analysis Reporting System

Table VIII contains summary data relating to the 102 backing incidents found in FARS in 2000 and 2001. Fourteen (14) of these backing incidents were located in LexisNexis as well. Table IX provides summary data relating to the location of the backing incidents found in FARS. Detailed information about each of the 102 backing incidents that was found in FARS may be found in Appendix IV.

Table VIII: Summary Data from Backing Deaths Identified in FARS – 2000, 2001

Year	Total Events	Multiples	Deaths	Injs.	<1	1-4	5-12	13-21	22-64	>64	Car	Pick up	Van, Minibus, SUV or station wagon	Gbge Truck	Truck-Other/	Other/ Unspecified
'00	57	4	57	4		18	4	1	12	26	15	12	19	3	5	3
'01	45	3	45	6*		12	3	3	8	22	11	9	12	5	1	7
Total	102	7	102	10*		30	7	4	20	48	26	21	31	8	6	10

*The age of three of the injured was not given. These three are therefore not included in the totals for any of the age groups indicated.

Table IX: 2000, 2001 Backing Deaths Identified in FARS By Location

Location	2000	2001
Driveway	24	20
Parking Lot	4	1
Road/Street	14	14
Other/Unclear	15	10
Total	57	45

4. Literature Review

Death certificate research and an examination of other sources confirm that the annual number of deaths resulting from vehicles backing up is small in comparison to deaths due to other types of vehicle crashes. In spite of these relatively small numbers, there are certain characteristics of these incidents that emerged from both the original research conducted for this report and in academic research examined. Very young children, particularly those between one and four years of age, seem especially vulnerable to being killed by a vehicle backing up. [10-15] Off-road locations, such as driveways and parking lots, are common locations where backing incidents occur. [11-14], [16], [17] The drivers of vehicles involved in these types of incidents are often parents, relatives or other people, such as neighbors, known to the family of the children involved. [10], [17] Larger vehicles for personal use, such as SUVs, van and pickup trucks, are often the vehicles involved in these types of incidents. [10]-[12]

Summaries of research articles reviewed for this report, and selected data from those articles, are provided in Appendix V.

5. Injury Databases

While a smattering of information relating to injuries and the issues under study was found in other sources, the National Electronic Injury Surveillance System (NEISS) of the Consumer Product Safety Commission (CPSC) and NHTSA's General Estimates System (GES) represented particularly good sources of data specifically relating to non-traffic and non-crash injuries, especially those resulting from backing incidents. The somewhat disparate results found in these two sources, however, make it difficult to make any but very broad statements regarding backing injuries.

Nearly 6,700 backing injuries were found in a recent year's worth (July 1, 2000 to June 30, 2001) of NEISS data. More than 85 percent of the injured were "treated and released." Nearly 2,400 average annual backing incidents were found in five years worth of GES data. More than 83 percent of these backing injuries were recorded as either "no injury," "possible injury," or "non incapacitating evident injury." The primary reason for the disparity in the data between the two sources is the completely different methods by which the data were gathered and the different people involved. NEISS gathers data from a probability sample of 100 hospital emergency departments. GES gathers its data from a representative sample of police reported motor vehicle crashes. Clearly there are backing incidents resulting in injury, usually minor, that cause the injured person to seek medical help, but that occur under circumstances that do not warrant a police report. In fact, several sources examined for this report suggested that about half the motor vehicle crashes in the country are not reported to the police. What seems to be true about vehicle-related backing injuries, based on the NEISS and GES data, is that there are several thousand such injuries a year and the majority of the injuries involved are minor. Data derived from NEISS and GES is contained in Appendix VI.

C. Vehicle Heat

1. 1998 Death Certificates

Passenger Compartment

As of this writing, a total of 22 deaths from heat exposure inside the passenger compartment of a motor vehicle have been located in the death certificates reviewed. A straight-line projection based on these results indicates that ultimately 29 vehicle heat deaths would be found in all the death certificates from the states. Six of the victims were adults. All of the other victims identified were four years old or younger. The study of 1997 death certificates found 25 passenger compartment heat-related deaths, which projects to a total of 27 such deaths. This is consistent with the 1998 findings.

Trunk

Seven of the 11 trunk entrapment deaths that were the impetus for the establishment of the new Federal Motor Vehicle Safety Standard, (FMVSS) No. 401; Internal Trunk Release were confirmed in 1998 death certificates received. Death certificates for the four other deaths were not received because no death certificates from the state in which those deaths occurred had been received at the time this report was finalized. Other deaths from trunk entrapment that were located in news accounts in LexisNexis are reported on in the next section. A complete listing of each passenger compartment vehicle heat incident along with basic information relating to each appears in Appendix VII.

2. LexisNexis

Passenger Compartment

A total of 117 deaths of persons who died inside the passenger compartment of a vehicle from excessive heat were located in LexisNexis for the five-year period 1998-2002. Of the 24 vehicle heat-related deaths found in LexisNexis for 1998, thirteen (13) matched deaths that were located in death certificates. Four 1998 vehicle heat deaths found in LexisNexis occurred in states from which death certificates were not received. The remaining deaths were not found in the death certificates selected for review according to the criteria previously described in this report. Data reflecting the vehicle heat deaths found in LexisNexis appears in the table that follows.

Table X:1998-2002: Vehicle Heat Deaths & Injuries Found In LexisNexis By Age

Age	1998		1999		2000		2001		2002	
	Deaths	Injs	Deaths	Injs	Deaths	Injs	Deaths	Injs	Deaths	Injs
<1	9	2	6	3	6	1	11	2	11	7
1-4	14	2	16	2	8	4	17	5	12	4
5-9			1	4					2	3
10 -Adult	1				2					
Total	24*	4	23	9	16	5	28	7	25	14

Note: Additional victims who suffered no injury were also found in LexisNexis articles.
*Includes 13 deaths for which death certificates were also found.

Trunk

A total of 16 incidents of unintentional trunk entrapment were found in LexisNexis dating back to 1987. These incidents involved a total of 25 deaths, one injury and one person who apparently did not sustain any injuries. The vast majority of the victims were young children ages six or younger with only four of the 27 victims outside that age range. The six incidents and 15 deaths, all involving children six years of age or younger, found for the period 1987-1998 is less than what was found by the Centers for Disease Control and Prevention (CDC) in similar LexisNexis research published in the December 4, 1998 issue of the Morbidity and Mortality Weekly Report. That paper, titled "Fatal Car Trunk Entrapment Involving

Children – United States, 1987-1998," found a total of 19 children six years of age or younger who died in nine incidents. As indicated earlier, seven of the 11 trunk entrapment deaths that were the impetus for the establishment of a new Federal Motor Vehicle Safety Standard, (FMVSS) No. 401: Internal Trunk Release were located in 1998 death certificates received. All of these deaths were also located in LexisNexis as were the four 1998 trunk entrapment deaths for which death certificates were not received because, for various reasons, death certificates from the state involved were not obtained as part of this study. These 11 trunk entrapment deaths were the only such deaths identified as having occurred in 1998.

The tables that follow provide information on the distribution of incidents and deaths by year and the distribution of the ages of the victims of trunk entrapment.

Table XI: Trunk Entrapment Incidents Found in LexisNexis: 1987 - 2003

Year	Incidents	Deaths	Injuries	No Injury
2003	1	1		
2002	1	1		
2001	3	3		
2000	3	4		
1999	2	1		1
1998	3	11*		
1995	1	2		
1994	1	1	1	
1987	1	1		

*Seven (7) of these deaths were also found in death certificates. Death certificates from the state in which the remaining four (4) deaths occurred were not received.

Table XII: Age of Trunk Entrapment Victims, 1987 - 2003

Age	Number of Victims
2	2
3	6
4	8
5	3
6	3
9	1
10	1
12	1
25	1

3. Literature Review

Only two articles relating to vehicle heat were located. Both of these focused on measuring the extent to which passenger compartments heat up under various conditions. There was no discussion in either article of victims of vehicle heat incidents. [18], [19]

D. Vehicle Window

1. 1998 Death Certificates

Only four (4) deaths as a result of interaction with a vehicle window have been located in 1998 death certificates received. The ages of the victims were 2, 3, 3, and 6. Two involved a power window. One apparently did not. Whether a power window was involved in the fourth case is unclear. In one incident a child was left fastened in a car seat while the child's parent went back into the house. The child somehow got out of the car seat and leaned on the power window switch, which caused the window to rise and strangle the child. Another incident involved a young child playing with other children. The child got into a vehicle, opened the power window to yell to the other children and then hit the power switch causing the window to go back up on the child's neck. In the third incident, a child apparently pulled itself up while on the outside of a vehicle, stuck its head through a partially open window, slipped, caught its neck between the window and the door frame and was strangled. The circumstances of the fourth incident were unclear beyond the fact that the child involved was strangled as a result of interaction with a vehicle window. The study of 1997 death certificates also found four (4) deaths of children that resulted from interaction with a power window. Only two of these could be confirmed as clearly involving a power window.

2. LexisNexis

For the years 1998-2002, a total of 12 vehicle window incidents were located in LexisNexis. Eleven children died as a result of these incidents. One of these eleven deaths involved a sunroof, the only such incident located as part of this research. One child was injured.

Summary information relating to these incidents appears in the table below.

Table XIII: 1998-2002: Vehicle Window Cases From LexisNexis

Year	Death/Injuries	Power Window	No Power Window or Unclear	Ages of Victims
1998	5*/0	3*	2	6, 3, 3, 2, 2
1999	1/0	1	0	2
2000	0/0	0	0	-
2001	2/1	3	0	3, 2, 2
2002	3/0	3	0	6, 3, 2

*Includes one vehicle sunroof incident

One of the power window deaths in the preceding chart involved an anomalous situation in which someone had apparently rewired the vehicle to allow the power windows to operate even when the keys were not in the ignition.

All four of the vehicle window incidents found in 1998 death certificates were also found in LexisNexis. The 1998 sunroof death occurred in a state from which death certificates were not received and therefore was not found in death certificates. As indicated earlier, this single sunroof incident was the only such incident found in any source as a result of the research conducted for this report.

3. Literature Review

Three articles were found relating to the hazard of strangulation in a vehicle window. Two of these reported on individual cases that occurred in the United States rather than on an evaluation and analysis of data derived from multiple cases. [20], [21] The third estimated that there are about 499 minor injuries annually, mostly to fingers and wrists, attributable to power windows with most of these, about 64 percent, involving children 14 years of age and younger. [22] These articles are more fully described in Appendix VIII.

V. CONCLUSIONS

This study determined that death certificates represent the best available source for identifying deaths that result from non-traffic and non-crash incidents involving a motor vehicle. However, even a comprehensive review of death certificates will not identify every non-traffic or non-crash death. This study, for example, found news reports of non-traffic or non-crash motor vehicle related deaths for which death certificates should have been found, but were not. A variety of factors can explain this, such as errors in coding on death certificates or a focus in the death certificate on the precise and immediate medical cause of death rather than the fact that the precipitating cause was motor vehicle related. As to the specific issues investigated, this study found the following.

- *Carbon monoxide* – The number of deaths found in 1998 death certificates suggests there are about 200 unintentional deaths a year, nearly all adults, from vehicle-generated carbon monoxide. Other sources examined found a similar, although somewhat higher number. These deaths most often do not involve moving vehicles, but rather vehicles left running in enclosed spaces. Some victims identified were under the influence of alcohol at the time of their death.

- *Vehicles backing up* – Based on deaths found in 1998 death certificates, about 120 deaths of persons struck by a vehicle backing up occur annually. Most of the victims are either very young (less than five years old) or elderly (60 and above), with most of the elderly victims over age 70. As many as 6,000 injuries, mostly minor, occur each year as a result of these types of incidents.

- *Excessive heat inside a vehicle passenger compartment* - Deaths found in 1998 death certificates project to a national total of 29 deaths annually of persons exposed to excessive heat inside a vehicle passenger compartment. A similar projected level of annual deaths (27) from this cause was found in the agency's previous study of 1997 death certificates.

- *Vehicle window* - Four deaths resulting from interaction with a vehicle window were found in 1998 death certificates. The agency's study of 1997 death certificates also found four deaths involving interaction with a vehicle window.

VI. APPENDICES

Appendix I - Vehicle-Generated Carbon Monoxide Deaths From 1998 Death Certificates

Table XIV: Vehicle-Generated Carbon Monoxide Deaths From 1998 Death Certificates

#	Age(s)	Location	Description	Found in LexisNexis™
1	38	parking lot	intake of alcohol; vehicle engine left running damaged exhaust system	yes
2	80, 82	in home, car in garage	one victim apparently forgot to turn off car after pulling into garage, victims found inside home	yes
3	29	garage	overcome by fumes in closed garage	yes
4	72	garage	sitting in car parked in garage with motor running	
5	91	residence	vehicle engine left running in closed integral garage	
6	76	home	car idling in garage below living quarters	
7	70	garage	motor home left running in garage	
8	28	garage	fell asleep in truck in closed garage	
9	51	barn	overcome by carbon monoxide while working on vehicle in barn	
10	82	garage	vehicle left running in integral garage	
11	53	garage	victim was found slumped over in auto parked in the garage	
			behind residence	
12	82	bedroom	decedent went to bed & left vehicle running	
13	49	garage	was working on car in garage with hose leading from exhaust to outdoors, but hose had leak	yes
14	68, 64	at home	inadvertently inhaled automobile gas fumes - accident	
15	64	residence	inhaled auto exhaust fumes	
16	84, 66, 37	Residence (car)	no further details available	
17	32	home	the subject inhaled exhaust fumes from a motor vehicle in a closed garage	
18	34	home	inhaled automobile exhaust	
19	83	at home	inhaled automobile fumes while inside of residence	

Table XIV: Continued

#	Age(s)	Location	Description	Found in LexisNexis™
20	83	home	left car running in attached garage	
21	4, 8, 9, 10, 21, 26, 29, 33	residence	eight died of apparent carbon monoxide poisoning – believed that poisoning occurred when two of victims left truck running in the garage as they listened to the radio – other victims in home	yes
22	32	garage	sat in running vehicle in enclosed garage listening to music while intoxicated with alcohol	
23	80, 72	at home	inhaled automobile exhaust fumes	
24	27	at home	inhaled automobile exhaust fumes – alcohol intoxication cited	
25	58	parking lot	CO poisoning	
26	46	Probably vehicle	unknown source of carbon monoxide	
27	70	home garage	decedent unexpected found down in garage	
28	26	at home	inadvertently left vehicle engine on	
29	34, 26	garage/in vehicle	deceased in car in closed garage with engine running—drinking apparently involved	yes
30	83	home	vehicle accidentally left running in garage	
31	48	in car in garage/home	subject inhaled auto exhaust fumes	—
32	34	dirt path	used drugs & inhaled exhaust fumes from car	
33	21	auto	subject inhaled auto exhaust fumes	
34	35	garage	inhaled car exhaust	
35	48	home-garage	was working on car and was overcome by carbon monoxide	
36	6	home	was placed in car in garage by parent and exposed to carbon monoxide	yes
37	52	home	was found in garage working on automobiles	
38	70, 71	home	inhaled exhaust fumes from car in garage	yes
39	36	home-garage	was found in automobile inside closed garage	
40	39	garage	was found in automobile in closed garage-diabetic, depression, alcohol abuse – accident	
41	40	home-auto	accidental exposure to carbon monoxide	
42	57	garage	working on car in closed garage	
43	26	home	sat in running automobile with garage closed up	
44	17	motor vehicle	auto exhaust	
45	30	garage	inhalation of auto exhaust fumes	

Table XIV: Continued

#	Age(s)	Location	Description	Found in LexisNexis™
46	26	garage	passed out in vehicle with engine running in enclosed garage - acute ethanolism	
47	41	garage	passed out in vehicle parked in garage while car was running	
48	33	garage	started vehicle in enclosed garage, apparently fell asleep after turning vehicle off – acute ethanolism	
49	97	garage	subject found in running car enclosed in garage	
50	41	residence	inhalation of exhaust fumes	
51	83	residence	auto exhaust fumes, vehicle left running	
52	22	parking lot	fumes from exhaust of vehicle	
53	48	home	exposure to carbon monoxide while working on auto in closed garage	
54	35	residence	in running vehicle with exhaust leak	
55	31	church assembly grounds	found in car, while painting car, with engine running, in closed garage	
56	36	garage	found in enclosed garage on floor with stalled car	
57	85	home	in motor vehicle in his garage motor running	
58	38	home	after drinking heavily, victim drove car into garage, closed door, apparently fell asleep at wheel with the car still running	
59	16	off-road	decedent found parked in vehicle with key on, all windows closed, body was in decomposed state	
60	31	garage	acute carbon monoxide intoxication	
61	64	car (in garage)	inhaled car exhaust fumes	
62	33	garage	sleeping in car inside garage after consuming large amounts of alcohol at party	
63	23	highway	decedent was riding in back seat of automobile with faulty exhaust system	
64	36	garage	breathed automobile exhaust fumes in enclosed garage	
65	39	residence - garage	inhalation of motor vehicle exhaust in an enclosed garage	
66	17, 18	street	the two died of carbon monoxide poisoning after apparently falling asleep in vehicle, which had been idling for hours with the windows closed	yes

Table XIV: Continued

#	Age(s)	Location	Description	Found in LexisNexis™
67	63, 58	at home	couple found in bed, which is directly over the house's garage-police said a car inside the garage had been running for some time	yes
68	51	garage	in auto in garage, carbon monoxide intoxication	
69	82	garage	running car in garage	
70	16	garage	running car in garage	yes
71	83	home	car running in garage	
72	75	home	happened in "own home - car left running"	
73	36	garage	fell asleep in truck in closed garage - acute alcohol intoxication	
74	76, 70	home	car accidentally left running in a closed garage killed an elderly couple when the deadly gases seeped into their bedroom	yes
75	73	home	accidentally left car running in house's attached garage	yes
76	21	garage	working on a truck in a closed garage	
77	49	garage	appears overcome by auto exhaust fumes in closed garage clouded judgment by alcohol	
78	90	garage	accidental fall near running car in garage	
79	38	residence	inhaled automobile exhaust while intoxicated with methamphetamine	
80	72	garage	overcome by car fumes in a closed garage	
81	84	residence	deceased accidentally left car running in garage and entered house to go to bed - passage door from garage was left open for pet to enter the house.	
82	76	residence	vehicle exhaust -carbon monoxide poisoning	
83	44	in auto in garage	asphyxia by carbon monoxide-inhaled auto exhaust fumes in closed garage	
84	24	in auto in garage	acute ethanol and carbon monoxide intoxication, sat in vehicle in garage listening to the radio drinking alcohol with the engine running & inhaled poisonous fumes	
85	91	garage	cause of death-carbon monoxide poisoning -auto exhaust	
86	80	residence	defective air handler blew automobile exhaust from garage and into home; died during sleep	
87	79	at home	acute carbon monoxide poisoning, inhalation of vehicle exhaust	
88	51	in auto in garage	found unresponsive in driver seat of car in enclosed garage: exposed to automobile exhaust fumes - acute alcohol intoxication	

Table XIV: Continued

#	Age(s)	Location	Description	Found in LexisNexis™
89	26	in auto in wooded area	subject abused ethanol and later inhaled exhaust fumes of auto, inadvertently, sitting in auto	
90	81	at home	apparently disoriented decedent left car running in garage- victim had Alzheimer's	
91	37	in auto at residence	found in auto – cause of death –carbon monoxide poisoning	
92	82	garage	subject inhaled automobile exhaust fumes	
93	23	in car, off road	decedent found parked in vehicle with key on, all windows closed, body was in decomposed state	
94	29	garage	inhaled motor vehicle exhaust	
95	84	garage	being in garage with motor running	
96	62	garage	victim was intoxicated, drove into garage, left car running, fell asleep, overcome by CO fumes	
97	34	home	carbon monoxide poisoning - in car with motor running	
98	89	home	left car running in garage	
99	52	garage	ran car engine in enclosed garage (of residence)	
100	24	street	defective exhaust system on car - carbon monoxide poisoning	
101	33	garage	found in van in closed garage with motor running	
102	51	garage	inhaled car exhaust fumes	
103	28	home	car running in garage - accident	
104	32	next to vehicle	inhaled carbon monoxide	
105	43, 41	residence	inside closed garage with car running - mixed drug and alcohol intoxication	
106	32	home/ garage/ vehicle	inhaled carbon monoxide, acute carbon monoxide poisoning	
107	21	home	found in auto at carport of home with motor on	
108	20	vehicle – on a road	fell asleep in enclosed vehicle with engine idling	
109	29	vehicle/ dwelling - driveway	inhaled car exhaust fumes	
110	37	home	mixed drug and carbon monoxide poisoning- drug usage and car exhaust	
111	43	home	working on vehicle in an enclosed building	
112	46	home	carbon monoxide fumes leaked from faulty exhaust thru rusted floor of vehicle	
113	42	garage	car running in closed garage	

Table XIV: Continued

#	Age(s)	Location	Description	Found in LexisNexis™
114	47	home	passed out due to migraine while car was running	
115	60	home	working under truck	
116	1	van in field	inhaled combustion fumes	
117	83	home	found lying next to auto	
118	70	garage	overcome by car exhaust while working on running car in closed garage	
119	38	garage	bundled up to sleep in running car – CO and ethanol intoxication	
120	38	garage	found in garage	
121	33	auto	accidental CO poisoning in auto	
122	96	garage	inhalation of auto exhaust	

Appendix II - Summaries of and Data From Articles on Poisonings from Vehicle-Generated Carbon Monoxide

The thrust of the research effort behind this report was to gather data, from whatever source, on selected non-traffic motor vehicle related safety hazards. The sources reviewed included academic research articles. The basic findings of the articles reviewed are presented in the body of this report. A brief summary of each article reviewed and selected data from each article is presented here.

Mott JA, Wolfe MI, Alverson CJ, Macdonald SC, Bailey CR, Ball LB, Moorman JE, Somers JH, Mannino DM, Redd SC. *National vehicle emissions policies and practices and declining US carbon monoxide-related mortality.* JAMA 2002;Aug 28;288(8):988-95.

This comprehensive study examined 31 years (1968-1998) of national mortality and motor vehicle emissions data. The study describes the reductions in overall carbon monoxide related deaths during this period and particularly the reductions in motor vehicle-related carbon monoxide deaths. While rates of reduction varied during portions of the 31-year period studied, overall unintentional motor vehicle-related carbon monoxide death rates declined from 20.2 deaths to 8.8 deaths per 1 million person-years, or about 57.8 percent. After 1975, the year in which catalytic converters were introduced into automobiles, the authors found a reduction in vehicle-related carbon monoxide deaths of 76.3 percent, a decline from 4.0 to 0.9 deaths per

1 million person-years. While not drawing any hard and fast conclusions, the authors nonetheless felt compelled to comment on this saying, "the concurrent decline in motor vehicle-related emissions and poisoning deaths that only occurred following the first national intervention to reduce CO in automobile exhaust appears unlikely to be coincidental." Two areas of data presented in this article are of particular value to the non-traffic research in this report. First, there were 238 unintentional motor vehicle-related deaths from carbon monoxide in 1998,, which is consistent with both other articles summarized below and the death certificate research conducted for this report. It adds to the certainty as to the magnitude and scope of the problem. Second, the data presented in the study (see table below) indicate that vehicle-related carbon monoxide deaths primarily affect adults, which is again consistent with information derived from death certificate research and other sources.

Table XV: (from Mott JA, et.al.) 1998 CDR (crude death rate) per 1 Million Person-years (No. of Deaths)

Age	
<5	0.16 (3)
5-14	0.13 (5)
15-34	0.97 (74)
35-64	0.99 (101)
>65	1.60 (55)

Shelef M. *Unanticipated benefits of automotive emission control: reduction in fatalities by motor vehicle exhaust gas.* Sci Total Environ 1994 May 23;146-147:93-101.

This article is simply noted here because it also documents what is more completely described in the article cited above.

Fatalities Associated With Carbon Monoxide Poisoning From Motor Vehicles, 1995-1997. Research Note, April 2000, National Highway Traffic Safety Administration.

Figures presented in this note are consistent with the article by Mott et. al. and the death certificate research conducted in support of this report. Of particular note is the fact that this note identified a consistent annual number of vehicle-related carbon monoxide deaths in moving vehicles, something that the researchers involved in this report did not find, although one such incident was located. Also, the note presented data that support the notion that carbon monoxide poisonings from motor vehicle exhaust are more likely to occur in the cooler months. Data from this article relevant to the research on which this report is based appear in the following tables.

Table XVI: (from NHTSA Research Note) Vehicle-Related Deaths Associated With CO Poisoning: 1995-1997*

	Nature of Deaths	1995	1996	1997	Total
Stationary vehicles	Accidental (%)	234 (11.9)	223 (12.4)	208 (12.9)	665 (12.4)
	Unknown (%)	67 (3.4)	61 (3.4)	41 (2.5)	169 (3.1)
Moving vehicles	Accidental	73	59	61	193

*Suicides were intentionally left out of this chart. Percentages are based on totals that include suicides.

Table XVII: (from NHTSA Research Note) Accidental CO Fatalities with Stationary Vehicles by Vehicle Location: 1995-1997

Vehicle Location	1995	1996	1997	Total
At home	126 (53.8)	149 (66.8)	122 (58.6)	397 (59.7)
On Public Roadway	6 (2.6)	7 (3.2)	7 (3.4)	20 (3.0)
Other Locations	102 (43.6)	67 (30.0)	79 (38.0)	248 (37.3)
Total	234	223	208	665

Table XVIII: (from NHTSA Research Note) All Accidental Vehicle-Related CO Fatalities in 1995-1997 by Season of Occurrence

Season	1995	1996	1997	Total
Fall	77 (25.1)	62 (22.0)	77 (28.6)	216 (25.2)
Winter	105 (34.2)	109 (38.6)	89 (33.1)	303 (35.3)
Spring	76 (24.7)	63 (22.3)	71 (26.4)	210 (24.5)
Summer	49 (16.0)	48 (17.1)	32 (11.9)	129 (15.0)
Total	307	282	269	858

Marr LC, Morrison GC, Nazaroff WW, Harley RA. *Reducing the risk of accidental death due to vehicle-related carbon monoxide poisoning.* J Air Waste Manag Assoc 1998 Oct;48(10):899-906.

Rather than focus on the numbers of incidents of carbon monoxide poisoning, this paper sets out measures of the risk of carbon monoxide poisoning in the typical settings in which most of the carbon monoxide poisonings continue to occur. Using various data sources and methods of statistical analysis, the authors came up with the relative risk of death in a number of situations. That is reflected in the table below.

Table XIX: (from Marc LC et. al.) Risk of Death for Four Accidental Poisoning Scenarios With All vehicles and With Pre-1975 Vehicles Removed

Location	Exposure Duration	All Vehicles	Post –1975 Vehicles Only
garage	1	3.5-7.7%*	1.7-5.6%*
garage	3	16-21%	12-16%
residence	1	0.0%	0.0%
residence	3	9.5%	3.1%

*A range in the risk of death in garages is presented because of uncertainty in garage air-exchange rates.

The garage size assumed in determining the risk factors above is 90 m^3. Changes in the size of the garage would affect the risks of carbon monoxide poisoning, the authors note. They also cite a number of other factors that would affect the risks involved. These include:

- The extent to which a garage is tightly sealed - "Oxygen depletion in a tightly sealed garage could perturb the air-to-fuel ratio in the engine and cause a clean vehicle to become a gross polluter."
- The effect of a cold start on CO emissions – A cold start would, initially at least, increase the amount of carbon monoxide released by a vehicle because "the fuel-air mixture is intentionally enriched to facilitate ignition and to improve cold-engine operation, and the automobile's catalytic converter is not warm enough to function efficiently."
- The effect of a vehicle idling for a long period of time – "the catalyst may never reach a high enough temperature to operate effectively."

Another factor that could confound the authors' results is "the distribution of garaged vehicles versus vehicle age." "This study has assumed that all vehicles tested in the random roadside emissions inspection are equally likely to be parked in an enclosed garage, but it is possible that a higher fraction of newer vehicles are kept in garages because of socioeconomic factors. It this were true, then the risk of death from CO poisoning has been overestimated because the older vehicles, which are responsible for a disproportionately high fraction of deaths, would be less likely to be parked in enclosed garages." What is interesting about the risk factors presented in this paper is that they are based on what is fairly prolonged exposure to the exhaust from an operating vehicle. As indicated earlier in this report, there have been significant declines in deaths from vehicle-generated carbon monoxide over the past 30 years. Also, the current numbers of vehicle-generated carbon monoxide deaths is quite small. With the addition of the risk factors developed by this paper, a picture emerges, which is consistent with information derived from other sources and provided in this report, that suggests that in the majority of cases of accidental carbon monoxide poisonings from vehicle exhaust, factors beyond the vehicle itself play a major role. These factors may include alcohol abuse or serious errors or lapses in judgment on the part of the victim, such as simply forgetting to turn off an operating vehicle in a garage that is attached to a home.

Girman JR, Chang YL, Hayward SG, Liu KS. *Causes of unintentional deaths from carbon monoxide poisonings in California.* West J Med 1998 Mar;168(3):158-65.

Based on unintentional vehicle-related carbon monoxide deaths in California over a 10-year period (1979 to 1988), this study supports certain characteristics of these types of deaths. Among the article's findings:

- 59 of the 136 unintentional deaths from vehicle-generated carbon monoxide were associated with alcohol use – "Typical cases involved drivers who, under the influence of alcohol, parked their cars in their garages and fell asleep without stopping their engine. Surprisingly, there were also cases involving decedents who experienced CO poisoning while drinking and listening to cassette tapes with the motor running, despite having parked their vehicles in the open."

- "California generally follows the national pattern with more deaths in the winter months and higher rates among males, African Americans and older persons."

Death from motor-vehicle-related unintentional carbon monoxide poisoning – Colorado, 1996, New Mexico, 1980-1985, and United States, 1979-1992. MMWR Morb Mortal Wkly Rep 1996 Nov 29;45(47):1029-32.

As with the articles reported on above, this article provides further supporting information relating to the circumstances most frequently involved in vehicle-generated carbon monoxide poisonings. Among the findings of this article are:

- For the period 1979-1992, national death rates from CO poisoning (in stationary vehicles) were higher in most states in the northern regions of the United States, where winter temperatures are coldest, than in states in southern regions, which have warmer winter temperatures.

- Most motor vehicle-related CO deaths in garages have occurred even though the garage doors or windows have been open, suggesting that passive ventilation may not be adequate to reduce risk in semi-enclosed spaces.

Yoon SS, Macdonald SC, Parrish RG. *Deaths from unintentional carbon monoxide poisoning and potential prevention with carbon monoxide detectors.* JAMA 1998 Mar 4;279(9):685-7.

This study, which basically advocates more extensive use of carbon monoxide detectors, includes findings similar to those found in the paper by Girman, et. al. Alcohol levels of greater than 0.01 percent were found in 53 percent of those identified in the study as having died from motor vehicle-related carbon monoxide. (The study examined a total of 136 deaths from CO poisoning that were investigated by the New Mexico Office of the Medical Investigator, 1980 through 1995.)

Rao R, Touger M, Gennis P, Tyrrell J, Roche J, Gallagher EJ. *Epidemic of accidental carbon monoxide poisonings caused by snow-obstructed exhaust systems.* Ann Emerg Med 1997 Apr;29(4):561.

Snow obstructed exhaust systems represent special circumstances that substantially increase the risk of carbon monoxide poisoning from vehicle-generated carbon monoxide. This article reports on the spike in carbon monoxide poisonings that resulted when on January 8, 1996, the New York City metropolitan area was blanketed by more than 24 inches of snow. The article focuses on 25 cases of carbon monoxide poisoning, 18 during the first 24 hours following the snowfall, that were referred to a medical center in New York for hyperbaric oxygen treatment to offset the effects of the patients having been exposed to CO in a stationary automobile with the engine running and the exhaust system obstructed by snow. Usually the patients involved were attempting to keep warm. There was one death from CO in the city that was not included in the study. Twenty (20) of the 25 patients included in the study arrived unconscious at the emergency department.

Baron RC, Backer RC, Sopher IM. *Unintentional deaths from carbon monoxide in motor vehicle exhaust: West Virginia.* Am J Public Health 1989 Mar;79(3):328-30.

This article again supports several tendencies inherent in motor vehicle-related carbon monoxide deaths:

- Involvement of older vehicles: "Of 64 episodes involving 82 deaths investigated by the West Virginia Office of the Chief Medical Examiner, 1978-1984, 50 occurred outdoors in older vehicles with defective exhaust systems..."
- Blood alcohol was detected in 50 (68 percent) of 74 victims tested.

Hampson NB, Norkool DM. *Carbon monoxide poisoning in children riding in the back of pickup trucks.* JAMA 1992 Jan 22-29;267(4):538-40.

This study identified circumstances that represent a particular risk of carbon monoxide poisoning in children. The authors examined, through follow up telephone interviews, 68 patients treated with hyperbaric oxygen for accidental carbon monoxide poisoning between 1986 and 1991. These patients were treated at a private, urban, tertiary care center in Seattle, WA and ranged from 4 to 16 years old. Twenty (20) of these cases occurred as a result of the children riding in the back of pickup trucks. In 17 of these, the children were riding under a rigid closed canopy on the rear of the truck. In three cases the children rode beneath a tarpaulin. Fifteen (15) of the children who had been riding in pickups had lost consciousness. One died, one had permanent neurologic deficits, and 18 had no recognizable after effects of the carbon monoxide poisoning. In all 20 cases, the truck exhaust system had a previously known leak or tail pipe that exited at the rear rather than at the side of the pickup truck.

Appendix III - Backing Cases from 1998 Death Certificates and LexisNexis

The following chart presents details of each 1998 backing incident that was identified in either death certificates or LexisNexis. Information from the two sources is combined here into this single chart to demonstrate that the two information sources complement one another. Despite best efforts to come up with criteria that would provide 1998 death certificates that included all backing incidents, there were still backing incidents that resulted in death that were found in news accounts in LexisNexis, but not identified through the death certificate research. It should be noted, however, that death certificates for many of the LexisNexis deaths may be found when the remaining death certificates are obtained.

Table XX: 1998 Backing Incidents Found in Death Certificates (DC) and LexisNexis (LN)

#	Age(s)	Vehicle Type	Location	Description	Source(s)	Death or Injuries
1	14 mos.	car	unclear	parent was parking car backing up	LN	injury
2	67	car	street	victim was crossing the street when hit by car backing out of store parking lot	LN	death
3	88	garbage truck	parking lot	pedestrian hit by garbage truck backing up, died next month	DC, LN	death
4	2	delivery truck	driveway of farm	truck was backing up in driveway of farm	DC, LN	death
5	7	pickup	parking space	driver was backing up pickup truck under tree, victim was on bicycle	LN	death
6	73	car	private property – probably parking lot	victim was struck by car backing out of parking space on private property	LN	injury
7	8, 5	truck	alley	victims were on skateboard, hit by truck backing down alley into condo complex	LN	8 – death 5 - injury
8	21 mos.	car	driveway	victim hit by car backing out of driveway - fractured skull	DC, LN	death
9	21 mos.	pickup	driveway	parent was backing out of driveway- pet ran under truck, someone scooted pet away, driver thought all the kids were out of the way	LN	death
10	31	truck	street	truck was backing up, hit and ran over victim crossing street in mid-block, beeper was working	LN	death
11	2	vehicle	driveway	elderly driver pulled into driveway to drop off residents of the home, as driver was backing out of the driveway, vehicle struck 2-year-old	LN	death
12	1	car	unclear	victim died after being accidentally run over by car, friend had been visiting family and was backing car up when the victim ran behind the car and was run over	LN	death
13	43	truck	unclear	43-yr-old victim died after being run over by friend who didn't realize was backing truck over friend, until police told driver, driver didn't know had run over friend	LN	death

#	Age(s)	Vehicle Type	Location	Description	Source(s)	Death or Injuries
14	1	car	driveway	parent thought three young children were safely waiting in front yard when backed out the car, felt a rear tire run over something and discovered that child had wandered into the path of the vehicle	LN	injury
15	19 mos.	pickup	driveway	parent accidentally backed pickup over victim in family's driveway	LN	injury
16	13 mos.	car	driveway	13-month-old died after being run over in driveway by parent backing out of driveway, parent did not know child was behind the car when backed up	DC, LN	death
17	18 mos.	car	driveway	run over in family's driveway, playing next to driveway when struck by sedan driven by family friend backing out, knocked under car when hit by bumper, then run over when the driver stopped, moved forward	DC, LN	death
18	adult	truck	street	crossing street, was struck and run over by a truck as it was backing up - driver apparently was unaware that there was anybody behind the truck.	LN	unclear
19	22 mos.	van	driveway	driveway of small apartment complex was play area for children - relative took victim outside to wave goodbye to parent, play w/children, before relative could react, victim walked behind a large van as it began backing out of driveway	LN	death
20	4	unclear	driveway	the accident occurred in a driveway, driver knew the child and was just backing up and thought the child was clear from the rear of the vehicle'	LN	death
21	86	unclear	driveway	driver accidentally ran over, killed friend, dropped friend off, began backing out of driveway, friend returned to passenger side, driver not aware of return, kept backing, struck friend then apparently accidentally accelerated instead of braking	DC, LN	death

#	Age(s)	Vehicle Type	Location	Description	Source(s)	Death or Injuries
22	2	car	driveway	backing up in car parent hit 2-year-old child, who was playing on the gravel driveway, police said	LN	injury
23	3	van	driveway	child killed when transit shuttle backed over child while child was riding tricycle, pedaled into neighbor's driveway just as 15-person van was backing out	LN	death
24	1	van	driveway	child was killed when relative accidentally ran over child while backing van out of a driveway in an apartment complex, pulled van out of a carport behind complex, backed vehicle around corner where child was sitting in driveway	DC, LN	death
25	18 mos.	vehicle	driveway	killed when parent hit child while backing a vehicle out of their driveway, police said - parent was not aware child was outside their home	LN	death
26	6	car	driveway	relative was backing car from driveway when child ran from house and jumped on the back of the car	DC, LN	death
27	19 mos.	car	driveway	driver was backing car out of a driveway when heard a loud thump from under the vehicle, child run over by car while parents watched.	DC, LN	death
28	4	van	driveway	parent was backing out of the driveway in the family van when child ran out of the family home and behind the van	LN	death
29	71	unclear	driveway	police said driver did not see victim as driver was backing out of the driveway	DC, LN	death
30	2 1/2	SUV	driveway	parent wanted to move vehicle to make room for a friend's truck in the driveway, as slowly backed out, felt impact	LN	injury
31	5	SUV	driveway	killed by the family Suburban while playing in the driveway – in article about dangers of backing	LN	death
32	1	unclear	unclear	parent backed over and killed his year-old child	LN	death
#	Age(s)	Vehicle Type	Location	Description	Source(s)	Death or Injuries

33	13 mos.	SUV	driveway	as parent backing vehicle out of garage, child had scampered out a side door (of house) into driveway into path of vehicle	DC, LN	death
34	3	pickup	driveway	sibling got in pickup truck didn't realize sibling was behind truck	DC, LN	death
35	5	unclear	driveway	sibling accidentally backed over victim in driveway	LN	death
36	2 mos.	pickup	driveway	parent brought baby outside in infant car seat, set it down in driveway while backed the pickup truck from garage	DC, LN	death
37	2	vehicle	driveway	2-year-old child was killed when a vehicle backed over that child in the driveway at child's home	LN	death
38	78	car	parking lot	victim walked behind a car that backed over victim in a parking lot	DC, LN	death
39	22 mos.	unclear	parking lot	was in the parking lot of apartments when driver backed over the child as driver was pulling out of a parking space	LN	injury
40	4	unclear	driveway	troopers said parent backed out of the driveway of a friend's home and didn't see child	LN	injury
41	8	car	street	was playing in a gutter when a car backed over leg	LN	injury
42	6	pickup	driveway/ street	was playing in a pile of sand in the street behind a pickup parked in a driveway - the driver came out of the home, which he had been visiting, but did not see the child and backed over child	LN	death
43	46	garbage truck	behind grocery store	victim was hospitalized in critical condition after a garbage truck backed over victim behind a grocery store	LN	injury
44	2	pickup with trailer	field	parent accidentally killed 2-year-old child when parent backed over child with a trailer	LN	death
45	2	van	driveway	2-year-old child died after parent backed over child with the family's minivan in the home's driveway	LN	death
46	3	truck	farm	3-year-old was killed Monday morning when parent accidentally backed over child with a truck	LN	death
47	19 mos.	van	driveway	parent thought child was in house accidentally backed over child in driveway	DC, LN	death

#	Age(s)	Vehicle Type	Location	Description	Source(s)	Death or Injuries
48	1	minivan	driveway	killed when backed over by a minivan	DC, LN	death
49	60	snow-plow	probably parking lot	snowplow backed over victim as victim left a store	DC, LN	death
50	7	truck	driveway	killed when parent - using plow-equipped truck - accidentally backed over child, didn't realize child was near truck when plowing driveway	DC, LN	death
51	3	unclear	driveway	parent backed over her child in the driveway	LN	injury
52	28 mos.	car	parking lot	parent buckled child into child seat, then went around car to load something, began to back out of a parking space when noticed child not in seat	DC, LN	death
53	64	auto-mobile	parking lot	pedestrian struck by reversing automobile	DC	death
54	1	vehicle	street	struck by vehicle-this was confirmed as a backing incident by FARS – point of first contact with vehicle, rear of vehicle	DC	death
55	85	vehicle	address given as location	crushed by vehicle - this was confirmed as a backing incident by FARS – point of first contact with vehicle, rear of vehicle	DC	death
56	77	car	driveway	victim struck when the car backed into victim while in own driveway - car driven by spouse	DC, LN	death
57	60	car	backyard	friend accidentally backed car into victim, pinning victim against wall of own house	DC	death
58	89	vehicle	driveway	neighbor accidentally struck victim while backing out of driveway	DC, LN	death
59	68	truck	farm	pedestrian that truck backed over	DC	death
60	81	recy- cling truck	street	deceased crushed by truck backing up	DC	death
61	89	truck	parking lot	truck backed over victim outside a retail business	DC, LN	death
62	91	pickup	street	was struck by a pickup truck that was backing out of parking lot, then pulled forward, running over victim again	DC	death
63	5	car	home	pedestrian backed over by vehicle (car)	DC	death

#	Age(s)	Vehicle Type	Location	Description	Source(s)	Death or Injuries
64	2	Auto-mobile	home	pedestrian backed over by automobile	DC	death
65	81	car	driveway	pedestrian struck by car backing out of driveway	DC	death
66	78	vehicle	driveway	run over while standing behind vehicle in driveway	DC	death
67	1	vehicle	home	vehicle backed over victim and struck head	DC	death
68	2	pickup	home	playing in side yard of residence - relative backed over child with a pickup	DC	death
69	1	vehicle	parking lot	hit by motor vehicle backing up	DC	death
70	3	vehicle	driveway	playing in driveway, decedent was run over by parent backing vehicle out	DC	death
71	1	car	driveway	child was backed over in driveway of home as driver was backing car into garage	DC	death
72	81	car	parking lot	victim was walking in the parking lot of grocery store, was run over by car backing out of parking space	DC	death
73	1	pickup	home	pickup backed over child	DC, LN	death
74	4	vehicle	home	child fell under a backing motor vehicle	DC	death
75	88	vehicle	driveway	victim struck by motor vehicle backing from driveway	DC	death
76	91	vehicle	parking lot	decedent was struck by a vehicle backing out of a parking space - occurred in an apartment parking lot	DC	death
77	17 mos.	car	driveway	car backed over the toddler's head	DC	death
78	41	tow truck	parking lot	tow truck backs up over pedestrian	DC	death
79	84	truck	parking lot	backed over by truck in parking lot	DC	death
80	1	vehicle	driveway	adults were distracted, child walked down street, neighbor backing out of driveway struck child	DC	death
81	82	pickup	driveway/ sidewalk	was walking down sidewalk, pickup truck was backing down driveway, did not see victim	DC	death
82	71	car	parking lot	82 yr.-old driver was backing out of parking spot, struck victim	DC	death

#	Age(s)	Vehicle Type	Location	Description	Source(s)	Death or Injuries
83	80	dump truck	unclear	victim was standing pretty far behind the truck, which backed up unaware victim was there	DC	death
84	1	pickup	yard of residence	victim was at the rear of the vehicle, driver backed up, hit victim, then went forward -	DC	death
85	79	car	parking lot	car was backing up from a parking space	DC	death
86	72	garbage truck	street	victim was throwing a bag of garbage into the truck, truck backed up into victim	DC, LN	
87	1	van or SUV	driveway	driver was backing out of driveway	DC	death
88	71	vehicle	field	person's vehicle backed over victim, happened in field behind person's business	DC	death
89	2	car	service station	fell out of car while backing up - occurred at service station	DC	death
90	2	pickup	at home	pickup truck was backing while victim was playing behind the truck	DC	death
91	82	auto	driveway	hit by auto in driveway - vehicle was backing out of driveway	DC	death
92	2	pickup	home	accidentally killed after crawling under parent's pickup truck when the parent backed the truck up to go to work	DC	death
93	53	garbage truck	parking lot	backed over by garbage truck	DC	death
94	1	car	driveway	car accidentally backed up over child	DC	death
95	1	truck	home	truck backed over child's head	DC	death
96	1	car	home	backed over by passenger car	DC	death
97	62	truck	yard	deceased lying behind truck that backed over deceased, happened in yard at an address- ethanol consumption a factor,	DC	death
98	1	pickup	driveway	from ME's office -deceased was reportedly backed over by a pickup truck	DC	death
99	77	delivery truck	alley	pedestrian struck by delivery truck in alley - was behind truck, no backup alarm referenced in report, driver didn't see victim	DC	death

#	Age(s)	Vehicle Type	Location	Description	Source(s)	Death or Injuries
100	1	van	driveway	driver of van owned by a shelter backed out of driveway and struck child	DC	death
101	1	car	driveway	accident occurred in front yard - from ME - car was backing out of driveway, child ran to left side of vehicle - left front tire ran over child	DC	death
102	1	car	parking lot	pedestrian run over by car - from ME's office - vehicle was backing	DC	death
103	2	car	home	apparently was backed over by car	DC	death
104	86	car	parking lot	driver attempting to back car out of a parking space	DC	death
105	2	vehicle	parking lot	was hit by driver backing vehicle up	DC	death
106	1	SUV	at home	spoke to police officer who remembered the incident, vehicle was backing up and it was an SUV	DC	death
107	17	dump truck	road repair site	deceased working as flagman on road repair job was distracted by a motorist, dump truck with no operating back-up alarm backed over deceased crushing head under the rear wheels	DC	death
108	58	dump truck	quarry	backed over by dump truck	DC	death
109	19	dump truck	highway	working on highway, dump truck backed over deceased	DC	death
110	42	dump truck	highway	struck by backing dump truck	DC, LN	death
111	34	truck	construction site	truck at construction site backed over decedent, crushing pelvis	DC	death
112	46	truck	construction site	truck backed over deceased at construction site	LN	death
113	47	dump truck	not indicated	municipal/construction foreman/victim was run over and killed by a dump truck deceased was guiding as it backed up	LN	death
114	41	dump truck	paving site	41-year-old construction worker died after an asphalt dump truck backed over worker - group of construction workers was paving part of a drive	LN	death
115	4	pickup	field	driver didn't see child relative dart behind truck as child - was backing from a field next to their house	LN	death

#	Age(s)	Vehicle Type	Location	Description	Source(s)	Death or Injuries
116	38	fuel truck	airport	killed when a truck backed into victim as victim waited to guide a jetliner to a gate, struck by a truck that had just finished fueling a departing jet	LN	death
117	35	water truck	construction site	as victim knelt down to inspect the soil, the truck driver backed over victim -	DC, LN	death
118	55	dump truck	construction site	victim run over by a dump truck - died after the truck backed over victim	DC, LN	death
119	40	pickup	median of interstate	truck's tailgate unexpectedly popped open and knocked victim down, truck's driver, was unaware victim had fallen, backed up	LN	death
120	78	dump truck	farm	dump truck backed into victim while victim was working on own farm	LN	death
121	67	dump truck	construction site	victim bent down to get some pipe when a dump truck backed over victim	LN	death
122	39	pickup	driveway	was killed when a pickup truck backed out of a driveway - truck's driver told police he did not see the pedestrian.	LN	death
123	41	truck	street/ workplace	backed over by truck	DC	death
124	55	truck	parking lot	truck backed over deceased	DC	death
125	52	farm truck	farm	was backed over by large farm truck -	DC	death
126	38	dump truck	landfill	dump truck backed over victim	DC	death
127	1	car	home	was backed over by car	DC	death
128	80	car	street in front of home	backed over by car	DC	death
129	57	plow truck	Road commission garage	plow truck backed over victim	DC	death
130	9	truck	Farm	truck backed over deceased	DC	death
131	88	pickup	parking lot	pedestrian struck by pickup truck - from police dept. - vehicle was backing up	DC	death

#	Age(s)	Vehicle Type	Location	Description	Source(s)	Death or Injuries
132	1	van	driveway	pedestrian run over by van - from ME's office - vehicle was backing up	DC	death
133	3	vehicle	driveway	from ME - child came from next door into path of vehicle backing out of driveway	DC	death

Appendix IV – Backing Deaths Identified in NHTSA's Fatality Analysis Reporting System (FARS) in Years 2000, 2001

Table XXI: 2000, 2001 Backing Deaths Identified in FARS

#	Age(s)	Vehicle Type	Location	Description	Found in LexisNexis™
				2000	
1	2, 10 (injured)	SUV	trailer park	playing children run over by truck backing up in trailer park - driver did not see children	Yes
2	16 mos.	car	driveway	driver in driveway to let off passenger and child, passenger put child down, child ran to back of vehicle, driver stuck child as driver was backing up	Yes
3	2	van	driveway	2-year-old died after was struck by a neighbor's van as it was pulling out of a driveway	Yes
4	22 mos.	small school bus	driveway	child was killed when run over by small school bus backing out of townhouse driveway, 3-yr- old sibling, & another student had just boarded bus, parent didn't know toddler had wandered away, no charges have been filed against the bus driver	Yes
5	22 mos.	car	driveway	22-month-old killed when run over, died at hospital after struck by car backing out of neighbor's driveway, was with parent and grandparent when ran down sidewalk, driver did not see the child behind vehicle, will not be charged	Yes

#	Age(s)	Vehicle Type	Location	Description	Found in LexisNexis™
6	22 mos.	pickup	driveway	child was struck and killed by a pickup backing out of a driveway near child's home	Yes
7	17 mos.	unclear	parking lot	driver who backed over and killed a 17-month-old has been indicted by a state grand jury on felony charges of leaving the scene of an accident involving death.-victim was walking across the parking lot with parent	Yes
8	7	tow truck	street	youth was pedaling bicycle behind the tow truck in evening on a private street at a mobile- home park when the truck driver stopped and backed over youth	Yes
9	20 mos.	van	alley	toddler was killed by a hit-and- run driver - van backed over the child, who was playing in an alley - van was ditched about a block away.	Yes
10	47	dump truck	unclear	two dump trucks owned by same company, parked with rears facing each other, one backed up, struck driver of the other who was standing behind other truck	
11	75	station wagon	driveway	driver backing out of driveway, did not see victim, heard bump, pulled forward, victim on ground conscious, but incoherent, victim died 10 days later from head injury sustain in accident	
12	55	van	driveway	driver backing out of driveway, began to drive down street, wasn't driving right, got out and checked twice, ultimately found victim under the van - was admitted to hospital in critical condition and later died	
13	67	pickup	apparently street	driver stopped, heard someone call, attempted to back up too fast, lost control, drove up on sidewalk hitting pedestrian and brick wall	
14	84, 80 (injured)	pickup	sidewalk	two pedestrians were walking on sidewalk when driver backed out of driveway and struck them	
15	76	van	driveway	driver backed vehicle out of driveway, didn't realize parent was out of the house (had gone to a mailbox), struck parent who was behind vehicle at time of accident	

#	Age(s)	Vehicle Type	Location	Description	Found in LexisNexis™
16	87	pickup	driveway	driver backed out of driveway and struck victim who was blind and using a cane	
17	79	pickup	parking lot	driver backed up in public parking lot, pedestrian entered path of vehicle and was struck and run over	
18	74	light truck	unclear	truck was stopped, started to back up, struck bicyclist who came into the path of the vehicle backing up	
19	74	car	driveway	driver was backing out of driveway, didn't see pedestrian on sidewalk, felt pressure on the car, pulled forward, saw victim on the ground	
20	mos. 32	pickup	driveway	parent was backing out of driveway when child tried to get parent's attention by beating on side of passenger side of truck running toward rear of truck, got to rear of truck and fell down at which time passenger rear tire ran over victim	
21	81	SUV	parking lot/street	driver backed out of parking lot into street striking victim who was crossing the street	
22	91	car	driveway	victim was helping driver back out of driveway, driver's door was open struck victim, victim died 12 days later	
23	36	car	street	vehicle, originally in parked position, backed up and struck victim who was crossing street, victim died approximately three weeks later	
24	71	??	unclear	vehicle backed up over victim	
25	2	pickup	driveway	driver was turning around in driveway, backed up looking over right shoulder, child ran into path of truck from the left was struck by vehicle backing up	
26	31	dump truck	unclear	no written description provided- drawing indicates truck backed up, did not realize struck pedestrian until dragging victim 61 feet	
27	90	van	apparently street	driver was backing vehicle, victim apparently stepped off curb into path of vehicle, victim was hard of hearing may not have heard beeper, van was owned by a business	

#	Age(s)	Vehicle Type	Location	Description	Found in LexisNexis™
28	6	recycling truck	apparently street	truck was backing up, with beeper and rear back-up camera working (driver didn't see anything in monitor), child on bicycle, apparently looking back at friend, rode into the back of the truck, truck then ran over child	
29	3	pickup	driveway	backing out of driveway struck victim, then pulled forward not knowing what had been hit	
30	89	pickup	alley	truck was backing out of alley, struck pedestrian	
31	7	garbage truck	street	backing from one street to another, truck struck bicyclist	
32	2	SUV	driveway	victim struck as vehicle was backing out of driveway	
33	1	car	driveway	driver backing out of driveway, child playing next door ran into path of car, fell to ground near rear left wheel of vehicle, which ran over child	
34	63	van	driveway	van backing out of the driveway struck victim who was apparently in the road	
35	4, 20(injured)	station wagon	unclear	PAR on this is very sketchy, it is clear that one vehicle backed up, pinning more than one victim between it and another vehicle-seems there were three victims, one died	
36	86	car	unclear	driver backed up, did not see victim or car victim was standing next to, victim was getting into vehicle, was pinched between door and interior of vehicle	
37	24	van	unclear	victim got out of passenger side of parked vehicle, was struck by van backing up-van left the scene	
38	70	pickup	unclear	vehicle struck victim while snowplowing	
39	40, 47 (injured)	car	apparently street	driver was backing up from gas station after dropping off friend, says she did not see pedestrians, hit them, dragged one across the street	
40	52	van	driveway	no written description - drawing indicates vehicle was backing up out of a driveway and struck pedestrian in street	

#	Age(s)	Vehicle Type	Location	Description	Found in LexisNexis™
41	85	SUV	street	vehicle backing up struck victim, who from diagram apparently entered the street from between two parked cars- driver said did not see victim, did not know where victim came from	
42	70	truck	parking lot	driver was plowing parking lot, was backing up, looking both ways at traffic, struck pedestrian who was walking on the sidewalk, didn't see pedestrian	
43	43	station wagon	parking space (street)	vehicle struck pedestrian while backing into parking space, pedestrian had stepped into the street	
44	55	vehicle	street	vehicle was backing southbound in the northbound lane, driver felt bump or thud, continued to back up, saw pedestrian in front of vehicle	
45	50	van	intersection (street)	driver was backing up vehicle near intersection, felt thump, stopped car, got out saw pedestrian	
46	89	car	driveway	driver backing out of driveway, saw pedestrian in side mirror, was stopped, driver continued to back out believing pedestrian had stopped to allow driver to back out	
47	85	car	driveway	driver backing out of driveway, struck victim who was walking on the sidewalk	
48	mos. 30	SUV	driveway	driver backing out of driveway, did not see victim	
49	66	SUV	street	driver backed up on street, struck victim who had been gardening and still had gardening blower on his back, victim died a week after the accident	
50	82	car	street	car backed down street across another street, struck victim who was in the intersection	
51	mos. 18	car	complicated scenario	vehicle was stopped by side of road, partly blocking driveway, 2nd vehicle backed out of driveway, apparently didn't look, struck 1st vehicle - child had been put outside of 1st vehicle between car and open door - 2nd vehicle struck door causing injuries to child	

#	Age(s)	Vehicle Type	Location	Description	Found in LexisNexis™
52	82	pickup	driveway	driver looked behind him prior to backing straight out of the driveway between church and rectory, did not see anything behind him, but two dogs were bouncing around in back (pickup w/camper shell), did not realize struck someone	
53	68	garbage truck	roadway (street)	after finishing a collection, driver backed into roadway, struck victim-truck had rear camera system that was not turned on and when turned on had dirt over lens so would have been ineffective anyway, also back-up alarm was too faint to be heard	
54	mos. 16	car	driveway	driver backing out of driveway, checked both side mirrors and rear view mirrors, didn't see anything, struck child who had been walking on sidewalk with her older sibling	
55	91	car	driveway	driver slowly backing out of driveway, looked both ways, proceeded, heard thump	
56	87	pickup	sidewalk	driver backed out of parking stall to enter road, as vehicle crossed sidewalk, people yelled that it had hit something, pulled back into parking spot-result - backed over victim then ran over victim again	
57	mos. 20	car	alley	car was attempting to back into an alley, driver did not see child and thought had run over a toy	
2001					
#	Age(s)	Vehicle Type	Location	Description	Found in LexisNexis™
1	6	truck, probably garbage	alley	child on bike was struck by truck backing out of alleyway	Yes
2	3	pickup	probably parking lot	3-yr-old was run over and killed yesterday by a pickup that was backing out of a parking space in the townhouse development where child's family lives	Yes
3	16 mos.	car	driveway	died after parent ran over child while backing out of driveway	Yes

#	Age(s)	Vehicle Type	Location	Description	Found in LexisNexis™
4	84, 80(injured)	SUV	driveway	victim was walking with neighbor around neighborhood, killed when driver backing out of driveway apparently didn't see victim and ran over victim	Yes
5	54	garbage truck	alley	disposal truck backed over a transient, who died at the scene from massive head injuries in an alley	Yes
6	39	pickup	median	pickup truck on interstate transporting furniture covered by plastic, but not tied down, sofa came off truck, driver pulled to median, ran back to pull sofa to median, victim got out of truck concerned for driver, another occupant of truck moved into driver seat, backed up truck, plastic blew up, blocked view, struck victim who originally seemed alright, but died	
7	mos. 33	pickup	driveway?	driver, possibly backing out of driveway, struck child on bicycle, child got stuck under truck, was dragged for some distance before driver realized, removed child from under vehicle and fled	
8	67	pickup	street	driver parked in front of residence, with a passenger in the vehicle, waiting to pick up spouse, backed up in anticipating of continuing down road, heard noise, perhaps scream, got out of vehicle, saw victim lying on the ground	
9	6	vehicle	street	parent was sweeping street with the vehicle, backed up to make another pass, struck child who was behind him on a bicycle	
10	77	vehicle	unclear	driver backed up in attempt to flee from fight, lost control, struck pedestrian-charged w/DUI for refusing to take test	
11	4	van	street	parent drove vehicle out of driveway, was attempting to turn around in street in front of house, backed vehicle up and unknowingly backed over child	

#	Age(s)	Vehicle Type	Location	Description	Found in LexisNexis™
12	adult	pickup	HOV lane	driver and victim were both workers on HOV lanes of an interstate highway - driver backed up vehicle in HOV lane to notify police of accident, struck victim, then went forward ran over victim again	
13	3	pickup	driveway	parent backed out of driveway, turned vehicle, did not see child approach vehicle from passenger side, vehicle struck child in area of front passenger side wheel and drove over child	
14	84	garbage truck	street	truck backing down street struck victim who was crossing the street (no crosswalk)	
15	80	SUV	driveway	driver backed at idle speed out of driveway, had looked before started, heard thump, got out of car, noticed victim in driveway bleeding - victim had gone to mailbox.	
16	80	SUV	driveway	driver backed out of driveway at high rate of speed, did not see victim who was on a mower mowing grass	
17	82	car	curb of road (street)	driver backed up along curb of road (from diagram) and struck pedestrian, was told by people what happened, then went forward for about 50 feet, dragging victim under the car	
18	71	car	driveway	driver was backing out of driveway, looked to rear on the sidewalk and street was clear, as backed up car was having trouble backing, driver got out of car, saw pedestrian laying under trunk area of car.	
19	79	garbage truck	unclear	truck driver was backing up, checking mirrors, was watching the right side because of parked vehicle there, said never saw victim, but felt two bumps, immediately stopped and got out to find victim lying on pavement.	

#	Age(s)	Vehicle Type	Location	Description	Found in LexisNexis™
20	77	car	street	driver had completed turn from shopping plaza exit to one-way street, then backed up and struck victim who was crossing the street to the shopping plaza - victim died 21 days later	
21	80	car	street	car pulled to side of street to drop off victim and groceries, passenger walked to rear of car after getting groceries out of car, driver asked victim if was okay, victim said was and it was okay to go, driver put car in reverse hit victim	
22	17	car	street	vehicle backed out of parking lot onto one way street very fast, victim, on bicycle, was traveling on shoulder in opposite direction of one way, was struck by vehicle which also struck another vehicle, which in turn struck another	
23	7	pickup	driveway	truck, backing out of driveway, struck victim	
24	37	van	driveway	vehicle was backing out of driveway, driver said "stopped and looked both ways twice," felt bump, stopped, got out, saw victim, who had headphones on	
25	72	??	unclear	only information in report is a drawing, which makes it clear it was a backing incident, but no other details of the incident were in the report because pages were missing.	
26	63	??	driveway	no written description received, drawing indicates vehicle backed out of driveway, struck pedestrian	
27	69	truck	driveway	driver backed out of driveway to allow another car to pull out of driveway, heard thump as drove forward to return to driveway, had apparently hit victim while backing up as pattern of victim's pants was found on bumper of vehicle	
28	89	??	driveway	driver was backing out of driveway when victim walked into path, driver stopped and avoided contact, but victim fell hitting head	

#	Age(s)	Vehicle Type	Location	Description	Found in LexisNexis™
29	83	van	street	driver backed up, apparently some distance (through an intersection) and struck victim who was crossing the street	
30	68	car	roadway (street)	driver was waiting for victim to give a ride, driver saw victim walking toward the vehicle, then lost sight of victim, driver began to back up when felt vehicle hit a bump, it is not known whether or not victim fell to roadway before accident	
31	90	SUV	driveway	driver backed out of driveway into passing pedestrian	
32	43	garbage truck	street	truck was backing up in residential street, victim initially walking in street and "then suddenly darted behind" truck, which ran over victim-driver said "looked at both mirrors and the camera in the back" saw nobody	
33	20	pickup	unclear	victim had gotten out of passenger side of parked truck, was headed away from truck - driver backed up, struck victim then left the scene	
34	89	SUV	driveway	driver backed out of driveway, didn't see victim, thinks may have been behind a tree on the same side of the street from which driver was backing	
35	1	car	driveway	driver ran over victim once as backed out of driveway, again upon reentering driveway- driver said thought had gone over the curb	
36	mos. 17, 4, 21 - 4 and 21 year olds injured	vehicle	driveway	vehicle backing out of driveway, in dark, street lights were flickering on and off, hit three pedestrians, youngest of whom was seriously injured and died	
37	mos. 22	car	driveway	backing out of driveway, looked, saw adult clear driveway, struck child	
38	47	SUV	unclear	backing up to enter vacant parking space, heard a thump, struck pedestrian	
39	67	van	street	vehicle backing up on street struck pedestrian	

#	Age(s)	Vehicle Type	Location	Description	Found in LexisNexis™
20	77	car	street	driver had completed turn from shopping plaza exit to one-way street, then backed up and struck victim who was crossing the street to the shopping plaza - victim died 21 days later	
21	80	car	street	car pulled to side of street to drop off victim and groceries, passenger walked to rear of car after getting groceries out of car, driver asked victim if was okay, victim said was and it was okay to go, driver put car in reverse hit victim	
22	17	car	street	vehicle backed out of parking lot onto one way street very fast, victim, on bicycle, was traveling on shoulder in opposite direction of one way, was struck by vehicle which also struck another vehicle, which in turn struck another	
23	7	pickup	driveway	truck, backing out of driveway, struck victim	
24	37	van	driveway	vehicle was backing out of driveway, driver said "stopped and looked both ways twice," felt bump, stopped, got out, saw victim, who had headphones on	
25	72	??	unclear	only information in report is a drawing, which makes it clear it was a backing incident, but no other details of the incident were in the report because pages were missing.	
26	63	??	driveway	no written description received, drawing indicates vehicle backed out of driveway, struck pedestrian	
27	69	truck	driveway	driver backed out of driveway to allow another car to pull out of driveway, heard thump as drove forward to return to driveway, had apparently hit victim while backing up as pattern of victim's pants was found on bumper of vehicle	
28	89	??	driveway	driver was backing out of driveway when victim walked into path, driver stopped and avoided contact, but victim fell hitting head	

vehicle backing up identified several distinct trends relating to backing incidents. Backing incidents tend to:

- Occur in residential driveways and parking lots,
- Involve sport utility vehicles (SUVs) or small trucks,
- Occur when a parent, relative or someone known to the family is driving, and
- Particularly affect children less than five years old.

Brison RJ, Wicklund K, Mueller BA. *Fatal pedestrian injuries to young children: a different pattern of injury.* Am J Public Health 1988 Jul;78(7):793-5.

This research examined Washington State death certificates from 1979-83 with ICD 9 E-Codes 814-825 (motor vehicle-related incidents) indicated as the cause of death. This study also reviewed coroners' reports when needed and if such a report was available as well as police reports if necessary to obtain details of the incidents involved. The study identified 71 fatal motor vehicle injuries to children less than five years of age during the five-year study period. Of these, 41 were found to be non-traffic related, with 30 incidents occurring in driveways and 11 having occurred in apartment or store parking lots.

The projected average annual death rate data presented in this study show that all of the non-traffic deaths involved children between the ages of 1 and 4. That data appear in the following chart:

Table XXII: (from Brison, et. al.) Average Annual Death Rates by Age and Sex of Child for Non-Traffic and Traffic-Related Pedestrian Incidents

	Non-traffic		Traffic	
Age(years)	Number	Rate/100.000 population	Number	Rate/100.000 population
0	0	--	2	0.6
1	19	5.8	7	2.2
2	11	3.4	4	1.2
3	7	2.2	10	3.1
4	4	1.2	7	2.2
1-4	41	3.2	28	2.2
Male	25	3.8	16	2.4
Female	16	2.5	14	2.2

The propensity for SUVs or small trucks to be involved in non-traffic incidents as well as for a parent or family member to be driving is demonstrated in the following data that was presented in this study.

Table XXIII: (from Brison, et. al.) Characteristics of Non-Traffic and Traffic-Related Pedestrian Vehicle Collisions to Children Less than Age Five

Characteristics	Non-traffic	Traffic
Vehicle Type		
Light Truck	16	1
4 x 4 Truck or Jeep	6	0
Van	6	3
Passenger Auto	9	25
Vehicle Direction		
Forward	9	29
Reverse	23	1
Fell/Jump from vehicle	3	0
Driver		
Father	10	0
Mother	4	0
Other family or visiting friend	6	0
Other	8	27

Winn DG, Agran PF, Castillo DN. *Pedestrian injuries to children younger than 5 years of age.* Pediatrics 1991 Oct;88(4):776-82.

Similar results were found in this study that examined the differences in pedestrian injuries between toddlers (children two years old and younger) and preschoolers (children three and four years old). The study found that toddlers more often die in non-traffic accidents than do preschoolers and it confirmed that children aged one to four are the ones most affected by driveway incidents. "In the entire sample of child pedestrians 0 through 14 years of age, all of the hospital admissions for driveway related events involved children younger than 5 years of age and all of the fatalities were younger than 2 years of age," the study reported. This study was based on data derived from a hospital-based monitoring system of motor vehicle-related injuries to children in Orange County, CA over a two-year period (April 1987 through March 1989). The monitoring system includes 9 of 38 hospitals in the county as well as the coroner's office. The sample examined in this study included 67 toddlers and 102 preschoolers either injured or killed in non-traffic events. Backing was the vehicle action most common among incidents involving toddlers, accounting for 32 or 57 percent of the incidents reviewed. In incidents involving preschoolers, on the other hand, backing was the vehicle action in only 13 or 17 percent of the cases. The data relating to this issue appear below.

Table XXIV: (from Winn et. al.) Action of Vehicles Involved in Non-traffic Accidents Involving Toddlers and Preschoolers

Characteristic	Toddlers(n=67)	Preschoolers(n=102)
Action of vehicle	No. (% of total)	No. (% of total)
Turning	2 (4)	6 (8)
Traveling Straight	22 (39)	57 (75)
Backing	32 (57)	13 (17)
Not ascertained	11	26

The majority of the vehicles involved in the 169 non-traffic events included in this study were automobiles, 35 or 71 percent of the incidents involving toddlers and 52 or 74 percent of the incidents involving preschoolers.

Of the 10 fatalities identified in the study, six involved toddlers and all of those involved a vehicle backing up. Four of these six incidents involved a van or pickup truck and five of the six incidents occurred in a driveway. All of the four deaths of preschoolers occurred mid-block and involved a vehicle (three cars, one motorcycle) proceeding straight. In addition to the 6 toddler and 4 preschooler deaths, the study identified 27 toddlers (40 percent) who required emergency department treatment only and 34 (51 percent) who were hospitalized. Some 44 (43 percent) of the preschoolers required emergency department treatment only and 54 (54 percent) required hospitalization.

Agran PF, Winn DG, Anderson CL. *Differences in child pedestrian injury events by location.* Pediatrics 1994 Feb;93(2):284-8.

This research compared "child pedestrian injury events occurring in driveways and parking lots and at mid-block and intersections with respect to the characteristics and activity of the child, injury outcome measures, and characteristics of the vehicle and roadway." Data for this study were derived from a large multi-hospital and coroner monitoring system for motor vehicle-related injuries to children in Orange County, CA. Data in the study cover the two-year period, April 1, 1987 through March 31, 1989. The sample consisted of 345 child pedestrians 0 to 14 years of age, who were injured during this period.

With respect to non-traffic events, the study found:

- 40 percent of the drivers involved in non-traffic events were driving vans, trucks, or four-wheel drive vehicles; most of these were backing up.
- Most of the children struck were under five years of age.
- Almost half were with adults at the time of the incident.
- The majority of those injured in non-traffic events sustained minor head injuries, but 8 percent of those in driveways sustained non-survivable head injuries, which was a much higher percentage than those injured at other locations.

Some of the data presented in the article and that supports these observations follow.

Table XXV: (from Agran et. al.) Location of Pedestrian Injury Events (N=345)

Location	N(%)
Midblock	182 (53)
Intersection	95 (28)
Driveway	39 (11)
Parking lot*	29 (8)

*The authors of the study found, "The results for events occurring in parking lots were similar to the driveway events."

Table XXVI: (from Agran et. al.) Movement and Type of Vehicle That Struck Pedestrian by Location of Injury, for Four Major Location Types

	Driveway (N=39) n(%)	Parking Lot (N=29) n(%)	Midblock (N=182) n(%)	Intersection (N=95) n(%)
Movement				
Backing	28(78)	16(59)	6(3)	...
Forward	6(17)	10(37)	162(93)	61(72)
Turning	2(6)	1(4)	6(3)	24(28)
Unknown	3	2	8	10
Type of vehicle				
Van, truck, pickup & 4-wheel drive	13(41)	11(39)	42(24)	17(19)
Passenger car	19(59)	17(61)	134(76)	71(81)
Unknown	7	1	6	7

Table XXVII: (from Agran et. al.) Gender and Age of Pedestrians by Location of Injury, for Four Major Location Types

	Driveway (N=39) n(%)	Parking Lot (N=29) n(%)	Midblock (N=182) n(%)	Intersection (N=95) n(%)
Gender				
Female	10(26)	7(24)	48(26)	40(42)
Male	29(74)	22(76)	134(74)	55(58)
Age in years				
0-2	22(56)	7(24)	17(9)	0(0)
3-4	8(21)	9(31)	42(23)	8(8)
5-9	5(13)	4(14)	87(48)	34(36)
10-14	4(10)	9(31)	36(20)	53(56)

Table XXVIII: (from Agran et. al.) Companions by Location of Injury, for Four Major Types

	Driveway (N=39) n(%)	Parking Lot (N=29) n(%)	Midblock (N=182) n(%)	Intersection (N=95) n(%)
Companions				
With adults	14(45)	14(50)	41(23)	21(24)
With other children	11(36)	13(46)	101(57)	43(49)
Alone	6(19)	1(4)	34(19)	23(26)
Unknown	8	1	6	8

Table XXIX: (from Agran et. al.) Disposition by Location of Injury for Four Major Location Types

	Driveway (N=39) n(%)	Parking Lot (N=29) n(%)	Midblock (N=182) n(%)	Intersection (N=95) n(%)
Fatality	4(10)	...	8(4)	4(4)
Admitted to hospital and Discharged home	15(38)	11(38)	103(57)	50(53)
Treated in emergency department and released	20(51)	18(62)	71(39)	41(33)

Duhaime AC, Eppley M, Marguilies S, Heher KL, Bartlett SP. *Crush injuries to the head in children.* Neurosurgery 1995 Sept;37(3):401-6.

While the focus of this article was on the clinical and treatment aspects of dealing with crush injuries to a child's head, it was nonetheless interesting and noteworthy for this NHTSA research effort that of the seven cases chosen to be reported in this article, four involved a child's head being run over by a motor vehicle backing up in a driveway or parking lot. Of these cases, three involved oversized vehicles --one van, one truck, and one small bus. One involved a car. The article does not indicate the years in which the cases occurred.

Partrick BA, Bensard DD, Moore EE, Partington MD, Karrer FM. *Driveway crush injuries in young children: a highly lethal, devastating, and potentially preventable event.* J Pediat Surg 1998 Nov;33(11):1712-5.

This study was based on a six-year review (1991 to 1996) of child (less than 18 years of age) pedestrian injuries treated at two urban trauma centers. In the study sample of 527 children who as pedestrians were injured by automobiles, the authors found 51 (9.7%) incidents that were driveway-related and in which the car rolled backwards over the child. Children under five made up the majority of the driveway cases (41 of 51, 80%). Six driveway cases involved children between the ages of five and nine. Four cases involved children older than nine. Of the children who died as a result of a driveway incident, all were in the 0 to 4 age group.

As with other studies discussed here, this study considered who was driving the vehicle in driveway incidents. A parent was the driver in at least 14 (34%) of the driveway rollover accidents. Siblings were the drivers in four cases (10%), a grandmother in one incident (2%), and neighbors in three (7%) incidents. The person driving the vehicle was not specified in 19 incidents.

Silen ML, Kokoska ER, Fendya DG, Kurkchubasche AG, Weber TR, Tracy TF. *Rollover injuries in residential driveways: age-related patterns of injury.* Pediatrics 1999 Jul;104(1):e7.

This research addressed rollover injuries in driveways and age-related patterns involved. From the medical records of 3,971 consecutive admissions to a single urban trauma service between March 1990 and October 1994, the authors found 26 children (0.7%) who sustained rollover injuries caused by a motor vehicle in a residential driveway. Eighteen (69%) of these injures occurred as the result of the child being struck by an adult driver in a vehicle backing up. The other 8 incidents involved either a sibling under the age of 16 rolling over the child (n=4) or the child putting the vehicle in gear then attempting to get out of the vehicle (n=4). Two of the children died as a result of their injuries and were excluded from the remainder of the study. Nineteen of the 24 survivors in this study were less than 5 years old. The study also determined that younger children were more likely to sustain more severe injuries as a result of these incidents, particularly those less than two years old.

Nadler EP, Courcoulas AP, Gardner MJ, Ford HR. *Driveway injuries in children: risk factors, morbidity, and mortality.* Pediatrics 2001 Aug: 108(2):326-8.

A study published in 2001 by Nadler et. al. focused on a cohort of 64 patients admitted to the Children's Hospital of Pittsburgh after having sustained motor vehicle-related injuries in a driveway. This cohort was derived from a total of 9,820 patients admitted to the hospital's trauma program between May 1986 and August 1999. The cohort was divided into two groups based on the types of events in which they were involved. Group 1 involved an adult driver striking a child because he or she was unaware of the child's presence. Group 2 consisted of children who were injured by a vehicle set in motion by a child. More than 85 percent of the incidents included in Group 1 involved a vehicle going in reverse. The findings of this study are consistent with those previously discussed with respect to the age of the children most affected by backing incidents in driveways (less than 5 years old) and the types of vehicles involved (more often an SUV or truck). Data supporting this presented in the study appear below.

Table XXX: (from Nadler et. al.) Age Distribution of Children Injured in Driveway Related Accidents and Types of Vehicles Involved

	Total(n=64)	Group 1	Group 2
Age in yrs (mean)			
<2		19 (43%)	3 (15%)
2-5		22 (50%)	9 (45%)
>5		3 (7%)	8 (40%)
Type of vehicle			
SUV or truck	31	28	3
Car	26	16	10
Not available	7	0	7

Di Scala C, Sege R, Guohua L. *Outcomes of Pediatric Pedestrian Injuries By Locations of Event.* 45th Annual Proceedings, Association for the Advancement of Automotive Medicine, Sept. 24-26, 2001.

This study by DiScala, et. al. focused on medical outcomes of pediatric pedestrian victims of motor vehicle accidents based on the location where the accident occurs. Data presented in this article relate entirely to the location of the incident. No data specific to backing incidents were presented. However, based on the review of the data involved, the following statement was made in the article with respect to incidents that occur in driveways, "Typically, a very young child is playing in the driveway, and is run over by a family member or a visiting friend reversing a vehicle out of a home driveway."

Nonoccupant Fatalities Associated With Backing Crashes. Research Note, *Revised* February 1997, National Highway Traffic Safety Administration.

The principal investigator involved in preparing this note retired from the agency several years ago. It was therefore not possible for the researchers involved in this report to clarify the methodology used in generating the data that are presented in this research note. The research note is based on 1992 and 1993 death certificate data from the National Center for Health Statistics (NCHS) and on traffic fatality data from police reports contained in NHTSA's Fatality Analysis Reporting System (FARS). The research note reports that data from these two sources "were used to obtain average annual estimates of the number of fatalities associated with off-road and on-road fatal backing crashes." The note makes clear, "Due to the lack of detailed information on death certificates (the source of NCHS data), it is not possible to determine the exact number of nonoccupants killed in off-road backing crashes. The NCHS data, therefore, provide an estimate of the maximum number of fatalities associated with these crashes." Data
presented in this research note confirm one of the patterns associated with backing fatalities that was identified in the research on which this report is based. The research note found that children ages 1-4 are particularly affected by backing crashes. The numbers presented in the note, however, are higher than were found either in counts made as part of the research done for this report or in projections of annual national totals based on those counts.

The disparity between the numbers presented in this report and those in this research note is likely rooted in the fact that different approaches were taken in the two research efforts. Those who did the work for the research note seemed to be addressing the question, "What is the maximum possible number of backing deaths that could be occurring annually based on NCHS death certificate and FARS data?" This may have caused those working on the research note to make certain assumptions concerning the data that were used to determine the maximum possible number of backing fatalities. On the other hand, the goal of those who did the work on which this report is based was to simply count the number of backing (and other) incidents that occur in a given time period and that can be verified through various sources.

There may be additional backing incidents that occurred in 1998, for example, the year that was the focus of death certificate research for this report, but only the incidents reflected in the counts presented in this report could be identified or verified.

In addition to the different research approaches, some of the disparity may result from the fact that the data used for the research note were from 1992 and 1993 while the years covered in this report are 1998 and later. Data presented in the research note appear below.

Table XXXI: (from NHTSA Research Note) Annual Estimates of Nonoccupant Fatalities in Off-Road Backing Crashes – 1992-1993 Average

Age Group	# of Fatalities	% of Total	% of Population
1-4	116	30	6
All Other Ages	274	70	94
Total	390	100	100

Table XXXII: (from NHTSA Research Note) Annual Number of Nonoccupant Fatalities in On-Road Backing Crashes – 1992-1993 Average

Age Group	# of Fatalities	% of Total
1-4	14	16
All Other Ages	71	84
Total	85	100

Appendix VI – Backing Injury Data

The National Electronic Injury Surveillance System (NEISS)

The following table presents data derived from an examination of the National Electronic Injury Surveillance System (NEISS) of the Consumer Product Safety Commission.

Table XXXIII: Injuries from Backing Incidents --National Projections Based on NEISS Data from July 1, 2000 – June 30, 2001

Age	<1	1-4	5-12	13-21	22-64	>64	All
Total(a)	125(a) (1 case)	1101	1089	1111 (a) (18 cases)	2394	860 (a) (13 cases)	6680
Disposition							
1	125 (a) (1 case)	483 (a) (16 cases)	1042	1086 (a) (17 cases)	2337	669 (a) (9 cases)	5742
2	--	--	--	--	--	28 (a) (1 case)	28
4	--	499 (a) (13 cases)	46 (a) (3 cases)	25 (a) (1 case)	56 (a) (2 cases)	161 (a) (3 cases)	787
8	--	118 (a) (1 case)					118
Total(a)	125 (a) (1 case)	1100	1088	1111 (a)	2393	858 (a) (13 cases)	6675

Any differences in totals result from rounding of national projections to the lowest whole number

(a) – Number of incidents found was below 20, which limits the reliability of the national projection

1 – Treated and released, or examined and released without treatment
2 - Treated and transferred to another hospital
4 – Treated and admitted for hospitalization (within same facility)
8 – Fatality including DOA

Backing Injuries in the General Estimates System

The following chart presents data on backing injuries derived from the National Highway Traffic Safety Administration's General Estimates System (GES).

Table XXXIV: Backing Incidents: Annualized GES National Estimates 1996-2000

	Leaving Parked Position	Entering Parked Position	Backing up (not parking)	Total ↔	No Injury	Possible Injury	Non incapacitating evident injury	Incapacitating injury	Fatal Injury	Unknown
Car	21.173	78.868	1248.4	1348.4	63.726	701.78	398.22	110.71	20.523	53.455
SUV	0	4.6268	158.92	163.55	0	51.437	42.408	69.703	0	0
Van	0	5	394	399	127.98	142.57	96.611	27.401	4.4368	0
Lt. Truck	9.0428	0	99.631	108.67	0	0	54.768	44.186	4.4928	5.2268
Other Lt. Veh.	0	53.11	133.5	186.61	0	157.64	5.6961	23.277	0	0
Single unit straight truck	0	0	40.343	40.343	0	14.862	16.153	4.8076	4.52	0
Truck-tractor cab only	0	0	6.8024	6.8024	0	4.484	2.3184	0	0	0
Unknown med./heavy Truck type	0	0	14.211	14.211	0	0	0	0	14.211	0
Other body type	0	0	43.514	43.514	0	0	38.706	4.8076	0	0
Unknown body type	0	0	79.148	79.148	0	59.386	19.762	0	0	0
Total	30.2158	141.6048	2218.4694	2390*	191.706	1132.159	674.6425	284.8922	48.1836	58.6818

*Rounded to the nearest whole number to reflect slight differences that occur in calculating the total using the various figures available for that calculation.

National Hospital Ambulatory Medical Care Survey – Data From Emergency Departments

The 2000 NHAMCS file for emergency department visits contains 25,622 records, 8,791 of which are for unintentional injuries. The text fields of the unintentional injury records were searched for certain words that would likely be used in describing one of the types of non-traffic motor vehicle-related incidents under study.

A total of five incidents involving a vehicle backing up were found in the NHAMCS emergency department file. Details of those incidents are provided below.

Table XXXV: Vehicle Backing Incidents Located In The 2000 NHAMCS (Emergency Department) File

Description	Patient Weight*
Walking across street and struck at low speed by a car backing up	2,041
MVC, truck backed into parked car	3,088
Passenger, restrained, car backed into their car and pushed their car back 5 feet	11,698
Jogging and ran into car that was backing up	4,302
Fell at 3 a.m. when she was standing behind her car and truck backed into her car which then pushed her	3,005

*When there are 30 or more similar incidents, the patient weights for all of the incidents can be added to together to create a projection of the national total of such incidents. The patient weights presented here are for information purposes only. They are of little or no predictive value since they each represent only one incident. Even if the incidents are considered to be similar, there are still only five such incidents here so no reliable predictions as to the national total of such incidents can be made.

Appendix VII – Passenger Compartment Vehicle Heat Deaths Found in 1998 Death Certificates

Some of the descriptions of passenger compartment vehicle heat deaths in the table below are supplemented by information contained in news accounts found in LexisNexis.

Table XXXVI: Passenger Compartment Vehicle Heat Deaths Found in 1998 Death Certificates

#	Age	Dscription
1	9 mos.	left strapped in child safety seat in a sweltering minivan for two hours - misunderstanding between child's parents resulted in the child being left alone in the van; one parent believed infant was at home with other
2	8 mos.	left in car - died of hyperthermia
3	6 mos.	child's parent had just returned from picking up victim and other children from the baby sitter - wasn't until an hour later, when other parent returned home, that they discovered child still inside car
4	6 mos.	baby died when accidentally left in hot car for 3 hrs, died when outside 90-degree temperatures rose to 130 degrees inside closed car, parents thought the other had carried the baby from the car to crib
5	34 mos.	toddler who recently learned how to open a car door apparently climbed inside family station wagon while parent and sibling were in house
6	23 mos.	relative babysitting child, put child in car for trip to store, went back in house having forgotten something, was distracted by something on television, sat on couch to watch, fell asleep, woke up two hours later
7	21 mos.	parents apparently forgot to remove child from car previous night
8	79	probable hyperthermia-exposure to heat inside vehicle
9	53	went outside to smoke accompanied by staff member of residential facility, missed dinner, employees searched van and found victim inside, doors were locked and windows were rolled up
10	51	exposed to extreme temperatures while in private vehicle - cause of death-hyperthermia, chronic ethanol abuse & emphysema
11	46	sleeping in closed van while intoxicated
12	45	hyperthermia - acute ethanol intoxication - happened in parked car
13	4	hyperthermia - left child in car - place of injury - child care center
14	4	found unconscious in closed vehicle - temp over 90 degrees
15	39	Exposure to desert heat in a vehicle without air conditioning - place of injury - automobile on highway
16	3	day care center workers overlooked a 3-year-old child who died of heat exhaustion after being accidentally locked in a van and left in the 95-degree heat for three hours
17	3	investigators believe victim could not escape because the car's rear door "child-proof" safety locks were engaged
18	2	found inside vehicle parked outside residence in 95-degree heat
19	2	parent left child in car after returning home from errand - was left for more than an hour
20	2	child apparently slipped away from parents and siblings, fell asleep atop blanket in unlocked car in driveway of home, oldest sibling found child 40 minutes later
21	2	siblings and parent were cooling off in a backyard pool when victim wandered out to the van, climbed in through an open door and got stuck when the door slid shut
22	2	found inside the car in extremely hot temperatures - place of injury – driveway

Appendix VIII - Summaries of Articles on Power Window Deaths

Simmons GT. *Death by power car window. An unrecognized hazard.* Am J Forensic Med Pathol 1992 Jun;13(2):112-4.

The case reported here was unusual in that it occurred while the vehicle was being driven. Also, those who investigated the case concluded that the power window was apparently activated by the driver of the vehicle rather than the child who died. The victim, a 26-month old child, was in the rear of an early 80s model passenger car being driven by an elderly relative. When the driver arrived at her destination, she found the child caught in a rear power window. The police determined that the position of the switch for the power window and the measurements of the child made it extremely unlikely that the child had activated the switch, although apparently the child might have done so by using her foot. Only the possibility that the child intentionally activated the switch with her hand is addressed and discounted in the article. There is no discussion as to whether or not the child might have inadvertently done so with her foot.

Strauss RH, Thompson JE, Macasaet A. *Accidental strangulation by a motor vehicle window.* Pediatr Emerg Care 1997 Oct;13(5):345-6.

The victim in the case reported here was a four year nine months old child. She was in the back seat of an early 90s model pickup truck with two siblings, one three years old, the other one year old. The vehicle was left running with the heater on while the driver (father) went into a neighbor's house. Five minutes later the victim was found trapped in the front seat passenger side power window. The author of this case report concluded that it was most likely that the victim or the three-year-old sibling activated the power window and neither was able to lower the window.

Injuries Associated With Hazards Involving Motor Vehicle Power Windows. Research Note, May 1997, National Highway Traffic Safety Administration.

Under an agreement between NHTSA and the Consumer Product Safety Commission (CPSC), the CPSC identified incidents from its National Electronic Injury Surveillance System (NEISS) in which injuries occurred as a result of several types of motor vehicle hazards, including motor vehicle power windows. NEISS is based on a representative sample of hospitals that provide emergency care on a 24-hour basis. A total of 10 incidents of injuries from power windows were found in the 12-month period, October 1, 1993 –September 30, 1994. These incidents project to an estimated 499 persons who were injured nationwide during this time. Most of the injuries were to the hand, wrist or finger. All of the injuries were either "minor" or "moderate." Most – 64 percent of the injuries – were to children 14 years old or younger, with 32% of the injuries to children 6-14 years of age and 32% of the injuries to children 0-5 years of age.

REFERENCES

[1]   Mott JA, Wolfe MI, Alverson CJ, Macdonald SC, Bailey CR, Ball LB, Moorman JE, Somers JH, Mannino DM, Redd SC. *National vehicle emissions policies and practices and declining US carbon monoxide-related mortality.* JAMA 2002;Aug 28;288(8):988-95.

[2]   Shelef M. Unanticipated benefits of automotive emission control: reduction in fatalities by motor vehicle exhaust gas. *Sci Total Environ* 1994 May 23;146-147:93-101.

[3]   Death from motor-vehicle-related unintentional carbon monoxide poisoning – Colorado, 1996, New Mexico, 1980-1985, and United States, 1979-1992. *MMWR Morb Mortal Wkly Rep* 1996 Nov 29;45(47):1029-32.

[4]   Girman JR, Chang YL, Hayward SG, Liu KS. Causes of unintentional deaths from carbon monoxide poisonings in California. *West J Med* 1998 Mar;168(3):158-65.

[5]   Rao R, Touger M, Gennis P, Tyrrell J, Roche J, Gallagher EJ. Epidemic of accidental carbon monoxide poisonings caused by snow-obstructed exhaust systems. *Ann Emerg Med* 1997 Apr;29(4):561.

[6]   Yoon SS, Macdonald SC, Parrish RG. Deaths from unintentional carbon monoxide poisoning and potential prevention with carbon monoxide detectors. JAMA 1998 Mar 4;279(9):685-7.

[7]   Baron RC, Backer RC, Sopher IM. Unintentional deaths from carbon monoxide in motor vehicle exhaust: West Virginia. *Am J Public Health* 1989 Mar;79(3):328-30.

[8]   *Fatalities Associated With Carbon Monoxide Poisoning From Motor Vehicles*, 1995-1997. Research Note, April 2000, National Highway Traffic Safety Administration.

[9]   Hampson NB, Norkool DM. *Carbon monoxide poisoning in children riding in the back of pickup trucks.* JAMA 1992 Jan 22-29;267(4): 538-40.

[10] Brison RJ, Wicklund K, Mueller BA. Fatal pedestrian injuries to young children: a different pattern of injury. *Am J Public Health* 1988 Jul;78(7):793-5.

[11] Winn DG, Agran PF, Castillo DN. Pedestrian injuries to children younger than 5 years of age. Pediatrics 1991 Oct;88(4):776-82.

[12] Agran PF, Winn DG, Anderson CL. Differences in child pedestrian injury events by location. *Pediatrics* 1994 Feb;93(2):284-8.

[13] Partrick BA, Bensard DD, Moore EE, Partington MD, Karrer FM. Driveway crush injuries in young children: a highly lethal, devastating, and potentially preventable event. *J Pediat Surg* 1998 Nov;33(11):1712-5.

[14] Nadler EP, Courcoulas AP, Gardner MJ, Ford HR. Driveway injuries in children: risk factors, morbidity, and mortality. *Pediatrics* 2001 Aug: 108(2):326-8.

[15] *Nonoccupant Fatalities Associated With Backing Crashes. Research Note*, Revised February 1997, National Highway Traffic Safety Administration.

[16] Silen ML, Kokoska ER, Fendya DG, Kurkchubasche AG, Weber TR, Tracy TF. Rollover injuries in residential driveways: age-related patterns of injury. *Pediatrics* 1999 Jul;104(1):e7.

[17] Di Scala C, Sege R, Guohua L. Outcomes of Pediatric Pedestrian Injuries By Locations of Event. *45th Annual Proceedings, Association for the Advancement of Automotive Medicine,* Sept. 24-26, 2001.

[18] Surpure JS. Heat-related illness and the automobile. *Ann Emerg Med* 1982 May; 11(5):263-5

[19] Roberts KB, Roberts EC. The automobile and heat stress. *Pediatrics* 1976 Jul;58(1):101-4.

[20] Simmons GT. Death by power car window. An unrecognized hazard. *Am J Forensic Med Pathol* 1992 Jun;13(2):112-4.

[21] Strauss RH, Thompson JE, Macasaet A. Accidental strangulation by a motor vehicle window. *Pediatr Emerg Care* 1997 Oct;13(5):345-6.

[22] Injuries Associated With Hazards Involving Motor Vehicle Power Windows. Research Note, May 1997, *National Highway Traffic Safety Administration.*

In: Automobile Industry: Current Issues   ISBN: 1-59454-686-X
Editor: Leon R. Domansky, pp. 195-209© 2006 Nova Science Publishers, Inc.

Chapter 6

COMPARISON OF DIFFERENCES IN INSURANCE COSTS FOR PASSENGER CARS, STATION WAGONS/PASSENGER VANS, PICKUPS AND UTILITY VEHICLES ON THE BASIS OF DAMAGE SUSCEPTIBILITY [*]

U.S. Department of Transportation National Highway Traffic Safety Administration

SUMMARY

The National Highway Traffic Safety Administration (NHTSA) has provided the information in this booklet in compliance with Federal law as an aid to consumers considering the purchase of a new vehicle. The booklet compares differences in insurance costs for different makes and models of passenger cars, station wagons/passenger vans, pickups, and utility vehicles on the basis of damage susceptibility. However, it does not indicate a vehicle's relative safety.

---

[*]Extracted from   http://www.nhtsa.dot.gov/cars/problems/studies/InsCost/2005CostofIns/index. htm

The following table contains the best available information regarding the effect of damage susceptibility on insurance premiums. It was taken from data compiled by the Highway Loss Data Institute (HLDI) in its December 2004 Insurance Collision Report, and reflects the collision loss experience of passenger cars, utility vehicles, light trucks, and vans sold in the United States in terms of the average loss payment per insured vehicle year for model years 2002-2004. NHTSA has not verified the data in this table.

The table presents vehicles' collision loss experience in relative terms, with 100 representing the average for all passenger vehicles. Thus, a rating of 122 reflects a collision loss experience that is 22 percent higher (worse) than average while a rating of 96 reflects a collision loss experience that is 4 percent lower (better) than average. The table is not relevant for models that have been substantially redesigned for 2005, and it does not include information about models without enough claim experience.

Although many insurance companies use the HLDI information to adjust the "base rate" for the collision portion of their insurance premiums, the amount of any such adjustment is usually small. It is unlikely that your total premium will vary more than ten percent depending upon the collision loss experience of a particular vehicle. If you do not purchase collision coverage or your insurance company does not use the HLDI information, your premium will not vary at all in relation to these rankings. In addition, different insurance companies often charge different premiums for the same driver and vehicle. Therefore, you should contact insurance companies or their agents directly to determine the actual premium that you will be charged for insuring a particular vehicle.

PLEASE NOTE: In setting insurance premiums, insurance companies mainly rely on factors that are not directly related to the vehicle itself (except for its value). Rather, they mainly consider driver characteristics (such as age, gender, marital status, and driving record), the geographic area in which the vehicle is driven, how many miles are traveled, and how the vehicle is used. Therefore, to obtain complete information about insurance premiums, you should contact insurance companies or their agents directly.

Insurance companies do not generally adjust their premiums on the basis of data reflecting the crashworthiness of different vehicles. However, some companies adjust their premiums for personal injury protection and medical payment coverage if the insured vehicle has features that are likely to improve its crashworthiness, such as air bags.

Test data relating to vehicle crashworthiness are available from NHTSA's New Car Assessment Program (NCAP). NCAP test results demonstrate relative frontal and side crash protection in new vehicles. Information on vehicles that NHTSA has tested in the NCAP program can be obtained by calling the agency's toll-free Auto Safety Hotline at (888) 327-4236 and through the NHTSA Web Page at: www.nhtsa.dot.gov.

COLLISION INSURANCE LOSSES
MODEL YEAR 2002 - 2004 PASSENGER
MOTOR VEHICLES

Mini Cars		
Make	**Model**	**Relative Average Loss Payment per Insured Vehicle Year**
Two-Door Models		121
Toyota	Echo	110
Hyundai	Accent	120
Four-Door Models		126
Chevrolet	Aveo	98
Toyota	Echo	119
Kia	Rio	125
Hyundai	Accent	130
Scion	xA	133
Station Wagons		119
Kia	Rio	120
Sports Models		110
Mazda	Miata convertible	95
Toyota	MR2 Spyder convertible	145
Specialty Models		121
Scion	xB 4dr	119
Honda	Insight 2dr	124

NOTE: Every model represents over 1,000 insured vehicle years and at least 100 claims. The experience for previous or discontinued models from 2002 – 2004 is included in the class averages.

Small Cars		
Make	**Model**	**Relative Average Loss Payment per Insured Vehicle Year**
Two-Door Models		142
Volkswagen	New Beetle convertible	74
Volkswagen	New Beetle	91
Mini	Cooper	99
Saturn	ION Quad Coupe	124
Pontiac	Sunfire	133
Chevrolet	Cavalier	135
Ford	Focus	142
Honda	Civic coupe	150
Mitsubishi	Eclipse	152
Volkswagen	Golf	156
Honda	Civic hatchback	186
Hyundai	Tiburon	201
Toyota	Celica	203
Acura	RSX	224
Four-Door Models		123
Saturn	ION	107
Volkswagen	Golf	112
Hyundai	Elantra	113
Volkswagen	Jetta	113
Honda	Civic	118
Chevrolet	Cavalier	118
Ford	Focus	120
Toyota	Corolla	120
Kia	Spectra sedan/hatchback	126
Volvo	S40	129
Dodge	Neon	131
Suzuki	Forenza	141
Nissan	Sentra	148
Mazda	3	151

Small Cars		
Make	**Model**	**Relative Average Loss Payment per Insured Vehicle Year**
Subaru	Impreza 4WD	155
Suzuki	Aerio	160
Mitsubishi	Lancer	165
Subaru	Impreza WRX 4WD	257
Dodge	SRT-4	287
Mitsubishi	Lancer Evolution 4WD	514
Station Wagons		110
Volkswagen	Jetta	80
Ford	Focus	87
Suzuki	Aerio SX 4WD	96
Volvo	V40	99
Pontiac	Vibe 4WD	104
Pontiac	Vibe	106
Subaru	Impreza 4WD	107
Toyota	Matrix 4WD	118
Toyota	Matrix	120
Suzuki	Aerio SX	129
Mazda	3	136
Subaru	Impreza WRX 4WD	154
Sports Models		143
Audi	TT Quattro roadster	106
BMW	Z4 Roadster convertible	107
Audi	TT roadster	110
Audi	TT coupe	111
Mercedes	SLK class convertible	119
Chrysler	Crossfire	121
Audi	TT Quattro coupe	124
Mitsubishi	Eclipse convertible	135
Porsche	Boxster convertible	181
Honda	S2000 convertible	225

Small Cars		
Make	**Model**	**Relative Average Loss Payment per Insured Vehicle Year**
Specialty Models		89
Toyota	Prius 4dr	74
Chrysler	PT Cruiser 4dr	86
Honda	Civic Hybrid 4dr	103

NOTE: Every model represents over 1,000 insured vehicle years and at least 100 claims. The experience for previous or discontinued models from 2002 – 2004 is included in the class averages.

Midsize Cars		
Make	**Model**	**Relative Average Loss Payment per Insured Vehicle Year**
Two-Door Models		117
Chrysler	Sebring convertible	77
Chevrolet	Monte Carlo	105
Oldsmobile	Alero	110
Pontiac	Grand Am	112
Toyota	Camry Solara	121
Chrysler	Sebring	125
Audi	A4 Cabriolet convertible	135
Honda	Accord	140
Dodge	Stratus	147
Infiniti	G35	164
Four-Door Models		104
Saturn	LS	75
Toyota	Avalon	82
Subaru	Legacy/Outback 4WD	84
Toyota	Camry	90
Saab	9-3	91
Mitsubishi	Galant	94

Midsize Cars		
Make	**Model**	**Relative Average Loss Payment per Insured Vehicle Year**
Honda	Accord	97
Oldsmobile	Alero	98
Chevrolet	Malibu	101
Hyundai	Sonata	104
Chrysler	Sebring	104
Pontiac	Grand Am	110
Volkswagen	Passat	111
Kia	Optima	112
Infiniti	I35	115
Nissan	Altima	115
Dodge	Stratus	115
Acura	TSX	118
Infiniti	G35	122
Volkswagen	Passat 4WD	124
Audi	A4	134
Nissan	Maxima	138
Mazda	6	141
Audi	A4/S4 Quattro	143
Mitsubishi	Diamante	143
Station Wagons		76
Chevrolet	Malibu Maxx	52
Saturn	LW	67
Subaru	Legacy/Outback 4WD	70
Volkswagen	Passat	86
Audi	A4/S4 Avant Quattro	107
Volkswagen	Passat 4WD	121
Sports Models		149
Chevrolet	Corvette convertible	71
Chevrolet	Corvette	113

Midsize Cars		
Make	**Model**	**Relative Average Loss Payment per Insured Vehicle Year**
Ford	Mustang convertible	126
Lexus	SC 430 convertible	126
Mercedes	SL class convertible	142
Ford	Mustang	156
Porsche	911 convertible	163
Nissan	350Z convertible	175
Mazda	RX-8	176
Porsche	911 Coupe	194
Nissan	350Z	206
Luxury Models		131
Saab	9-5 station wagon	82
BMW	3 series station wagon	84
BMW	3 series station wagon 4WD	88
Acura	TL series 4dr	95
Lexus	ES series 4dr	100
Saab	9-5 4dr	104
BMW	3 series 4dr 4WD	105
BMW	3 series convertible	111
Mercedes	C class 4dr	116
Mercedes	C Class 4dr 4WD	116
BMW	3 series 4dr	117
Volvo	S60 4dr	121
Volvo	S60 4dr 4WD	128
Mercedes	C Class station wagon	133
Mercedes	C Class 2dr	136
Jaguar	X-Type 4dr 4WD	141
Mercedes	CLK Class 2dr	177
Lexus	IS 300 Sportcross station wagon	178
BMW	3 series 2dr	183

Midsize Cars		
Make	**Model**	**Relative Average Loss Payment per Insured Vehicle Year**
Mercedes	CLK Class convertible	199

Midsize Cars		
Make	**Model**	**Relative Average Loss Payment per Insured Vehicle Year**
Lexus	IS 300 4dr	229

NOTE: Every model represents over 1,000 insured vehicle years and at least 100 claims. The experience for previous or discontinued models from 2002 – 2004 is included in the class averages.

Large Cars		
Make	**Model**	**Relative Average Loss Payment per Insured Vehicle Year**
Four-Door Models		80
Buick	LeSabre	55
Buick	Century	65
Pontiac	Bonneville	67
Buick	Regal	68
Chevrolet	Impala	76
Ford	Taurus	83
Mercury	Sable	85
Chrysler	Concorde	85
Pontiac	Grand Prix	96
Dodge	Intrepid	102
Chrysler	300M	104
Hyundai	XG350	107

Large Cars		
Make	Model	Relative Average Loss Payment per Insured Vehicle Year
Station Wagons / Minivans		70
Pontiac	Montana SWB	57
Mazda	MPV	58
Pontiac	Montana LWB	61
Ford	Taurus	62
Oldsmobile	Silhouette	63
Chevrolet	Venture LWB	69
Dodge	Caravan	71
Mercury	Sable	76
Chevrolet	Venture SWB	76
Sports Models		103
Ford	Thunderbird convertible	60
Jaguar	XK series convertible	248
Luxury Models		116
Buick	Park Avenue 4dr	62
Audi	A6 4dr	80
Cadillac	DeVille 4dr	88
Volvo	V70 station wagon 4WD	93
Volvo	V70 station wagon	97
Volvo	S80 4dr	98
Acura	3.5 RL 4dr	102
Cadillac	Seville 4dr	102
Lincoln	LS 4dr	111
Audi	A6/S6 Quattro station wagon	112
Lexus	LS 430 4dr	112
Lexus	GS series 4dr	115
Audi	A6/RS6 Quattro 4dr	122
Volvo	C70 convertible	122
Jaguar	S-type 4dr	125
Mercedes	E class 4dr	127

Large Cars		
Make	**Model**	**Relative Average Loss Payment per Insured Vehicle Year**
BMW	5 series 4dr	133
Infiniti	M45 4dr	134
Cadillac	CTS 4dr	137
Infiniti	Q45 4dr	152
Jaguar	XJ series 4dr LWB	193
Jaguar	XJ series 4dr	205

Large Cars		
Make	**Model**	**Relative Average Loss Payment per Insured Vehicle Year**
Mercedes	CL Class 2dr	305

NOTE: Every model represents over 1,000 insured vehicle years and at least 100 claims. The experience for previous or discontinued models from 2002 – 2004 is included in the class averages.

Very Large Cars		
Make	**Model**	**Relative Average Loss Payment per Insured Vehicle Year**
Four-Door Models		71
Ford	Crown Victoria	72
Mercury	Grand Marquis	76
Station Wagons / Minivans		70
GMC	Safari	54
Chevrolet	Astro 4WD	63
Pontiac	Montana LWB 4WD	65
Chevrolet	Astro	65
Oldsmobile	Silhouette 4WD	65
Honda	Odyssey	66

Large Cars		
Make	**Model**	**Relative Average Loss Payment per Insured Vehicle Year**
GMC	Safari 4WD	67
Nissan	Quest	68
Chrysler	Town & Country LWB	69
Dodge	Grand Caravan	71
Toyota	Sienna	72
Chevrolet	Venture LWB 4WD	72
Toyota	Sienna 4WD	76
Ford	Freestar	77
Chrysler	Town & Country 4WD	81
Dodge	Grand Caravan 4WD	82
Kia	Sedona	83
Chrysler	Town & Country SWB	86
Luxury Models		139
Lincoln	Town Car 4dr	84
Mercedes	S class LWB 4dr 4WD	105
Audi	A8 L Quattro 4dr	133
BMW	7 series 4dr LWB	150
BMW	7 series 4dr	167
Mercedes	S class 4dr LWB	181

NOTE: Every model represents over 1,000 insured vehicle years and at least 100 claims. The experience for previous or discontinued models from 2002 – 2004 is included in the class averages.

Pickups		
Make	**Model**	**Relative Average Loss Payment per Insured Vehicle Year**
Small Pickups		97
Chevrolet	Colorado series	85

Chevrolet	S10 series 4WD	85
GMC	Sonoma series 4WD	85
Nissan	Frontier series	87
Mazda	B series	93
Dodge	Dakota series	93
Toyota	Tacoma series	96
Ford	Ranger series	97
Dodge	Dakota series 4WD	101
Nissan	Frontier series 4WD	102
Chevrolet	Colorado series 4WD	103
Mazda	B series 4WD	106
Ford	Ranger series 4WD	108

Pickups		
Make	Model	Relative Average Loss Payment per Insured Vehicle Year
Toyota	Tacoma series 4WD	110
Large Pickups		86
Ford	F-150 series 4WD (NEW)	63
Nissan	Titan series 4WD	67
Ford	F-150 series (NEW)	70
Dodge	Ram 1500 series 4WD	79
Chevrolet	Silverado 1500 series 4WD	79
Ford	F-150 series 4WD (OLD)	80
GMC	Sierra 1500 series 4WD	81
Dodge	Ram 1500 series	85
GMC	Sierra 1500 series	89
Chevrolet	Silverado 1500 series	90
Ford	F-150 series (OLD)	90
Toyota	Tundra series	91
Nissan	Titan series	97
Toyota	Tundra series 4WD	105
Very Large Pickups		89

Ford	F-250 series	71
Ford	F-350 series	72
Chevrolet	Silverado 2500 series	73
Dodge	Ram 2500 series	75
Chevrolet	Silverado 2500 series 4WD	81
GMC	Sierra 2500 series 4WD	82
GMC	Sierra 2500 series	83
GMC	Sierra 3500 series	86
Chevrolet	Silverado 3500 series	86
Dodge	Ram 2500 series 4WD	88
Dodge	Ram 3500 series 4WD	93
Ford	F-250 series 4WD	96
Pickups		
Make	**Model**	**Relative Average Loss Payment per Insured Vehicle Year**
GMC	Sierra 3500 series 4WD	99
Dodge	Ram 3500 series	100
Chevrolet	Silverado 3500 series 4WD	105
Ford	F-350 series 4WD	106

NOTE: Every model represents over 1,000 insured vehicle years and at least 100 claims. The experience for previous or discontinued models from 2002 – 2004 is included in the class averages.

INDEX

D